The Racial Middle

The Racial Middle

Latinos and Asian Americans
Living beyond the Racial Divide

Eileen O'Brien

NEW YORK UNIVERSITY PRESS
New York and London

NEW YORK UNIVERSITY PRESS
New York and London
www.nyupress.org

Library of Congress Cataloging-in-Publication Data
O'Brien, Eileen, 1972–
The racial middle : Latinos and Asian Americans living beyond the
racial divide / Eileen O'Brien.
p.   cm.
Includes bibliographical references and index.
ISBN-13: 978-0-8147-6214-1 (cl : alk. paper)
ISBN-10: 0-8147-6214-X (cl : alk. paper)
ISBN-13: 978-0-8147-6215-8 (pb : alk. paper)
ISBN-10: 0-8147-6215-8 (pb : alk. paper)
1. Hispanic Americans—Ethnic identity. 2. Hispanic America—
Attitudes. 3. Asian Americans—Ethnic identity. 4. Asian Americans
—Attitudes. 5. Racism—United States—Public opinion. 6. Public
opinion—United States. 7. United States—Race relations.   I. Title.
E184.S75O275 2008
305.800973—dc22   2007051507

New York University Press books are printed on acid-free paper,
and their binding materials are chosen for strength and durability.

Manufactured in the United States of America

c 10 9 8 7 6 5 4 3 2 1
p 10 9 8 7 6 5 4 3 2 1

Contents

Acknowledgments

Like no other "sole-authored" project I've worked on before, this book is a collaborative effort that I never could have accomplished on my own. The support and assistance I have received along the way has been so overwhelming, that I apologize in advance if I have missed anyone. Truly the circle of sustenance around me during this project has been boundless and immeasurable. But a few deserve special mention.

First and foremost, I am grateful to the fifty men and women who so generously gave their time to speak with my student interviewers or me. Most refused what little compensation we offered, and the rest accepted little more than the cost of lunch or a drink. It is my hope that this gift of your time will contribute tremendously to our collective knowledge about the racial middle and help pave the way for you to soon inhabit a more open society than currently exists.

The fact that I even arrived at a total of fifty respondents is due in large part to the able assistance of three undergraduate student interviewers who worked hard for this project—Jennifer Conlon, Annie Hirschman, and Leah Adams. Additionally, two other students assisted with transcribing and coding—Emily Gates and Catherine Estevez. I am especially grateful to Catherine for her constant and candid feedback in the later stages of the project. Her keen observations on patterns in the data led to her collaboration with me on the writing of chapter 2, and I am so proud of her work. Data collection was also enhanced by the generosity of Michael Armato and Sheera Olasky—Mike's willingness to circulate my announcement for summer housing in New York, together with Sheera's willingness to donate her Harlem apartment for next to nothing, by Manhattan standards, were both indispensable in securing the first phase of the interviewing for this project.

The financial support that allowed me, as well as a majority of the abovementioned students, to spend summers collecting data was provided by the Arts and Sciences Dean's Office at the University of Richmond. Special thanks to Andy Newcomb and Kathy Hoke, who both played roles in securing that support. Sociology department chair Joan Neff was patient with scheduling, travel reimbursement, and approving student independent studies, among other things, which helped things flow more smoothly. Kerran Kempton, the administrative assistant, was equally patient in helping to order tapes, recorders, transcribers, and to serve as a go-between to get such materials between the students and me when I was away from the office. Now that I have moved on to Christopher Newport University (and special thanks to Joe Healey for the needed push that helped me make that leap), I can fully appreciate the meaning of departmental support.

Outside my own academic environment, support has also been boundless. Extra special mention in this category goes first and foremost to Deirdre Royster. Aside from those for whom reading this manuscript was part of their job description, Dee is the one who pored over the manuscript most thoroughly (although any errors that remain are most undoubtedly my own). There are a couple of chapters that she completely overhauled, coming up with new section titles and so forth. I am a great admirer of her work; I was honored that she took the time to give such detailed feedback on my writing, but our relationship went even further than that. Our meetings became not only a source of writing support, but seemingly naturally and effortlessly flowed into pedagogical support, the emotional stumbling blocks of being on sabbatical, parenting, relationships, bodily functions, and everything in between. Although I feel as if she were coauthor on this book, I look forward to us being "real" coauthors on a future project. We work well together! Thanks also to Deenesh Sohoni who helped direct me to various references on Asian Americans and intermarriage, one of his specialties.

Being also an admirer of the work of Eduardo Bonilla-Silva, Joe Feagin, and George Yancey, I very much appreciated their informal feedback on earlier stages of the project. As I was entering the book publishing market again after years away, I turned to their advice, as well as other admired colleagues—Kathleen Korgen, David Brunsma, Pamela Perry, Melanie and Rod Bush, and others who I am sure I am forgetting—for whose help I am grateful. I also especially thank Leanne Andersen and Kate Wahl, who showed a steady and unwavering support in this project—I am sure our paths will cross again in the future.

At NYU Press, where I found my home, I am grateful to "the other Eileen," executive editor Ilene Kalish, whose support at every stage has been phenomenal. Also thanks to everyone else at NYU Press, including

Gabrielle Begue and Despina Papazoglou Gimbel, whose attention to the details was much appreciated. I am certainly indebted to the comments of two thorough and insightful anonymous reviewers who worked on behalf of the press.

While those mentioned above formed much of the intellectual support for the work, there are many other sources of social and emotional capital in my life, without whom this book quite surely would never have been completed. Although I completed three books before this one, I underestimated how much being a parent would affect the work pace to which I had formerly been accustomed. To that end, I am especially indebted to my step-grandmother-in-law, better known as my daughter's great-grandmother, Essie James. For close to nothing each week, she took good care of Kaya and was gracious in attempting to understand why, even though I'm not going to Richmond, I still have to work. This is also a difficult truth for one's live-in family to swallow, so I am also grateful to both my daughter, Kaya, and my partner Kendall, for tolerating all the times I was hopelessly glued to my computer screen. Many a paragraph was written through Kaya's steady pleading of "click on the X, Mommy!" between being babysat by the PBS or Nick Jr. morning lineup. And I know that Kendall's over-sixty-five-hour-a-week work schedule leaves little time for much else, so I appreciate his willingness to occupy Kaya while I transcribed or went to a coffeehouse to write, even though he would have much preferred us all spending the time together, or going off and doing his own thing. His steady encouragements in the most stressful moments —"you'll get it done, honey, you always do"—are always appreciated. Other at-a-moment's-notice free child care has been provided by Aunt TuTu (my sister-in-law, Kathy Roache), her daughter, Jameshia Roache, and Gramma (my mom, Jean Kelly)—who once took care of Kaya overnight in Boston so I could continue on to Montreal to meet with book publishers. I am so fortunate to have family around—there is no such thing as an isolated superwoman, to be sure.

And then there's my free therapy staff, consisting of Elizabeth Ransom, Doug Godfrey, and my second/stepmother, Shari O'Brien. In many an exasperated moment where I have felt the need to completely walk away from my job, my partner, my parenting responsibilities, or all of the above, one or more of the above wonderful people came through for me. Liz must graciously listen because she's stuck in the carpool with me and can't escape! I love her down-to-earth advice and type A professionalism/pragmatism, which brings me back to reality when I'm on the edge.

Doug, whom I have known since sixth grade, will eventually pick up his phone, daily and sometimes more than daily (and even while at work), to become listener, travel agent, concierge, personal comedian, and everything in between. How he reliably brings me to laughter by the end of every tearful conversation I will never know, but I am eternally grateful. Shari, actually a "real" therapist, though, is first and foremost my friend, knows how to calm down my dramas, put them in perspective, and gives right-on perfect advice every time (my personal favorite: "bring food!"). I could have never been in any state to come back to this computer on a regular basis without their consistent and unwavering support.

Countless people inquired at various points how the book was going and showed an interest in its ideas, especially members of the Williamsburg Unitarian Universalist Church (particularly Jessica O'Brien, David Wilcox, and the reverends Jennifer Ryu and Preston Moore). I am so grateful for, and humbled by, the enormous network of assistance I have encountered throughout this project. Though I am sure I have only touched on a fraction of the love and support that surrounds and sustains me, just to reflect on this alone reminds me how truly blessed I am. I hope I have done you all proud.

1

The Panethnic Racial Middle

They say, if you's white, you's all right,
If you's brown, you can stick around,
But if you black, oh brother, get back, get back, get back.
— Big Bill Broonzy, "Black, Brown, and White" (1951)

The experiences of persons in the racial middle in the United States have always been framed by those on the racial poles of white and black. As the above song lyric makes plain, those in the "brown" ambiguous middle category have often been juxtaposed against a "white" category that is favored and a "black" category that is not. Thus, a "brown" person is anyone conditionally accepted as "not black" (and thus can "stick around") but still not completely favored as "white." They hover in a middle that subverts the simple characterizations in this dichotomy of "right" and "wrong," "front" and "back." This is undoubtedly a precarious position and begs the question: How have those in the racial middle negotiated this position, framed largely by the poles on either side of them? How do they navigate this middle territory?

If one studies in detail the social construction of racial categories and the ideologies attached to them in the United States, one soon realizes that virtually everyone in the society actually fits into a middle category, because the idea of a "pure" racial stock is an absolute scientific fallacy.[1] There are indeed many Americans, however, who either think of themselves as "white" or "black," and perhaps more important, Americans who are treated as "white" or "black" in social, economic, and political institutions. This ever-present reality fuels modern racism as we know it. History shows that the U.S. government has attempted at all costs to fit all persons into this seemingly clear-cut white/not-white dichotomy, making it difficult for those who did not fit it to assert their own exceptionalities.[2]

Yet there are two "middle" demographic groups in particular whose proportions in the U.S. population are growing at such unprecedented rates that changes to this simplistic dichotomy could very well be on the horizon. Those two groups are Latinos and Asian Americans. Indeed, as of the 2000 census, those categorized as Hispanic have already outnumbered those in the black/African American category.[3] By the middle of this century, the percentage of Latinos in the U.S. population is expected to double, amounting to almost 25 percent of the entire nation, and Asian Americans' proportion is also expected to more than double, from 3.6 to 8.9 percent.[4] This means that, taken together, Latinos and Asian Americans will soon constitute about 35 percent of the U.S. population, while African Americans would be at only 13 percent. Whereas previous numerical realities meant that challenges to the hegemonic white-over-black racial order were contained enough not to disrupt it, many experts are now questioning whether such a status quo can be maintained, given these massive population shifts.

The racial middle groups of Latinos and Asian Americans exhibit interesting characteristics that are not completely reducible to the patterns typical of whites or blacks. Asian American families earn incomes and attain educational levels that are equal to and sometimes even higher than whites.[5] Latinos and Asian Americans both tend to feel most "warm" (on feeling thermometer indicators) toward whites and least warm toward blacks.[6] These sentiments, coupled with greater social contact with whites, have led to Latinos' and Asian Americans' higher intermarriage rates with whites than blacks. They are less likely to support race-related policies like affirmative action, and less likely to vote Democratic, than are African Americans.[7] Yet they continue to earn lower returns on their education than similarly educated whites, facing glass-ceiling barriers to promotion in their occupations.[8] Both groups are severely underrepresented politically.[9] Many Latinos are segregated residentially, particularly when they are darker skinned.[10] Some Asian Americans are targets of cruel hate crimes, often becoming the racialized scapegoats for the instability of the working class in a globalizing national economy.[11] Both groups also cope with the internalization of cultural images that marginalize their phenotype, some even undergoing plastic surgery to emulate European physical features.[12] Some of these patterns mirror African American historical experiences in the United States, while others are more reflective of white experiences. Latinos and Asian Americans are thus sociopolitically an "up-for-grabs" group in the United States, because they do not consistently ally with blacks or with whites. They defy simplistic categorizations in a society that has insisted on operating along such dichotomous lines for the greater part of its history.

History of the Not-So-New Racial Middle in the United States

Although the exponential growth of the racial middle has been largely a post-1965 development, members of certain racial middle groups have been present in the United States for as long as it has existed as a nation. This means that some members of the racial middle, whose claims to being "American" are sometimes challenged by white Americans, can have longer generational histories in the United States than some white Americans themselves. In the mid- to late nineteenth century, as the United States was transitioning from an agriculturally based to an industrially based economy, three groups from the racial middle played a key role in providing the labor power that built the nation—Mexicans, Chinese, and Japanese. These groups arrived in a racially polarized society, between the bifurcated poles of black and white, and the society struggled to make political, legal, and social sense of where these middle groups should "fit" and what their rights should be, if any.

The Mexicans had an interesting experience because some of what was formerly Mexican land eventually, despite resistance, became U.S. territory. Thus, in some ways, their experiences of conquest and broken treaties were similar to those which had already been experienced by Native Americans. The same kinds of cultural disparagements that were created to justify the takeover of Native American land were created by those in power to rationalize the westward expansion onto Mexican ground.[13] The influence of European colonization, however, and the more fluid boundaries between skin tones among Latin American peoples, meant that some persons of Mexican nationality were deemed "white" and allowed to experience the privileges attached to that racial designation. Indeed, up until 1980, census takers were instructed to mark Mexican Americans down as "white" unless their phenotype appeared to be "Negro, Indian, or some other race."[14] Thus, gradations in skin tone made a difference for Mexican Americans' access to privileges, in a way that was not similarly experienced by their African American peers.

African Americans, in contrast, were forced to follow the law of hypodescent (known as the "one-drop rule") when categorizing their "race."

Whether they appeared visibly lighter skinned or not, if they had even "one drop" of "black blood," they were to be considered racially black. This existence of "black blood" had nothing to do with biological blood testing or even phenotype, but was based on the legal records of racial assignment for all of the distant generations of the person's family. Thus, if even one parent or great-grandparent (and in some states, great-great-great-grandparent) was considered "black" on paper, no matter how many other "whites" existed in that person's family, they would still be deemed black. This rule worked effectively to maximize the percentage of the population who would be legally forced to provide free labor to the U.S. economy, consigned to lives of chattel slavery. This one-drop rule continued as the basis of the racial dividing line for legal segregation, however, long after slavery was outlawed in 1865. As a case in point, the landmark separate-but-equal U.S. Supreme Court case *Plessy v. Ferguson* ruled in 1896 that a "black" man who seemed visibly "white" to most still had to ride in the "colored" car of the train, legally solidifying the salience of the one-drop rule for at least another half century.[15] This state-created racial category of "black" neglected the myriad ethnic differences among Africans that existed on their forced transport to the Americas as slaves, and then continued to neglect the vast diversity of class, skin color, educational attainment, and other factors among them long after slavery had been abolished.

That system of chattel slavery that predated the century of legal segregation for African Americans had itself been in place for over a century when the first Chinese arrived on U.S. soil. The arrival of this mostly male cohort began with the California gold rush of 1849 and continued throughout the following three decades, as they labored in mining, railroad, irrigation, and manufacturing industries, sending remittances home to their families in China.[16] As was also the case with Mexican laborers, Chinese workers were paid less for the same work than workers who were considered "white."[17] Americans who had previously considered themselves along more ethnic lines (as Irish, Italian, Polish, and so on), much like the Chinese and Mexicans, began to abandon some of these ethnic affiliations, as it became more materially expedient for them to identified with the privileged "white" class.[18] This pattern of labor exploitation pitted white workers against others, and sprouted white resentment of the other groups. In contrast to the Mexican workers whose homeland was either formerly part of the United States or very nearby, however, the Chinese workers could be more easily eliminated as a labor threat by banning their continued immigration from China, which was accomplished by the Chinese Exclusion Act of 1882.[19] The Chinese in the United States did not have much say in such policy matters, because, not deemed legally "white," they were ineligible to be voting citizens.[20] While Mexicans were often tragically disenfranchised due to the refusal to recognize their rightful property claims (and one had to own property to vote), they were never legally barred from voting as an entire group due to their "race" in the same fashion as the Chinese.

The Chinese Exclusion Act of 1882 created some space for Japanese workers to begin migrating to the United States, beginning in the late nineteenth century. Japanese officials worked with the U.S. government to come up with an arrangement that would hopefully subvert the negative representations and backlash that the Chinese laborers had experienced before them. They worked out the Gentlemen's Agreement, which would allow the Japanese to bring their wives with them, unlike the Chinese who were forbidden to do so. This allowed the Japanese to eventually move out of the low-wage job sector to an extent that the Chinese had been unable to do.[21] This still could not withhold the eventual backlash, however, and immigration acts of 1909 and 1924 prevented further generations from immigrating.[22] Even the second generation that was already permitted to remain in the country, and worked hard to be deserving of the designation of "American" (after all, the United States was their birthplace), could not escape hostility. The U.S. courts also still held that persons of Japanese descent could not be considered white, as evidenced by the case of *Ozawa v. United States* (1922), where a Japanese American man unsuccessfully petitioned the courts for a white racial designation.[23] The backlash was felt even harder when the United States placed members of the second generation into internment camps during World War II. They were under suspicion as "the enemy," despite the fact that most of them knew nothing of life in Japan and felt more allegiance to the United States.

When the internment camps began, it may surprise Americans today to find that Chinese Americans—who now are included in the same "race" category as Japanese Americans—proudly wore buttons stating "I'm not a Jap."[24] At this point in its history, the United States dealt with each of these three "middle" groups as distinct ethnic categories, with varying rights and privileges depending on the sociopolitical circumstances (but never at the level as esteemed as whites). As such, the divergent policies and national sentiments applied to the Chinese, and then the Japanese, illustrate how meaningful ethnic distinctions remained to Americans in the racial middle, at a time when ethnic differences were rapidly declining in significance for those on the racial poles of black and white. These ethnic distinctions in the racial middle, however, were still circumscribed by the ultimate racial categories of black and, more important, white. The U.S. courts have played a significant role over time in policing the boundaries of race, especially guarding the boundaries of whiteness, due to the material and social privileges that come along with it.[25] Thus, in the early U.S. history, we see policies that protect the borders of whiteness, largely preventing Mexicans, Chinese, and Japanese from fully penetrating them.

Post–Civil Rights Era: The Panethnic Racial Middle

As the civil rights movement began to put the United States squarely in the international spotlight, threatening its global reputation as a beacon of freedom and equality for all, the nation necessarily became a bit more flexible on race and ethnicity than it had been in the past. After intervening on the global scene in World War II in the name of anti-Semitism and antifascism, it became difficult for the United States to continue to stand behind certain of its own policies which ran counter to such ideals. One such policy concerned immigration. A national-origins quota system had been in place since 1924, severely restricting flows from Africa, Asian, and Latin America, and the United States repealed those racist quotas with the Immigration Act of 1965. Although the United States did not set out to invite large numbers of non-Europeans to its shores by enacting this newer policy, it is indeed what happened. Well-educated immigrants from Korea, Hong Kong, Taiwan, the Philippines, and India began arriving in much larger numbers than they had previously.[26] This mid-twentieth century period also expanded significantly the ethnic diversity of Latin American immigrants. Beginning in 1917, Puerto Rican American immigration became unrestricted due to their status as U.S. citizens, but a subsequent project called Operation Bootstrap (1948–65) dramatically increased the "push factors" drawing them to the mainland; consequently, between 1950 and 1960, the average number of Puerto Rican Americans migrating to New York annually more than doubled. Further, Cuban immigration peaked dramatically in the 1960s after Fidel Castro took over.[27] Immigrants from Latin America, the Caribbean, and Asia began significantly outnumbering those from Europe, representing many more nations than are listed here.

The U.S. civil rights movement, happening concurrently, undoubtedly set a model for other disenfranchised and exploited groups in the nation. African Americans and their allies raised additional unwanted global attention for the United States as mass media became more easily transmittable across the world, and the brutality of white terrorism, particularly in the southern United States, could longer be ignored. As African Americans began to gain concessions from the state in the form of Supreme Court decisions, support from the National Guard in the South to enforce these rulings, and civil rights acts enacted by the president, other oppressed groups began to take note of their successful organizing tactics and sought to put them into practice for themselves. The Black Power movement of the late 1960s gave rise to the Native American "Red Power" movement, the Asian "Yellow Power" movement, and the Latino "Brown Power" movement.[28] These movements were some of the first efforts of Latinos and Asians to organize across ethnic lines into panethnic racial groupings. Because no single ethnic group (e.g., Chinese, Japanese, Mexicans, Puerto Rican Americans) possessed numbers by itself to come close to the total population of African Americans, it became a necessary organizational move for Latinos and Asians to bridge across their ethnic differences for the sake of forming these race-based groups. By 1980, the United States exhibited a further degree of racial flexibility in its record keeping, as for the first time, respondents filled out their own racial designation on the census as opposed to census takers choosing it for them.[29] It was the beginning of a bit more agency and the ability to shape racial categories "from below."

It is not the whole story, however, that Latinos and Asians, through simply their own volition, came across ethnic differences to form larger panethnic racial groups. A variety of external factors exerted pressure on them to acknowledge the reality of their shared fates. Ye Len Espiritu's work on Asian panethnicity does an excellent job of outlining how such factors operated in the lives of Asians in the latter part of the twentieth century. She points out that community activists who provided necessary services to their respective ethnic communities found that access to valued resources was at stake, because agencies realized that they had more access to grant money if they reported to serve the larger sounding "Asian" population, rather than just one or two specific Asian ethnic groups.[30] Moreover, the brutal race-related killing in 1982 of Vincent Chin (a Chinese American attacked by whites who were upset that Japanese had allegedly taken their jobs) underscored the fact that Asians were interchangeable in the eyes of many Americans, despite their distinct ethnic differences.[31] Responding to these external factors, Espiritu argues that Americans of various Asian Pacific Islander ethnicities came together strategically under the panethnic "API" (Asian Pacific Islander) racial category. The post–World War II period was the earliest time at which such a coalition was possible, due to native-born Asian Americans outnumbering foreign born (at least in California, the state with the largest number of Asian Americans) and the younger generation sharing a common language (English) for the first time. This younger generation also was not particularly attached to the historical animosities among Asian nations that had separated the allegiances of their parents, paving the way for a smoother transition to a panethnic Asian identity.[32]

The Asian Pacific Islander category, which I will sometimes refer to as API and most other times simply as Asian American, was an attempt at self-naming on the part of the members of the group. They were already being lumped together by outsiders as homogenous in a way that did not mesh with their diverse realities. This juncture, however, required some thoughtful strategizing. To respond to this overgeneralization "from above," would they continue to allow others to define them, or would they respond as a collective voice that shaped the direction of how others henceforth would regard them? As with the civil rights movement before them, student activists played a major role in defining the movement. Over one hundred students attended an "Are You Yellow?" conference at the University of California-Los Angeles in the summer of 1968, and the first Asian American national conference was held just four years later in 1972. Students rejected the term "Oriental" because "while Oriental suggests passivity and acquiescence, Asian Americans connotes political activism."[33] The continent of Asia is "the Orient" only in reference to those in the Western Hemisphere for whom it is the "other." Further, while "yellow power" was gaining some credence with students, a Filipino caucus at the 1972 meeting did not feel that the term "yellow" applied to their own experiences, identifying more with Brown Power instead. So the term Asian Pacific Islander took precedence to encompass the ethnic diversity of the group and to re-center the continent away from the position of an exoticized other that Oriental suggests.[34]

The cooperation and temporary setting aside of ethnic, cultural, geographic, religious, class, status, and phenotype differences that had to be accomplished to arrive at this panethnic coalition cannot be overstated. As early as the 1880s, in an attempt to distinguish themselves from the Chinese, the Japanese had appeared to assert an air of superiority that other Asians, particularly the Chinese, resented. Further, Koreans had their own negative sentiments toward the Japanese due to Japan's occupation of Korea. The longer history in the United States and the larger size, relative to other Asian groups, of both the Japanese and the Chinese was a source of friction between them and other, smaller Asian groups. Due to the language, religion, and phenotype differences that the colonization of the Philippines by Spain created, Filipinos had been particularly ambivalent about their relationship to the Asian Pacific Islander category. As one Filipino activist is quoted as saying: "we are lumped together with Asians because of a geographical accident."[35] Americans from India likewise have their own experiences that separate themselves from the larger grouping, including phenotype, religion, and colonization by Great Britain. Many are English speaking and were not even included as an Asian Pacific Islander ethnicity on the U.S. census until 1980. Before that time, they were either marked as "white" or "other race"—an option that was not available to most other Asian groups during that time period.[36] This brief summary only scratches the surface of all the differences that were bridged to in order to create Asian panethnicity.

The genesis of an official Asian Pacific Islander category on the census by 1980 should not be taken as an indicator of a moment at which all individuals who might be considered in this category ceased to regard themselves as a particular ethnicity and began magically at that moment to be only Asian Americans. In fact, as many other constructionist scholars of race have shown, and as will be evident throughout the data presented here, racial and ethnic identities are quite fluid, taking shape and changing depending on one's particular circumstance. As we shall see throughout the following chapters, both Asian and Latino Americans may regard themselves primarily with ethnic identifiers at times, and at other times through more panethnic racial lenses. There are some respondents that feel so little in common with the others in their panethnic racial umbrella that they prefer to refer to themselves only ethnically, while others feel so alienated from a distant ethnic cultural past that they feel more comfortable with a racial identity like Asian American, emphasizing their primary connection to the United States. Clearly, these identities are highly relational and take shape according to one's relation to others, in family, neighborhood, and geographic context. Espiritu cites an example of a panethnic Asian coalition successfully organizing to get a bill passed in California that would require agencies to report separately their social service needs and participation rates by specific ethnicity.[37] Thus, while acknowledging that they would wield more political power as a unified Asian voice on this particular issue, they also understood that there were distinct ethnic differences within this category with vastly different resources and needs to be taken into account. There is tremendous interplay between race and ethnicity, and one does not get erased because another takes precedence at a particular time and place. While it is a minority of whites who assert their ethnic differences from their racial group at times (with no significant structural penalties or benefits for doing so), and a minority of American blacks who emphasize ethnic differences (e.g., West Indians, Haitians, Jamaicans, Africans) so as to separate themselves from the negative cultural stigma of African Americans, for Latinos and Asians in the racial middle, the interplay between race and ethnicity is more characteristically and consistently on center stage.[38]

Like Asian Americans, those who would describe themselves as being of "Hispanic origin" on the census are contending with a sizeable amount of ethnic diversity, and racial/phenotype differences as well. As Clara Rodriguez points out, how Latinos categorize themselves racially depends on who is asking and answering the question, the format of the question, and the context in which the question was asked. Because Latin Americans are weaving their own indigenous (and more fluid) concepts of race together with the more rigid U.S. racial protocol—which is in some ways similar but in others quite different—Rodriguez argues that much of the community would prefer being able to identify themselves both racially and ethnically, rather than having to choose one Hispanic or Latino "race."[39] Thus, as it stands now, the U.S. census states that "Hispanics can be of any race." That is, there is a separate question in which respondents can indicate whether they are of Hispanic origin but still choose from one (or more) of five standard racial categories: white, black/African American, Native American Indian, Asian Pacific Islander, or other. In 2000, 48 percent of persons who stated they were of Hispanic origin selected the "white" race, while 42 percent said they were some "other" race, and two percent chose the "black" race.[40] While there have been some discussions to move Hispanic from an "origin" to a "race" on the census, Rodriguez writes that most of that discussion has been initiated from outside the communities themselves, and most agree that rephrasing these questions that count Latinos could only result in lower counts of whites, lower counts of Hispanics, and an increased movement toward checking the "other" box, a choice that census officials highly discourage due to the difficulty of aggregating its results.[41]

Thus, the line between race and ethnicity is particularly blurry for those considered Hispanic or Latino. On the census, Hispanic is considered more of an ethnic identity than a racial one. The Hispanic/Latino category, however, is much like the panethnic racial umbrella of API in that it encompasses a variety of nationalities and backgrounds, without any unifying repertoire of cultural traditions. Latin America is a bit more of a geographically contained and linguistically similar region than that represented by the API racial category. But it is important to stress that even these linguistic and religious connections assumed among Latinos are not unanimous. There are an increasing number of Protestant Latinos, and one can point to the case of Brazilians who speak Portuguese, or Puerto Rican Americans who inhabit a territory of the United States and are only taught English in the public schools.[42] Political and economic experiences also have led to some Latinos preferring to identify along ethnic lines (separating themselves from their other, less-prestigious Hispanic counterparts) rather than racial ones. Further, phenotype differences in the context of widespread European colonialism in Latin America have resulted in distinct status differences between lighter- and darker-skinned Latinos. In the U.S. context, however, many have rallied around a common Latino experience, being perceived as a unit despite their differences, in much the same way that Asian Pacific Islander Americans have done. They have organized under the Latino panethnic umbrella to fight restrictive immigration laws as well as to obtain better bilingual education and interpreting services.[43]

In this work, I generally use the term Latino rather than Hispanic to describe this panethnic group. As with the conscious choice of the name Asian Pacific Islander as a more inclusive term, the term Latino is more inclusive than Hispanic because it seems to include persons whose origins are in Brazil and Portugal, in a way that Hispanic does not. Further, in much the same way that the derogatory Oriental de-centers the continent of Asia from a Western perspective, the term Hispanic asserts the centrality of the European Spanish colonizers, as opposed to Latino, which more aptly puts Latin America at the center.[44] Hispanic is also sometimes understood as expressing the "desire to achieve white status," while the term Latino suggests more of an awareness that "systems of the United States are unfair and should be changed."[45] Because I approach this work from the latter perspective, I generally prefer the use of the term Latino over Hispanic when I am speaking from my own voice. I privilege my respondents' usage of racial and ethnic terms, however, to describe themselves whenever I analyze the particular quotes they have contributed to the study.

Whitening, Browning, or Something "Other"?

The fact that Latinos and Asians are now interpreted on the national scene as two sizeable and significant racial groups allows them, especially when put together, to become the fodder for a national conversation about a changing future for race relations in the United States. Given the diverse ethnic peoples that make up these two groups, the pivotal question is how will they see themselves? Will they continue to be defined by the racial poles of black and white, or will they forge new kinds of race-related conversations and policy questions for the nation? As scholars debate what will be the outcome of these significant changes in the racial-ethnic composition of the United States population, their theorizing often continues along dichotomous options. Rather than reflecting a white/black dichotomy, however, this new theorizing posits a majority/minority dichotomy. There are two major schools of such dichotomous thought, and I will call them the "whitening thesis" and the "browning thesis."

The whitening thesis expects a black/nonblack dichotomy to emerge as a result of the growth of the Latino and Asian American populations. In this model, blacks will experience chronic alienation and powerlessness in the social order, while the racial identities of Latinos and Asians will initiate a process of "thinning," declining in salience for them as they increasingly access the privileges of whiteness, much like Irish, Italian, and Jewish Americans before them.[46] For these assimilated groups, one's racial identity as "white" begins to take primacy over one's ethnic connections, and ethnicity becomes largely symbolic.[47] This prediction is based on the classic assimilation model, as proposed by Milton Gordon, which postulates that immigrants move through a series of stages, incorporating them into various aspects of mainstream life in a relatively linear fashion. That is, once a group undergoes cultural, structural, and marital assimilation, respectively, we would expect the final stage of identificational assimilation to occur. When this happens, the group would no longer racially identify itself separately from the majority group.[48]

George Yancey has tested the whitening thesis on a national data set (the 1999–2000 Lilly Survey of American Attitudes and Friendships), which examines residential segregation, interracial marriage rates, and views on several political questions that tend to sharply divide white and black voters (e.g., welfare, affirmative action). Yancey's analysis places Latinos and Asian Americans in the middle stages of assimilation, because their residential patterns, marital patterns, and several key political beliefs align more closely with white Americans than they do with black Americans.[49] If Gordon's model holds true, then the next step over the next few generations is that Latinos and Asian Americans would move to identificational assimilation; that is, becoming white.

Focusing on Mexican Americans specifically, Edward Murguia and Tyrone Forman document how Mexican Americans tend to prefer spouses, neighbors, coworkers, and friends who are either Puerto Rican American or white, but not black. They also discuss the 1990 Latino Political Survey, which uses a 100-point feeling thermometer (from warm to cold), and Latinos consistently feel warmer toward whites than toward blacks. Interpreting these results, Murguia and Forman explain the "immigrant hypothesis," which asserts that "the shared immigrant ideology of Latinos and Asians . . . [leads to] distaste for blacks, whom they perceive as not embracing the achievement ideology."[50] To the extent that they align with this immigrant hypothesis, Latinos and Asian Americans both reflect the dominant color-blind ideology in the United States, which asserts that racism is not much of a barrier to the success of people of color, who bring their hardships on themselves.[51] This alignment with the dominant color-blind ideology positions them well on the whitening path. These authors point out that Latinos, however, and even Mexicans themselves, are a diverse group, and one's skin tone and educational level makes a significant difference in whether or not one rejects alliances with blacks. Mexican Americans with darker skin, higher educational levels, and those who are born in the United States are less likely to buy into the antiblack stereotypes of the larger culture than their counterparts, and recognize the significance of racism in their lives. But although certain segments of the Latino whole may be less likely to "whiten" than others, there are many attitudinal and behavioral variables that seem to support a transition toward whiteness for a substantial sector of the group.

It is important to note that, although it is closely related to theories of assimilation, the whitening thesis is not identical to the classic assimilation perspective. The whitening thesis defies the idea of a smooth assimilation process for all groups, and instead asserts that access to such privileges only comes to those who are allowed to step into the nonblack side of the black/nonblack dichotomy. Those left on the black side are prevented from achieving full access to the "American dream." The assimilation perspective tends to deemphasize the kinds of power differentials that have historically been so crucial in structuring black-white inequality, placing a group's attempts at becoming like the majority group at center stage to the neglect of the structural barriers that might prevent it from doing so.[52] As we can see from the above studies, as well as studies of other formerly not-quite-white groups (e.g., Irish Americans, Jewish Americans), an important part of the whitening process in the United States is distancing oneself from the perpetually stigmatized black group.[53] Advocates of the whitening perspective can document so many instances of such distancing that they predict that the logical next step would be for members of these groups to identify as, and become, "white."

The browning thesis, on the other hand, argues that majority-group power cannot be maintained in the face of the exponential growth of the racial middle. This thesis predicts that soon whites will no longer have a corner on the market. Whether this loss of dominance of the white majority is seen as a positive or negative change for the society depends on the version of the browning thesis one consults—the doomsday version or the optimist version. The doomsday version of the browning thesis, most notably publicized by Samuel Huntington, makes the argument that Latinos are "unassimilable" due to their alleged unwillingness to learn English and other cultural aspects of the United States.[54] The doomsday perspective on the browning of America is based largely on nativist xenophobia, coupled with nostalgia for a bygone industrialist society altogether different from the service-based global economy of today. This position is not given credence by most sociologists. Indeed, prominent immigrant experts Portes and Rumbaut write that it "runs against all empirical evidence and hardly deserves consideration."[55] Yet it has gained some momentum in popular culture and even in some political decisions, particularly with respect to U.S. immigration policy and the movement to make English the "official" language of the nation. Immigration history in the country demonstrates that if enough public fear exists about the perceived threat immigrants pose to a society, it can have deleterious policy consequences (and even violent hate-crime consequences) on the groups it demonizes.

On the other hand, there is a more optimistic version of the browning thesis that has taken hold amongst some sociologists, and in popular culture as well. Joe R. Feagin and his colleagues put a positive spin on the idea of the declining white majority. They believe that as the numerical base of those considered "minority" increases, more demands will be placed on the dominant white majority to share power in a more democratic and egalitarian fashion.[56] The historical examples of Red Power, Yellow Power, and Brown Power movements that organized in solidarity with the Black Power movement discussed previously are good illustrations of how cross-racial coalitions can raise demands for a more racially inclusive society. Further, studies of generational differences in the racial attitudes of immigrants that compare the foreign born with the native born have shown that with increased time in the United States, certain members of Latino and Asian American communities are more likely to express solidarity with African Americans than their recently arrived counterparts.[57] As opposed to the espousal of the color-blind ideology that the whitening thesis predicts, this optimistic browning thesis expects Latinos and Asian Americans to embrace a more color-conscious worldview.

The optimistic version of the browning thesis not only takes its cue from the U.S. context, but also adopts a more global perspective. The world as a whole is occupied by many more "people of color" than by European-descent whites. To the extent that the United States would begin to view its people of color as a resource in the global marketplace, the optimistic version of the browning thesis would be more realistic than the doomsday version. Further, the United States is in the minority on the global scene as far as its largely monolingual society. Many European citizens, for instance, who speak two or three languages, position themselves at an advantage in a global marketplace that values linguistic diversity. If the United States encouraged the "fluent bilingualism" of its Latino and Asian American citizens, scholars predict that it could have a decisive edge in the globalizing economy.[58] Thus, a combination of color-conscious (on the national political scene) and culture-conscious (on the global scene) outlooks is predicted by the optimistic browning thesis.

Still another group of scholars challenge both the browning and the whitening theses by foreseeing a three-way racial dynamic. These scholars, while not discounting either the idea of browning or whitening, instead focus on the tremendous diversity within both Latino and Asian American communities in the United States.[59] For example, the racial category of Asian Pacific Islander (API) includes ethnic groups whose incomes are above the U.S. average (e.g., Indians, Koreans, Filipinos) as well as groups who are well below that average (e.g., Laotians, Cambodians). The same is true for Latinos, whose Brazilian, Peruvian, Colombian, and Cuban members are close to the U.S. average income while Mexicans, Dominicans, Salvadorians, and Guatemalans are well below that average.[60] Facts like these income levels, combined with the various skin tones, religions, and nations represented within these groups, have led some to conclude that a partial section of Latino and Asian Americans may begin to "become white," while others will not. Eduardo Bonilla-Silva and his colleagues have even begun to sketch out a futuristic racial "trichotomy" that will separate out three categories: white, honorary white, and collective black. This schema challenges the notion that the more well-off and light-skinned Latinos and Asians would simply "become white," but rather would occupy a transitional "honorary whites" status. This intermediate status would afford them much of the privileges and esteem not widely accorded to people of color, but it would still be a conditional status, with the potential to be revoked in times of economic crisis or any other time in which those in power would deem them no longer worthy. Bonilla-Silva predicts groups like Chinese, Japanese, Koreans, Asian Indians, and lighter-skinned Latinos would fit into the honorary white category, while Cambodians, Hmong, Laotians, and darker-skinned Latinos would fit into the collective black category, along with, of course, American blacks.[61]

An earlier forerunner of this trichotomous perspective appears in Edna Bonacich's theory of middleman minorities. Bonacich argues that "middle" groups, such as Korean storeowners in Los Angeles, stand as a buffer between the exploited African American group and the white capitalist class.[62] Korean store owners occupy a privileged position relative to most urban blacks with whom they share the urban landscape, in that they have become entrepreneurs and thereby hold some measure of wealth, which local blacks have largely been unable to access. They are, in turn, able to turn a profit off the wages blacks in their community spend in their stores. Koreans, however, face their own obstacles. They still are beholden to the banks that hold their mortgage loans, or to the property owners to whom they pay their rent (most often members of the white capitalist class). They are also unable to break into the more mainstream markets for store ownership due to prejudice and discrimination.[63] Moreover, they become the scapegoats in times of racial/ethnic tension, like the 1995 riots in the aftermath of the Rodney King verdict, where Korean storeowners who had nothing to do with the all-white jury verdict became targets of looting and burning. African Americans, angry at a grave miscarriage of justice, focused their costly property damage efforts largely on other exploited groups in their vicinity, much to the benefit of the white capitalist class, who lost little in the incident. Although Bonacich does not refer to the middle category as "honorary whites," she captures a similar idea that members of middle groups might be elevated to a provisionally privileged status that would not be completely the same as that of "white," emphasizing the material differences between them.

Rarely has in-depth qualitative or ethnographic data been brought to bear on the question of both Latino and Asian Americans' perspectives on whether they are whitening, browning, or remaining in a distinct middle, as a group. Research that has asked Latinos and Asian Americans who their friends are, who they live near, who they marry, who they vote for, and so on, and then compares it to how whites and blacks have answered these questions at a nationally representative level, has made a valuable contribution by providing *some* generalizable patterns about these groups' attitudes and behaviors.[64] In order to fully investigate the color-blind ideology that facilitates the process of whitening, however, and the color-conscious ideologies that would accompany the browning process, qualitative methods need to be brought to bear on the topic. Although such methods invariably yield a smaller sample, and one that cannot necessarily be generalized to a wider population, they ask key questions that large-scale surveys cannot.

Such an approach becomes especially crucial for a topic where racial meanings are undergoing a process of transition and renegotiation. For instance, just because someone might not check the "white" box on the census form does not mean that they do not essentially think of themselves as white or even nonethnic and go about their lives in ways that position themselves as indistinguishable from whites. Their Latin-ness or Asian-ness, in this case, might only come out in the foods they enjoy on one or two particular holidays, much like Italian or Irish Americans. In contrast, a Latino or Asian American who *does* check the white box on the census, lives in a predominantly white neighborhood, and so on, may conceive of themselves very much Latino or Asian American and see themselves as more aligned with communities of color than they do with whites. In other words, the specific variables that certain social scientists have identified (e.g., political views, marriage patterns, residential patterns) may not necessarily be the same variables that Latino and Asian Americans have in mind in their understandings of who is white/American and who is not. Further, these understandings might shift for any given respondent depending on the context, an option seldom allowed for in survey research. Using qualitative data—in-depth interviews with fifty Latino and Asian American respondents—allows me in this study to explore the thought processes behind the negotiation and renegotiation of racial understandings for two groups rarely studied in this way.

In brief, what these Latino and Asian American respondents reveal is that the racial middle does not fall neatly in line with the whitening thesis, nor the browning thesis, even as some dimensions of both receive limited support. The trichotomy perspective, while it does acknowledge a distinct middle ground between whites and blacks, posits the third racial category as a watered-down version of whiteness—"honorary whites" —which needs to be further clarified by empirical data. The data for this study show that there is indeed a distinct racial middle that is not simply a lighter shade of brown, nor a darker shade of white. In asking respondents whether they face the kind of discrimination that blacks do, or whether they receive the same privileges that whites do, prior research has limited itself from finding out the unique ways in which the racial middle experiences discrimination, as well as the distinct ways that the racial middle perpetuates and participates in majority-group privilege. My aim in this book is to identify the particular experiences that are unique to the racial middle as they describe it. While the sample is not necessarily generalizable to the wider population, it represents a segment of the racial middle that other social scientists would probably expect to confirm the whitening thesis—college educated, fluent in English, and mostly raised in the United States. The extent to which my findings do not confirm the whitening thesis will hopefully raise new directions in studying these questions on a larger and more generalizable sample.

Sample and Methods

The data I use for this project come from fifty in-depth interviews with self-identified Latinos and Asian Americans. Twenty-three of the respondents are Latinos and twenty-seven are Asian Americans. The respondents were selected using a purposive snowball sampling method that had several different points of departure. The first attempt at gathering data began in New York City in the summer of 2005. Flyers were circulated via e-mail to student and community organizations that were Asian American or Latino in membership (e.g., student clubs, genealogical societies); these flyers were also posted in neighborhoods known to have higher

TABLE 1-1
Selected Demographics of the Sample

Race: Latinos = 23   Asians = 27

U.S. Census Race for Latinos: Other = 61% (14)   White = 35% (8)   Black = 4% (1)

Gender: Males = 22   Females = 28

Age: Under 30 = 32% (16)   30–50 = 50% (25)   Over 50 = 18% (9)

Generation: First = 32% (16)   "1.5" = 26% (13)   Second = 36% (18)   Third or Fourth = 4% (2)

Geographic Residence Experience: California = 20% (10)
                                   Other U.S. West[a] = 6% (3)
                                   New York/New Jersey = 42% (21)
                                   Greater Washington DC SMSA = 10% (5)
                                   Florida = 4% (2)
                                   Other U.S. East[b] = 18% (9)

[a] includes Texas, Utah, and Colorado
[b] includes Tennessee, Virginia (excluding northern Virginia), Kentucky, Pennsylvania, North Carolina

ethnic concentrations (e.g., Chinatown and East Harlem in Manhattan, Kew Gardens in Queens). Only seven of the respondents came from this process. Because it utilized "cold contacts" with no prior rapport established between interviewer and interviewee, and the budget was not such that we could pay the respondents except for that which would buy them a coffee or lunch (when interviews were held in eateries), there was no major draw for respondents to participate. The first set of interviews was conducted by me and an undergraduate student, Jennifer Conlon. Jennifer and I also each did one pilot interview, both included in the sample, with someone we knew who was willing to be interviewed for the study.

The second wave of gathering data occurred throughout the academic year of 2005–6. In the late summer of 2005, after returning from the New York trip, I attended a community event focusing on issues of concern to the local Latino community. Two respondents were recruited from the audience of this event, and several more resulted from the recommendations of these two interviewees. The sample continued to proliferate from the snowballing out from these respondents. At social events, whenever people would ask me about my research, often these people would recommend others who might be appropriate for the study. Because this word-of-mouth method created more rapport between interviewer and interviewee (we had a mutual contact person whom we both knew), it seemed to yield greater success than the "cold contact" method from the previous summer, so I continued with this approach. The following

TABLE 1-2
Ethnicities in the Sample as Compared to
Their U.S. Population Proportions

	Sample	National
Latinos (n = 23)		
Mexican	30% (7)	64%
Puerto Rican	22% (5)	9%
Cuban	9% (2)	3.5%
Other Caribbean	13% (3)[a]	4%
Central American	9% (2)[b]	7%
South American	17% (4)[c]	5%
Asian Pacific Islanders (n = 27)		
Chinese	30% (8)	28%
Indian	18.5% (5)	16%
Filipino	11% (3)	18%
Korean	11% (3)	10.5%
Vietnamese	4% (1)	11%
Pacific Islander	7% (2)[d]	4.4%
Japanese	4% (1)	7.7%
Cambodian	4% (1)	2%
Thai	4% (1)	1%
Bengali	4% (1)	less than 1%

[a] Includes 2 Dominicans and 1 Dominican/Honduran
[b] Includes 1 Guatemalan and 1 Salvadorian
[c] Includes 3 Brazilians and 1 Argentinean
[d] Both are Macanese

summer (2006), I had two new undergraduates assisting me (Leah Adams and Annie Hirschman), so I asked them to return to their hometowns for the summer to follow their own contacts and preestablished rapport to recruit qualified respondents. This yielded ten respondents who resided in the Northern Virginia/greater Washington DC area at the time of the interview, and thirteen respondents who resided in the vicinity of the Princeton, New Jersey, area at the time of the interview. I also continued following my own local contacts during this time. By September 2006, fifty total interviews were completed—twenty-one conducted by me, and twenty-nine spread among three different student interviewers.

Because the last wave of interviews was conducted simultaneously among three different locations and interviewers, there was not an exactly even 25/25 split between Latinos and Asians, and between men and women, as I would have liked. Coordinating communication among everyone as far as when to stop interviewing people from a certain demographic group when the "25 quota" was filled was a challenge across the miles, and I found it inappropriate and inconsiderate for interviewers to cancel out on a person who was already scheduled to be interviewed. Also, all the interviewers were female, which may have contributed to our difficulty with recruiting comparable amounts of men. The balance of 23/27 of Asians/Latinos and 28/22 of women/men, although not completely equal, provides a fairly sizeable and roughly comparable balance in terms of race and gender. Because it was not my goal in this project to attempt statistically significant comparisons, the ethnicity and gender breakdowns of the sample serve my purposes well for being able to take note of any particular patterns that may be heightened for one particular ethnicity or gender category over another.

Another area where demographics of the sample fall slightly short is geographic location, due to the east coast location of all three waves of interviewing. Only a fifth of our sample either grew up in or currently reside in California, while fully 30 percent of the nation's total immigrant population resides there.[65] Although none of us traveled to California, we were able to conduct interviews with a few people who were visiting from California, and with others who had grown up there. Additionally, three other respondents grew up in Texas, Utah, and Colorado, so there are a total of thirteen respondents (26 percent of sample) with a western U.S. frame of reference. While I was careful to attend to what might have been east coast/west coast differences in any of the major patterns I examined for this study, I actually found that the biggest regional difference in the data usually had to do with patterns that distinguished respondents from New York City *and* California from the rest of the sample. This seemed to be connected to the relatively larger concentration of both Latinos *and* Asian Americans in one place that most of the rest of the sample had not experienced. Thus, because a majority of our sample has connections to either California, New York, or New Jersey, and at a national level those three states hold about half of the country's total immigrant population, the totality of the sample does a pretty good job of capturing the geographic variation in the United States, for the purposes of this study.[66] Moreover, the vast majority of the respondents (41 out of 50, or 82 percent of the sample) either grew up or currently reside in one of the six largest population concentration areas: Washington DC metro area (including northern Virginia), California, New York, New Jersey, Texas, and Florida. Because these six states account for two-thirds of the total U.S. immigrant population, and four-fifths of our sample has connections to these areas, it is actually fairly representative on the whole.[67]

The sample also represents a variety of age groups. One's worry when conducting an interview study that originates in academe is that young adulthood will be overrepresented, due to the readily available student population. Only about a third (32 percent) of the sample, however, is under the age of thirty; exactly half of the sample is between the ages of thirty and fifty; and 18 percent of the sample is over the age of fifty. The immigrant population as a whole tends to have a younger age pyramid than the U.S. average, so this age distribution is fairly reflective of Latino and Asian American populations as a whole. Related to age (but certainly not identical to it) is the issue of generation. An important goal of the sampling strategy was to have a mix of generations represented. Thirty-two percent of the sample (sixteen respondents) came to the United States as adults and are considered first generation. Twenty-six percent of the sample (thirteen respondents) came to the United States either as babies or very young children—the "1.5 generation."[68] This includes three respondents who were born in Korea but adopted as infants by white families in the United States. It is important to distinguish these folks from the usual categorization of "foreign born" and thus first generation, because spending one's formative years in the United States is significantly more salient to the socialization process than one's place of birth. Most such respondents have limited memories of their country of birth, unless they have returned to visit it regularly in adulthood (more the case with Puerto Rican American foreign-born respondents than others). Thirty-six percent of the sample (eighteen respondents) were in the first wave of their families to be born in the United States, rendering them second generation. Unfortunately, only two of the respondents were of subsequent generations (third or fourth), but this is largely reflective of the total proportions of Latinos and Asian Americans in the United States (with the exception of a couple of specific ethnic groups within those categories, such as Japanese).

Perhaps the most central goal of the sampling strategy was to obtain a variety of ethnicities within the two racial groups. Nine different ethnicities are represented among the twenty-three Latino respondents: Mexican, Puerto Rican American, Dominican, Cuban, Honduran, Guatemalan, Brazilian, Salvadorian, and Guatemalan. Likewise, eleven different ethnicities are represented among the twenty-seven Asian American respondents: Chinese, Taiwanese, Indian, Filipino, Japanese, Korean, Thai, Bengali, Vietnamese, Cambodian, and Macanese. While ethnic diversity was the utmost goal, over and above having their proportions reflect their share of their panethnic group's population, it is indeed the case that the most heavily represented ethnic group in each category is also the most sizeable group in the overall U.S. population. Thus, the sample has more Mexican Americans (seven total) than any other Latino ethnicity (as is the case nationally), and there are more Chinese American respondents (eight total) than any other Asian ethnicity in the sample (also true on a national level). With five Puerto Rican American respondents being the sample's second largest Latino group, this also matches up with national patterns, because Puerto Rican Americans are the second-largest Latino group in the United States. The sample's second- and third-largest Asian ethnic groups are Indians and Filipinos respectively, while the next largest Asian ethnicities are Filipinos and Indians, respectively. Thus, the sample's top three Asian ethnicities match up with national patterns, even though the second and third positions are reversed.

With Latino ethnicities in particular, it is not as crucial that the percentages of ethnicities in the sample match exactly their proportion in the overall U.S. population, because Mexicans actually make up 64 percent of the total Hispanic population.[69] Thus, with a sample size of only twenty-three Latino respondents, this would have required that fifteen respondents be Mexican, and left us with only eight persons to represent a host of other Latin American ethnicities. Because diversity of ethnic representation was a key goal, it is necessary that all of the other Latino ethnicities besides Mexican are represented in slightly higher proportions in our sample than they would be in the overall Latino population in the United States. In fact, this diversity provides the study with some rich points of interethnic comparison among the sample.

Examining the Asian ethnicities in more detail, in most cases the percentages in our sample of each ethnicity are actually quite close to what they are in the total Asian American population. This was easier to do, because unlike Mexicans for Latinos, there is no one Asian ethnicity that account for more than 28 percent of the Asian Pacific Islander category.[70] Thus, in pursuing an ethnically diverse Asian American sample, we could also attend to national proportions. One additional Japanese respondent would have been helpful, because there is only one in the sample (although they do make up less than 8 percent of all Asian Americans); and with Vietnamese making up 11 percent of the total Asian population, we could have had more than one Vietnamese respondent as well. This could have been done by cutting down one or two on the South Asian (Indian and Bengali) respondents in our sample, who are represented in slightly higher proportions here than they are nationally. Because all this is a matter of one or two persons here or there, however, on the whole the sample is an excellent reflection of both the ethnic diversity within both racial categories and of the proportions that they actually exist in the larger U.S. population.

At its outset, an important goal of this study was to further explore the whitening thesis—substantiated in quantitative data—with in-depth interview data, which would elucidate the meanings behind what it meant for respondents to "become white." As I have clearly argued from the beginning, upon analyzing the data it became evident that the whitening thesis is only partly substantiated with these data. This conclusion could not be made, however, until after the data were collected. As a result, part of the purposive sampling strategy followed the whitening thesis by collecting respondents mostly on the higher end of the socioeconomic ladder. That is, fully *all* of the sample has had at least some college education, which, although reflective of national patterns for *most* Asian ethnic groups, actually places the Mexican, Cambodian, Dominican, Guatemalan, and Salvadorian respondents well above the national marks for their ethnic peers.[71] Because possessing a relatively higher socioeconomic status than the rest of one's group is a key factor in the "becoming white" process, the sample is chosen well insofar as the key purpose is to explore the whitening process alone.[72] Future research is necessary, however, to explore whether the same patterns I find in this work would evidence themselves in a sample that included greater variation in educational achievement.

Further exploring the "whitening" connection, I attempted to select respondents who did have intimate connections with whiteness when possible. Thus, fully 32 percent of this sample has an ethnically different partner or spouse, usually someone who is a non-Hispanic white. This may seem slightly higher than the rate of intermarriage in the general population; for instance, according to the 2000 census, one out of every five marriages (20 percent) for Hispanics include someone who is not of Hispanic origin.[73] By including unmarried partners and ethnicity differences, however, my own count is more inclusive and thus higher than that of the national census. Intimate connections with whiteness in this sample also includes having one or two (in the case of adoptive or step-) white parents—nearly a quarter of the sample (24 percent) has experienced this. Notably, all three Korean respondents were adopted and raised by white families in the United States; thus, we might expect these respondents to have a greater likelihood to confirm the whitening thesis than the more typical first- or second-generation Korean immigrant. One might even, at first glance, argue that this sample selection stacked the deck in favor of confirming the whiteness thesis. Indeed, I did not set out to confirm it; rather, I set out to explore it in more depth, actually taking the thesis as a given.

As data analysis progressed, however, it became evident that even among this highly educated group of Latinos and Asian Americans, there were some aspects of their narratives that did not fully jibe with the whitening thesis. Such aspects included experiences with discrimination, some racially progressive ideologies, and some views on intermarriage with whites (especially among Asian Americans). It may have been the case that these patterns could have been explored in more depth with a sample that was more diverse in terms of educational attainment. Thus, the reader may want to keep in mind that the reports of experiences with discrimination, negative views on intermarriage with whites, and the extent of racially progressive outlooks that I have explored in these pages may be *conservative estimates* of the extent to which these patterns exist in the wider, more socioeconomically diverse population. Because it was not my overall goal to estimate which percentage of the racial middle is whitening, browning, or doing something else, I believe I have explored as best I could in these pages the patterns that do not substantiate the whitening thesis. I will leave it to future research on more socioeconomically diverse populations to investigate whether these and other as-of-yet-untapped dimensions of the racial middle may exist to a greater extent on the whole than I have reported here.

Other aspects of the interview process itself may have yielded overestimates of the usual "whitening" indicators as well. Over half of the interviews (thirty-four) were completed by two interviewers who appear "white" to most U.S. observers. I was one of these interviewers, although throughout the interviews I made use of rapport-building strategies like mentioning specific examples of other persons of color who had experienced negative treatment from whites, and used other techniques to demonstrate that I would not be offended, and perhaps would even wholeheartedly agree with, certain critiques of whiteness or of whites in general. I am not convinced that the other "white" interviewer I refer to here made these efforts. Although in one interview she did mention at the outset (and a bit out of context) her recently discovered racially mixed background, on the whole this student interviewer remained relatively passive and did not engage in enough rapport-building strategies to offset the potential effect of her "race" on the interview. While this did not seem to affect the rapport of her interviews with several white Latino respondents, several of her interviews of Asian American respondents did not include the kind of give-and-take flow of conversation characteristic of most of the other interviews. This result could be due not only to her phenotype, however, but also her generally deferent personality, coupled with the older, first-generation, English-as-a-second-language respondents that were overrepresented in her particular set of interviews. Because of these factors, she may have been more willing to accept their responses at face value and not draw them out or give them more related experiences to react to.

The other two student interviewers were able to elicit particularly good rapport with respondents, due both to their interviewing skills and perhaps also their ambiguous phenotypes. The first student interviewer on the project has a Japanese American mother and an Irish American father. The interviews she conducted were all through cold contacts in New York City, but she was often asked during the interview about her own ethnic background. She explains that she (and especially her brother) is often mistaken for Hawaiian, an experience that several of the respondents (both Latino and Asian) also report. Her candor about her own experiences with the respondents, as well as her willingness to submit to my critiques after each interview and work hard at improving her technique, resulted in some interviews that include quite forthright, seemingly uncensored comments. The other nonwhite interviewer on the project has an African American father and a white American mother, though she is most often mistaken for South Asian. This phenotype, coupled with her selection of age peers, many of whom were either friends or shared a mutual friend, resulted in strong rapport in her interviews as well.

In all cases, respondents were interviewed using an interview guide[74] with thirty "questions." As can be observed in appendix A, many of these numbered "questions" actually include several interrelated questions under one number. As a result, most of the interviews took over an hour, and in some cases two to three hours. The normative length of an interview was about ninety minutes. The interviews usually took place at a public place such as a coffee shop or restaurant, or in the respondent's office or home. Interviews were taped and later transcribed without specific person or place names. This process yielded interview transcripts that were anywhere between six and forty-four single-spaced pages. Although this process included most of the demographic information about the respondent contained in the transcripts, information about the respondent's skin tone and English-language proficiency was recorded by the interviewer in a separate place, using a four-point scale for both. I did not examine coder reliability for these scales, however, because it was impossible for all researchers to view all the respondents. More than one researcher being present at the time of the interview would have significantly damaged interviewer-interviewee rapport. As a result, I do not attempt to do any systematic analyses or comparisons with this information. In the text, this information about a respondent is discussed only when it is relevant for analyzing particular quotes (most often accompanying anecdotes about times a respondent is mistaken for something she or he is not).

While no qualitative research project ends with a sample that completely matches the ideal visions with which the researcher began, the reader will find that the data analyzed for this particular study do provide a diverse assortment of Latinos and Asian Americans with rich experiences and views on a variety of race-related matters. For the purposes of this project, which explores in detail the meanings that respondents have attached to their race-related experiences, the sample and its methods provide an ideal starting point. Most respondents have provided quite candid comments that allow for some intriguing analysis of the complexities, and even contradictions, of life in the racial middle. I look forward to future research testing the utility of the concepts and frameworks I have developed from these data on other larger and more nationally representative "racial middle" populations. Indeed, I advance such ideas with the conviction that they would be useful to such ends.

Exploring the Racial Middle

As I present the data in the following chapters, I will first explore the meaning of racial and ethnic categories in the racial middle in chapter 2. As I have suggested here, the panethnic racial categories of Latino and Asian American are meaningful in some contexts for some respondents, but not so for others, who feel more allegiance to their particular ethnic communities, or alternatively to a more generic cultural category of "just American." Chapter 2 analyzes the particular diverse life experiences than bring respondents to such various racial and ethnic positions, and how the various meanings of different categories either repel or attract them as a result. Chapter 3 delves more specifically into the respondents' racial ideologies; that is, how they make sense of racial differences among groups and why certain groups are doing better than others. Whites and blacks have been shown to differ dramatically in how they make sense of such racial matters, and chapter 3 will investigate the extent to which Latinos and Asian Americans follow the typical white or black patterns, or their own unique racial ideologies. The next chapter (chapter 4) examines respondents' outlooks on racial intermarriage, which have been important indicators of racial attitudes and ideology throughout the history of research in racial/ethnic relations; they are no less significant as we consider the experiences of those in the racial middle. Preferences of whites over blacks as mating partners, in particular, give some insight into how the dominant racial ideology is internalized by nonwhites, and how they adapt it to fit with their middle position.

In chapter 5, I turn to the unfortunate reality of racial discrimination that permeates the lives of those in the racial middle. I focus particularly on the unique forms of discrimination that are typically not as prevalent in the lives of African Americans, such as language discrimination and the assumptions of "foreignness." I also examine the minimization strategies used to cope with these negative experiences. Those who are suspected of being un-American are caught in a double bind, for if they accentuate the difficulties they have had with being treated as fully "American," they run the risk of being viewed as all the more un-American in the eyes of the dominant majority. Therefore, I explore how they negotiate this precarious position in their dealings with prejudice and discrimination. In chapter 6, I consider a progressive subsample of Latinos and Asians, which alternatively does not minimize the significance of racial discrimination in the racial middle, and consider the life experiences that have enabled them to adopt such a critical eye toward the racial status quo in the United States. Finally, I conclude in chapter 7 by reconsidering the browning and whitening claims in light of the evidence presented. What does it mean to become white, or to be part of a larger community of Americans of color —not according to criteria used by prior researchers, but rather according to the voices of these particular respondents? Do they see themselves as negotiating between two sides of a racial dichotomy, or are they envisioning a society that is more multifaceted than that? To the extent that the latter is true, I will explore what such a multifaceted society might look like, by privileging the voices of Latinos and Asian Americans in the racial middle.

2

The Meanings of Race and Ethnicity from the Racial Middle

(*with Catherine Estevez*)

The racial categories of Latino and Asian American studied in this book are panethnic categories that only have meaning in the U.S. context. Persons living in South America or the Caribbean do not tend to refer to themselves as Latino or Hispanic, nor do residents of various Asian nations think of themselves as Asian where they are. Yet those living in the United States for a particular length of time, in the post-1960s context, have united together under these panethnic labels to give voice to their common experience. A distinct shift took place when the U.S. census used the racial category of Asian Pacific Islander (API) beginning in 1990, combining previously separate categories like Chinese, Japanese, and Hindu that had been offered as options over the previous century. And although the U.S. census itself does not allow for a Latino option for race, there is a separate "Hispanic origin" question that assumes a shared Latino collective identity. But as Omi and Winant point out, racial formation can be a project of those in power just as well as it can be shaped by those "from below."[1] So what do Latino and Asian American respondents think of these racial categories? Are these the categories that form the bases of their identities, or do other categories (ethnic, religious, national, generational) have more relevance for them? What experiences unite these two groups in the racial middle, and what are the perceived or real barriers between them? How do their relationships, perceived or real, with members of other racial groups, affect their sense of self?

Previous attitudinal research, which relies largely upon quantitative survey data, reveals a complex picture about how Latinos and Asians feel about whites, blacks, and themselves. Several studies show that Latinos and especially Asians may be likely to adopt the antiblack prejudices that permeate U.S. culture, particularly when they are foreign born. They are likely to see themselves as more like whites than like blacks, particularly to the extent that the dominant racial ideology upholds whites as most reflective of the American dream.[2] This type of research often, however, asks respondents to place themselves into a racial dichotomy of white and black, to which they themselves may not necessarily relate. Indeed, our research shows that in their conversations about race and ethnicity, Latino and Asian American respondents are most likely to discuss other ethnic groups within their own racial category more than any other group. Those in the racial middle become more salient for them as reference groups than most others, followed by whites. Although some would argue that there is a black/nonblack divide in the United States, the data show otherwise, at least from the vantage point of Latinos and Asian Americans. While upon mentioning blacks they are much more likely to react negatively than positively, the overall pattern is that blacks are absent from their explicit conversations. (That blacks might be unspoken but implied in other conversations is a topic we shall explore more in the next chapter.) The results show that there is a definitive racial middle, both for those who occupy it and for those who perceive it from the outside. It is a middle that tends to overlap with whites more than blacks, to be sure, but not to the point of respondents actually "becoming white."

Perhaps the most striking finding is that racial and ethnic categories operate more as sliding scales or continuums in the mind of respondents rather than as hard and fast classifications. That is, one could conceive of race and ethnicity as continuous variables rather than categorical. Race and ethnicity appear to be "relative" designations that take shape for respondents as meaningful or salient categories for them depending on the context or who is surrounding them. Respondents often evaluate themselves and others around them as "more Asian" or "less Mexican," for example, such that there is a wealth of additional meaning that lies behind a simple check mark in a box on a form. These shifting meanings are based in large part on perceived expectations—both those of their "own group" and of outsiders—of how someone who occupies a particular racial or ethnic category "should" act. Thus, how respondents see themselves, as well as how they perceive others to be seeing and interpreting their behavior, has relevance in this process.

How Latinos and Asians See Themselves and How They Are Seen by Others

In naming themselves, some respondents use racial and ethnic labels interchangeably, while others prefer ethnic terms because they cannot fathom relating to the whole gamut of nationalities incorporated into their racial umbrella (particularly the foreign born). Still others prefer the racial umbrella terms to describe their experiences, particularly when generations and upbringing have removed them significantly from many of the cultural practices of their specific ethnicity. Upon examining the respondents' reports of both the groups they feel closest to themselves and the groups they are most often mistaken for, it becomes evident that the panethnic racial categories of Latino and Asian are salient for Americans both in and outside the labels. Members of Latino and Asian American groups are often mistaken for other ethnicities within their own racial groupings, and they even more often report feeling similarities to those other ethnic groups themselves.

Taking a look at table 2-1, the most frequently mentioned category by far is respondents who cite another ethnic group within their own "race" as the group toward which they feel the most closeness. Although Latinos often make clear distinctions among Caribbean, Central American, and South American groupings, they are most likely to choose one of those "different" groups as the next closest to them upon reflecting on all of the other groups present in the United States. Similarly, East Asians and South Asians are quick to point out what they perceive as major differences

TABLE 2-1

Respondents' Perceived Relationships to Other Racial/Ethnic Groups

	Feels closest to	Feels furthest away from	Is most often mistaken for
Another ethnic group within one's same "race"	31	8	15
Whites, white ethnics, white Europeans	16	2	12
Latinos to Asians; Asians to Latinos	4	13	18
Middle Easterners, Arabs, Muslims	5	5	8
Blacks, African Americans	6	12	1

Note: Totals do not add up to 50 because some respondents cite more than one group they feel closest to, furthest away from, and/or are mistaken for, or alternatively insist that they could not answer questions that ask them to interpret their relationships through such racial/ethnic lenses.

among them, yet still find areas of commonality with other Asians in the United States context. Outsiders are less clear about such interethnic distinctions, in even broader strokes than one might expect. Although as respondents pointed out, Americans are famous for holding such prejudices as "all Asians look alike" or "all Hispanics look alike," the truth is actually that many Asians *and* Latinos look "all the same" to outsiders, because each gets misperceived for the other more than any other misperception —even more frequently than being misperceived as another ethnicity within one's own racial group. Thus, while Latinos and Asians themselves may be three times as likely to see themselves as diametrically opposed to each other than as comrades, those outside their groups may have a tendency to lump them all together regardless.

Looking outside these racial middle groups, the next group Latinos and Asians feel closest to and are most often mistaken for is whites. Sometimes respondents do not mention whites specifically but instead name particular white ethnic groups, like Italians, Greeks, and Jews, as groups that they feel are most similar culturally to their own. Other times, they actually point to their own predominantly white social circles and networks to explain why they feel most comfortable with whites. Whites are much more likely to be the group respondents feel closest to than the group from which they feel distant.

In contrast, blacks are much more likely to be thought of as a distant group from Latinos and Asian Americans than they are to be thought of as similar. Interestingly, when I analyzed each count in this table to see whether Latinos or Asian Americans were more likely to mention a particular group positively or negatively, I found that each count was pretty evenly spread between Latino and Asian American respondents, even for those who felt most distant from blacks. This seems surprising given that the survey data often posits Asian Americans as holding more antiblack attitudes than Latinos. There was one category in the table, however, that was unevenly split between Latinos and Asian Americans—those who feel closest to African Americans. Five out of the six who chose blacks as the group they felt closest to were Latino respondents (one Guatemalan, two Mexicans, and two Puerto Rican Americans). The sixth respondent, Levan, who is Cambodian, is an exceptional case because her discussion of blacks during her interview could just as well count as a testament to antiblack prejudice as it could be a statement of affinity toward African Americans. So by and large it is only Latinos who decisively count blacks in their "inner circle" of racial and ethnic similarity.

Even though these results, indicating a more positive read of whites than of blacks, confirm what survey data show about the "feeling thermometers" Latinos and Asian Americans tend to hold, it is important to note that neither whites nor blacks are ever mentioned by a majority of the respondents consistently. The one category mentioned consistently by a majority of the sample is that which includes the other various ethnic groups making up the respondent's own racial category. Thus, while race-relations scholars have often conceptualized the social location of Latinos and Asians from the vantage point of blacks and whites (because this is also often the lens from which whites interpret them), it seems crucial to also give voice to Latinos and Asians themselves. Their frame of reference is firmly based in that racial middle.

Panethnic "Races": Different but Similar, Relatively Speaking

Although respondents regularly find fault with U.S. racial categorizations that combine vastly different Latino and Asian cultures all under one pan-ethnic umbrella, they still tend to cite the groups within that umbrella as those to whom they feel closest before all other racial groups. Their responses highlight the acute distinctions between ethnicity and race, with Latino and Asian "races" being U.S. social and political constructs. Culturally, for instance, South Asians (Indians, Bangladeshis), Southeast Asians (Filipinos, Vietnamese, Cambodians), and East Asians (Chinese, Japanese, Koreans) frequently agree during interviews that they have little to nothing in common with one another. When they consider their relationships and/or comfort levels with other U.S. racial groups such as blacks and whites, however, they often admit that those "other" Asians would still be the group they gravitate most to, relatively speaking.

Debie, a Filipino respondent, highlights clearly this relational evaluation process in the following quote:

Sometimes if I'm at a party, and it's like all Asians, they're not Filipino, they're all Chinese, I'll find that I always relate to like the white person, [laughs] it's totally weird. And then when I'm at a party and it's like all white people, and there's like one like Chinese person there that I don't even know, I like relate to the Chinese person. I don't know what it is. Maybe it's because like I just, I identify best with Filipinos. But yeah, it goes both ways, sort of either way. I feel like, uncomfortable among too many Chinese or too many Koreans, because when there are a lot of them, I realize that I'm different. And like the same as like when I'm in a group with a lot of white people and I realize that I'm different, so I go to the closest person which will be an Asian of any sort.

As a Filipino American, Debie believes she has little in common with Chinese or Korean Americans. The panethnic racial category of Asian seems to encompass far too many foreign variables to which she cannot relate. In situations where there are enough Asians to where she feels comfortable —she does not stand out or feel overwhelmed by whites—she feels more confident in rejecting other Asians in favor of whites. In settings where whites are numerous (making her lack of racial power more noticeable to her), however, she ends up recognizing a shared experience of marginalization with other Asian Americans that is more racial than cultural.

A Chinese American respondent named Scott explains that there exist antagonisms among Asian American groups that are more attached to the histories of their countries of origin, which tend to evaporate or take on less meaning the longer one inhabits the United States. Being from a southern region of China (his father's family is Cantonese), he reasons that he feels more of a connection to Southeast Asian groups, while other northern Chinese may feel that primary connection toward East Asians, such as Koreans and Japanese:

Filipinos, I feel, are relatively similar to Chinese, and that's really, that's it. I would say, being from southern China, there's some affinity to Burmese and Malay, the Hmong, for example, and like Koreans and Japanese are sort of like those second cousins that you don't like, [laughter] you know what I mean? They're you're—they're related—now the northern Chinese are much closer to them, so, does that make sense? So it's kinda like, Northerners [American] feel more affinity towards Canadians, and as an American [from Texas], I'm much more comfortable around Mexicans than Canadians, so the southern Chinese really dislike the Koreans [laughs] and the Vietnamese, and the Japanese . . . nowadays I don't have any of that, but if I had to really rank them, so—although Vietnamese I would probably feel more personal affinity towards.

Pointing out "nowadays I don't have any of that," Scott compares the differences among the various Asian ethnicities to the differences between

Northerners and Southerners in the United States—there are cultural differences and antagonisms, perhaps, but none that would trump their collective identity as Americans.

Charlene also connects the distinctions she makes among Asian ethnicities to the "older" generation that was historically closer to those countries of origin. Specifically, she connects her own anti-Japanese prejudice to her elders' socialization of her:

> I think the only ethnic group that I have problems, and this is a clear prejudice on my part, is Japanese. Just because . . . well, truthfully, the Japanese invaded the Philippines, and during World War Two and repeatedly throughout history, and then there's some antagonism, it's sort of, it's much like the antagonism between the Japanese and Koreans and you know, I have very vivid memories of my grandmother and my mother and my dad saying very disparaging things about the Japanese, how they're violent, militaristic, colonial, that's not the way Asians are supposed to be, you know that sort of, people they killed, you know all sort of stemming back from those experiences. Well, my grandmother was a young woman during World War Two, of course my parents were just little kids, or just babies, or basically little, little toddlers and babies at that time, but they sort of inherit those opinions from their parents, and then they talk about it and so it, it is a prejudice that I have. And it's not like, you know, when I meet people who are Japanese, it's not a problem that I have, but you know, you hear something in the news about them wanting to strike references about World War Two from the textbooks and you're like, "Ah, such a Japanese thing." And, you know, this is probably really bad, but I have a really good friend who's Korean, and she and I, we get going about oh, "The Japanese," and we would just go and go and go about how awful they are. So I think, I don't think it affects the way I relate to people on an individual level, but it's definitely a prejudice that I have.

This history of Japanese efforts to colonize several other Asian nations has profoundly affected how members of the various Asian American groups feel toward each other, at least on an abstract level.[3] In an interesting off-tape conversation between two of the respondents, Brian, a fourth-generation Japanese American, and April, a Korean American adopted by whites, two close friends lightheartedly observed that there was actually what they believed to be a distinct hierarchy among Asians due to this history of conflict and colonization. Perhaps because both respondents were more removed, culturally speaking, from their biological families' countries of origin, they were more willing to engage in joking banter about this hierarchy. They asserted that the Japanese were probably considered most prestigious, followed by the Chinese, and then the Koreans. Thus, even though some interethnic tensions among Asian Americans may go both ways, there is a clear sense, even from the perspective of an "outsider" (generationally), that some groups are more positively regarded than others due to these various historical relationships.

Likewise, some Latino respondents assert that there exist status hierarchies within their own panethnic racial category. For Latinos, interestingly, at least two status hierarchies are identified across the interviews —one is organized by the particular ethnicity/country of origin (like that of Asians) while the other follows along skin tone, with the lighter the better. The latter type of hierarchy should sound painfully familiar to blacks in the United States, which may be one factor behind why more Latinos than Asians identified African Americans as a racial group to whom they felt similar. The skin-tone hierarchy is rooted in a history of slavery that both groups share, although arguably the Latino experience was not to the same extent as the chattel slavery of blacks in the United States.[4] According to Joe, a Cuban/white respondent, such labor/exploitation relationships, as well as socioeconomic status and political situations, are among the factors that delineate a Latino hierarchy. This discussion ensues in the context of Joe's primary assertion that other Latino ethnicities are the ones that he feels closest to, among all U.S. racial groups:

> Obviously the other groups, the ones that would be more closely is [sic] the other Latin denominations—whether it be Puerto Ricans or Dominicans or Mexicans or Colombians or Venezuelans. You can even break it down from there. I think with Cubans you find very industrious folks from South America, whether it be the Colombians, very good business- hard-working. It's funny because there's kind of a rivalry, a rivalry amongst you know like the Cubans like to bad mouth the Puerto Ricans, the Puerto Ricans and the Cubans both like to bad mouth the Dominicans, and then everybody likes to bad mouth the Mexicans. . . . So I would [say] if you're asking me who they most closely—are similar—obviously the other Latin groups. [Interviewer: And you said some of the South Americans within that?] Yeah, probably like the Colombians, Venezuelans, Chileans.

When taken together with the rest of his interview (see especially chapter 3 for more), Joe prides himself on an "industrious" work ethic that he believes other minorities, including some Latinos and blacks, do not necessarily share. Thus, he includes his own group (Cubans) with some Central and South American groups as those he believes are most high status, like himself, due to this perceived work ethic difference. For him Caribbean Latin groups seem to come next in line in the hierarchy, followed lastly by Mexicans, who "everybody" seems to "bad mouth." Elsewhere in his interview he ridicules the political situation in Mexico as "corrupt" and suggests that anti-Mexican stereotyping may be in part deserved due to such politics. (We will turn more critically to all the racist ideology inherent here in the following chapter).

While some ethnic hierarchy is discussed as politically based, other respondents, especially those from the Caribbean, discussed hierarchies that had to do with skin color. For example, Wanda, a Puerto Rican American woman and the only respondent in the sample who identified racially as black, recalls:

I know that some of my friends used to say, talk about blacks, you know they call them "*morenos*," you know, and then I'd say, "Well, you know, I'm *morena* too!" You know, and "oh no no, you're different. You're Spanish. You're Spanish, you're Puerto Rican!" and I said, "But my skin is still the same." I said, "It's a race." And you know, ancestry came from the same place—Africa. Because that's where the Africa . . . the blacks came to Puerto Rico. Africans, mixed with the . . . Indians, yes, and mixed with the Spaniards, and even the French . . . that's how you get some Puerto Ricans who are blond and blue eyed. There aren't many. But you go to Ponce, and you'll see some that still are there. I also remember when I was little hearing that you needed to advance the race. That's where I got the sense that, "You know, you need to do something about not being this black." [laughs] And your family is supposed to marry somebody who's a little bit more white than you, or have feature, I mean, they get into the features, and the hair! I go to Puerto Rico and they say to me, "Oh, you need to do something with your hair. . . ." [laughs] "Why do you do, why do you do this mess [wear your hair natural, without straightening it]?" "Because I like it the way it is!"

Other scholars have observed that there is much more of a mixture between the racial poles of black and white in Latin American cultures than there is in the United States. This in no way, however, renders such cultures racial utopias. There are clear values placed on lighter-skinned children even within the same family, and they, too, propagate white supremacist notions of "advance[ing] the race."

Several respondents discuss the desire among such Caribbean groups to claim European/Spanish/Castilian ancestry in order to assert a certain prestige. Michael explains:

> Every time I've been to Puerto Rico, I've noticed that with some of the Puerto Ricans down there, some of them, that kind of is a big deal with them too, that they're white Puerto Ricans. You know what I mean? And I think it's a socioeconomic status thing, just like over here. . . . In fact, this last time we were down there . . . we went to that famous fort, and the lady was talking, she was telling us, she said, well, on this side of the island is where you find all the blue eyes. And then I was describing this one part, and then she said, that's a very poor area. And [pause] as I was describing it, it was a very beautiful place, and I said, we went through there, and she said, well it's a very poor area, and that was where all the plantations were years ago, and that's where all the black people are. And this one, along the, this one area, and we went through there, and it was very very—you know apparently that is the black section of the island and it's near San Juan, and it's—but they got the prettiest, [laughs] the prettiest section [both laugh] but that's the one black section. . . . The trying to claim the European [heritage] . . . I even heard them, "Well such and such, her great-grandparent was from Ireland," there was always this being able to say that your ancestry was from Spain. Spain would be the number one . . . and then England and Ireland, because even the English came down there, and the Dutch, actually. Learned that the last time I was down there, they tried to conquer the island . . . the whole, that social status thing.

Elsewhere in the interview, this U.S.-born respondent discusses expecting Puerto Rican Americans not to harbor prejudices because they should be able to know how it feels to be stereotyped and not want to do the same to others. Although he too observed more interracial mixing and less racial tension when visiting Puerto Rico than he knew on the U.S. mainland, Michael still expresses a degree of dismay that skin-color hierarchies exist among Puerto Rican Americans.

Another Puerto Rican American respondent, Alfonso, agrees that there is a tendency to draw on the lighter-skinned ideal by claiming a closer connection to Spain in one's lineage than may actually exist:

> In Puerto Rico, we are all Puerto Ricans. But still there are some associations that are more cultural, or more—there are some associations that are more, there, showing appreciation for things, not so much Hispanic, but Spanish. That's what we would see as our roots there, they say our roots are Spanish roots. And many people classify themselves, "Oh, my grandfather is Spanish." They will say, "I'm black, but my grandfather was Spanish." And it could not have been the grandfather, it had to have been the great-great-grandfather, because there weren't that recent of migrations for the most part, so people tend to abuse that a little bit, and claim more recent Spanish heritage.

The opening of this quote, "We are all Puerto Ricans," reaffirms this recurring notion in the interviews that there may be a common connection that transcends divisions among Latino peoples, but there nevertheless exist various factors that make such a racial affiliation not nearly as homogenous as some outsiders may think.

Claudia, a Dominican respondent, likewise connects skin color and socioeconomic status to divisions among Dominicans themselves:

> Well we have different skin colors in our country. And . . . [some think] that they are white. I just feel shame for them. [laughs] . . . In my country, people are racist, discrimination. And we discriminate in two different ways: economic and because of skin color. [Interviewer: Oh, so those people who are wealthier are associated with lighter skin normally, or—] Yes. And it's associated with money, yeah, and [they say,] "Me, I have this position, and my skin color is lighter and [I] discriminate against poor people and people that have really dark [skin]. . . ." [Interviewer: Do you feel like that's here too?] Oh yes, definitely yes.

There are real divisions within various Latino ethnicities due to this skin-color and socioeconomic-status ordering, and these were most readily discussed by Caribbean Latino respondents during the interviews. Most respondents, however, link discussions of these divisions back to their family's country of origin. While Claudia admits that the hierarchies continue to exist in the United States, she still feels most affinity toward other Dominicans, and to other Latinos in general. (She specifically cites Puerto Rican Americans and Mexicans as other ethnic groups to which she feels closest.) Like the Asian respondents discussed earlier in this section, they feel that the tensions among their groups, whether between ethnicities or even within one's own ethnicity, do not trump the connections they have across the larger racial grouping, particularly in the U.S. context.

"Estranged from My Own": Degrees of Asian-ness or Latin-ness

Not every respondent, however, feels the closest connections toward his or her own racial group. Others feel estranged from their particular ethnicities, and thus from their respective racial categories, because of what they perceive to be their own "Americanization." What this process might mean depends on the respondent. For some who no longer (or never did) speak fluently the language of their family's origin, this "language barrier" is the primary reason they feel more comfortable among members of other groups. For others, simply having a majority of friends who are white, or living what they identify as a "Westernized" lifestyle, is what makes them feel they have less in common with their own ethnicity and race. The particular group that they feel most affinity toward due to this perceived estrangement depends on the respondent. Some cite being most comfortable around whites, some cite feeling closer connections to other nonwhites (Asians feeling closer to Latinos, Latinos feeling closer to blacks, and so on), and some say they can still connect to other members of their groups who are also "Americanized" like them.

As one fourth-generation Japanese American respondent, Brian, points out, "My great-grandparents came here in the early part of the twentieth century." As a result, he insists that he bonds with others on the basis of shared interests that rarely have to do with anything ethnic. Brian does not feel a particularly strong affiliation with either the category "Asian" or "Japanese" and indeed would refuse to even fill in the racial or ethnic questions on the census. He probably would not have even volunteered to participate in this research project of his own volition, but his (white) wife suggested we might be interested in interviewing him, during some casual conversation about our research interests at a party. In his interview, he asserts that there is only a small fraction of Japanese Americans that he feels he would have any connection with whatsoever:

> Just speaking for myself, I don't think I could really identify, I don't really identify with other Asian groups that are my age that are—I mean I can

identify with like other Japanese Americans in my age groups who have the same experience and family history, just because it's kind of similar in that way. [Interviewer: Right, but outside of that, would you say there are any others that are closer or no?] Outside of that, I don't, I don't think so, no.

Interestingly, Brian speaks a little Japanese, but only because he chose to take it up as a high school language in his California hometown. He likens his knowledge of the Japanese language to other Americans' knowledge of a language like Latin—he learned it as an academic subject and not through his family or any other ethnic connections.

A common pattern among the portion of the sample that were born and/or raised in the United States is that they describe no stronger connections toward their "own" ethnic group than with other folks who share their age and other "experiences." Several respondents reflect that the only set of people who share their ethnicity that they feel more comfortable with than any other group are their family members. Thus, it is not an ethnic connection as much as a family comfort level. Reena, a Bengali American respondent who was "foreign born" but raised in the United States, observes:

> The only Bengalis I would say I feel—I won't even say more comfortable, as comfortable being with than people of other backgrounds—is my family. I feel very comfortable with them, I feel as comfortable as I feel with my friends. But in situations other than that, I don't really feel more comfortable being with Bengalis, especially those who have more traditional values than I do because I feel like I'm an outsider with them. Even though I have other ethnic backgrounds than most of my American friends, I feel like much more of my values and my culture are in tune with that so I feel more comfortable with them than I do with other Bengalis. . . . I go to [names college]. There are a lot of them [whites]. And I don't feel any less comfortable with them than I do with my friends of other backgrounds. Like I feel more comfortable when I'm hanging out with a group of my friends who happen to all be white than I would with people who were all Bengali.

Reena is still fluent in Bangla and uses a mixture of Bangla and English ("Banglish") with her parents at home. So in this case it is not necessarily her lack of knowledge of the language, but other cultural factors that put her less at ease with other Bengalis outside her own family than with white Americans. Some respondents even feel they may be looked down on by those in their own group for not having a stronger connection to "their heritage." As Lisa, who also speaks fluent Vietnamese, notes: "Sometimes I feel like they know more about Vietnam than I do. I don't know if I have to be embarrassed because I don't want them to think, 'oh she's a disgrace' or anything."

In these discussions of what makes respondents uncomfortable around people of their same ethnicity, their perceived expectations of what it means to be more (or less) Asian or Latino emerge. Whether these expectations are perceived or real on the part of the respondents, they become the reality against which they measure how closely they identify with particular racial or ethnic categories. As one Macanese-Irish respondent named Crystal surmises: "When I'm around all Asian people, it's usually fine unless they're doing a real cultural thing, sometimes I feel a little bit out of place, like I'm not as Asian as they are." What does it mean to be not "as Asian" or not "Asian enough"? Clearly, respondents consider this racial category as more of a continuum than any sort of biological or genetic mandate. These discussions come up particularly (but not solely) among respondents whose parents are of different ethnic backgrounds, even when such ethnicities are both Asian, because the respondents' parents decided to stress the English language in the home and American customs, holidays, and so forth as the common denominator in the family. As Charlene states:

I certainly had friends, . . . acquaintances or people that I knew . . . who, I hate to say it, did the stereotypical good Asian thing, like went to med school, married the Asian doctor, had good little Asian kids, and never questioned all those stereotypical things that Asians are supposed to do. Like never question the decisions that their parents made for them, studied all the time, majored in chemistry or biology . . . My Asian friends are not like that, they're more like me, where you have a lot of white friends, you do things that are not stereotypically Asian, like major in English. We sometimes make fun of those people who are the "good" Asians about how "Asian" they were. And that's the adjective we used to describe that, and I don't know, it's really different. So, now that I think about it, when I think about those kids, almost the first thing that I perceive about them are them being Asian, whereas when I think about my friend [name removed] who did political science, like I did, and has a mixed group of friends, I never think of her as Korean. In fact, didn't think of her as Korean until . . . she sent out the wedding announcement and it has her formal Korean name, and it sort of struck, "Oh yeah, that's right, she is Korean." She just married a guy who's Italian, so it's not your stereotypical Korean. So I guess it's sort of the context who you surround yourself with, but then I guess even among me and my Asian friends, like how Asian, stereotypically Asian you act . . . and particularly, sort of your relationship to your family. Do you try to assert your own identity, and just tell your parents that this is not the way things are going to be, sort of question the decisions of your parents, which is not something that's traditionally done, or they don't, it's frowned upon in Asian societies to disrespect your elders in that way. It's sort of those people who don't break the mold . . . they look much more Asian.

Clearly, Koreans, Thai, Filipino, Vietnamese, Bengalis, Macanese, and Japanese all speak different languages. Asian Americans thus do not necessarily look to particular languages to assess whether someone is particularly "Asian," nor do they look at phenotypes. Rather, as the above respondent puts it, it is a combination of who one surrounds oneself with (in terms of friends, marital partners, and neighborhood) and how one orients oneself toward one's parents and fields of study. Because both Charlene and the friend she mentions here married white men and studied fields that are not typically associated with Asians (such as English and political science), they register on her continuum of evaluation as "not as Asian." It is important to note that the descriptor is "not *as* Asian" or "*more* Asian" as opposed to not being Asian at all. According to our respondents, there are *degrees* of Asian-ness.

Similar discussions emerge among Latino respondents. Although Roberto feels comfortable with his own family, and his Spanish language ability is "free flowing" with them as well, he feels uncomfortable with heavily Mexican American areas because he no longer feels Mexican enough for them:

There are some Mexican Americans, that, when I go back home, it's uncomfortable. And they're trying to make sense of me, and I'm trying to make sense of them, and when I'm uncomfortable around Mexican Americans, my Spanish becomes more choppy. And I know it does.

Because I struggle to find words, and I have to say, "How do you say," you know, in Spanish. But when I'm around my parents, my family, it's free flowing . . . so there are a lot of times when I feel uncomfortable in Mexican American areas, Mexican American districts. . . . I think my uncomfortableness has to do with my own—I've been [pause] [sigh] in the white world too many years. Like I said, everybody in grad school is white, when you go to conferences, everybody's white, I've grown a comfort around white people, that when I go back to a Mexican American community, I feel like a stranger. I've been estranged from it. . . . also my socioeconomic status, look where I live. I didn't choose to go find a barrio somewhere and live there. And I think it has to do with my education. . . . So the irony is that I'm uncomfortable amongst my own people when they're numerous.

Roberto agrees with the previous Thai-Filipino American respondent that part of the evaluation process of belongingness in one's group involves the people one surrounds oneself with (his spouse is also white but he does not mention that as a factor here). In short, he characterizes himself as "in the white world" too long. Considerations are also given, however, to socioeconomic status. This is where whiteness and higher socioeconomic status get fused in Americans' minds. Because he "didn't choose to go find a barrio" to live in, he describes himself elsewhere in the interview as someone who made an economic decision about where to live that has had racial-ethnic consequences on his life. Other Latino respondents cite similar class-related decisions that they feel have estranged them a bit from their ethnic group. Another Mexican American respondent, Peter, states: "Most Mexicans [who] know that I work in the law enforcement call me coconut or sell out, whatever you wanna call it, because I'm working for the white guy, which to me is just plain stupid." And a Puerto Rican American respondent named Maria says: "Since I'm getting my education sometimes you feel like you have less in common with them because your life is going in a different direction."

Here is where the Asian and Latino narratives about not fitting in with one's group differ—when considering the socioeconomic stereotypes of what it means to be "more Asian" or "more Latino." This Macanese-Chinese-Portuguese respondent, Rebecca, also felt estranged from her respective category (here "Asian") *not* because she her socioeconomic status was perceived as high/white, but because it was considered to be low/not Asian *enough*:

I actually don't feel comfortable being around Asians except for my family. . . . I couldn't relate to any other Asians there cause they grew up in [names wealthier areas]. I couldn't relate to the whole "I live in a mansion" were wealthy kind of—the Asians, and this summer I worked in the media company and it was kind of hard to relate to them because we all grew up in a different place—some grew up in California, some grew up in the Upper West Side, and, the look I would get when I say, "Yeah I'm from [New York neighborhood]," they're like, "Oh, oh," like, "That's unfortunate for your parents, I'm sorry they didn't make it."

Rebecca considers herself to be solidly middle class (her father is a police officer and her mother is an accountant), but because she did not hail from a more affluent neighborhood, as did most of the Asian students in her high school, she could not relate to them as well. She is one of the rare (four) respondents in the sample who feels closest to the other "racial middle" group.

In fact, all three of the Asian respondents in that particular subgroup (that feels closest to Latinos) discuss these types of feelings of not really meeting the expectations of their respective Asian group. And all three have lived in either New York City or California, where there is a relatively high concentration of both racial middle groups. All three of those Asian respondents also have a close friend or romantic partner who is Latino. As one Filipino-white respondent, Heather, observes:

I'm less comfortable around Asians and it's because I feel like an outsider, because, yeah, I feel like an outsider. So usually, like if I was hanging out with just all white people, then that would make me uncomfortable too because I would have judgments about some of them, I'm sure. And, yeah, so I don't like that feeling either. But especially the Asian people, like even if it's a bunch of Korean people and me, I still feel a little uncomfortable because I feel like an outsider. That I don't have the entire enrichment of the culture, so, yeah.

Although some respondents who do not feel Asian or Latino enough find comfort in the white community, this seems an equally uncomfortable prospect for some. While some of those folks just contend they would simply prefer a "mixed" or "diverse" group with many backgrounds represented, this handful named a specific nonwhite group with whom they would feel comfortable—but not blacks. Their precarious "middle" status in terms of the type of racism they experience sometimes made them feel less akin to African Americans. As Heather notes:

> Well, I think that for myself, I think I got into this last night with a black man. It's harder for me to identify with black people because sometimes it annoys me that they don't see the difference in me too. And it's really hard to argue that point sometimes. [Interviewer: You mean that they assume that you're just a white person?] Yeah. Yeah, or even, or even can't understand the trials that somebody who's of a mixed race might have. That bothers me.

Feeling not connected to other Asians, but also not connected to whites that do not share certain experiences of being "in the minority," Heather opts for the middle ground of Latinos. This relationship is particularly heightened for Asian Americans who are Filipino because of the Spanish Catholic history of the Philippines. As she points out: "See, I would like to believe that Asians are close to Hispanics. That's what I believe. The language that my mother speaks is similar to Spanish; the skin complexions are similar. They cook similarly. Yeah, I would say it's close to that."

Indeed, the one Latino respondent in the category who feels closest to the other racial middle group cites Asians because of some Filipino family members. This Salvadorian respondent, Mateo, reasons: "I have some Asians in my family—Filipino—I could identify myself close to them because of the culture, they're mainly Catholic and stuff like that." But even aside from the Philippines-Spain connection, the more crucial factor seems to be feeling estranged from one's "own" community, as evidenced by April, a Korean respondent who was adopted and raised by a white family (that she admits just "didn't get it" in terms of exposing her to any part of her Korean heritage):

> I don't know, I feel like I kind of fit in everywhere except for with Korean people, when I think it's hard. [Interviewer: Because there's more of that expectation there and you feel like you're not meeting it?] Uh-huh, yeah. And I feel like I'm not meeting it and that I am expected to meet it. Versus like when I hang out like with my friend, you know, she's from Iran, and of course at their house they're speaking Farsi, but nobody expects me to speak Farsi, you know, there's no expectation that I'm going to speak Farsi and then so people speak English to me.

April cites Mexicans as the group she feels closest to, in part because she lives in a predominantly Mexican community, speaks Spanish, and now has a Mexican husband and stepchildren. Part of this comfort level, however, seems to be with any group *but* Koreans, due to the fact that she perceives that she is not meeting the expectations of how someone from her "own group" should act.

These expectations for behavior for members of particular ethnic groups can sometimes be laden with gendered assumptions as well. As another Korean respondent, Sarah, who was adopted by whites, observes: "I think for women, Asian women, I think that they expect them to be docile, and quiet, and I'm not. So I don't know if that ever takes people aback." Such a discomfort level due to perceived unmet expectations of one's ethnic group, however, is not unique to those who are adopted or of subsequent generations. Even respondents who were born outside the mainland United States have a sense of not living up to cultural expectations. As Mya reflects:

> I don't know whether it's me uniquely, or other people, other Asians, but I actually [pause] feel more comfortable around non-Asians than Asians sometimes. Not because that I identify with white people, I don't identify myself as white, it's just because—it's because a lot of traditions, that's why what I am saying is a restriction, because of Asian females makes me, I don't necessarily agree with that, and non-Asians, they don't expect anything, so they don't see anything beyond the box. But with an Asian, they see me, they go out of box, they know I'm out of the box, you know what I'm saying?

There is a repeated theme in the interviews of feeling safer with "outsiders" because "they don't expect anything." Whether expectations are seemingly "positive" or "negative," they can be daunting to live up to, and respondents tend to use a process of elimination to figure out which group will have the fewest expectations of them, drawing from their own diverse experiences as to who that group might be.

These gendered expectations affect Latina women as well. Wanda, a black Puerto Rican American respondent, who attributes her outspokenness mainly due to her age (she is retired and done with "pleasing others"), observes: "I think a lot of the Spanish people think, when I'm in the group, they consider me probably a rebel and pretty outspoken. I don't know my place." Not "knowing one's place" is where the expectations of the majority culture also come into play. When respondents talk about all the expectations they are or are not meeting, they are addressing several different types or levels of expectations. There are the perceived expectations of one's ethnic group, which include speaking the language, marrying within the group to preserve the heritage, practicing the religion (if there is one), respecting one's elders, and so on. Then there are racialized expectations, which are often perceived as coming from *outside* one's own ethnic group—that Asians will be smart, that Asian women will be "docile," that Latinos will have a darker phenotype, and so on. In this case, members of this group may feel "outside the box," that they are not meeting such expectations, but often they also recognize that members of their ethnic group realize, from experience, that people from their particular group come in all shapes, sizes, colors, personalities, and ability levels. Racialized expectations of one's group from outside one's own culture, however, can also become internalized and operate to constrain one's own actions and sense of self.

Michael describes why, in the past, he was uncomfortable sometimes to be among other Puerto Rican Americans:

> When I was younger, I was more comfortable around people that were the same social status. Which—we grew up somewhat poor—but I didn't like, there are the stereotypical Puerto Ricans that are loud, and blah blah blah . . . and they make, they bring attention. And that used to embarrass me when I was younger. That really embarrassed me when I was younger. Because I knew how everybody, you know, I knew. [pause] [Interviewer: How everyone was perceiving it?] How everybody around us was perceiving it, right—when I was younger. Now [pause] it doesn't even—when I'm around Puerto Ricans it doesn't even—although there's not a lot around here. But when I'm around people that speak Spanish, whenever, no big deal.

In his youth Michael distanced himself from his own group to achieve a greater sense of security, thinking that he could protect himself from the negative racial stereotypes applied to it. Through this distancing process, he came to develop some contempt for "his own" people. Although he has since grown more comfortable "in his own skin," so to speak—he has developed self-confidence in part by achieving a prominent position in the community and upper-middle-class status—he still inhabits a predominantly "white world," as evidenced by his comment that "there's not a lot [of Puerto Rican Americans] around here." Notice also that the stereotype being reacted to here places Latinos at a lower socioeconomic status and as "loud," in contrast to the racializing of Asians at a higher socioeconomic status and quiet. In the next chapter, on racial ideology, we will pay more attention to these different stereotypes and what function they have typically served for each group. For the purpose of this chapter, however, it is evident that regardless of the particular content of the stereotype, Latinos and Asians both negotiate their identity evaluation process (how Asian or Latino am I?) by evaluating themselves against these preexisting notions about their respective groups.

Who Is "American"? Negotiating Race, Ethnicity, and Nationality

As we have seen in table 2-1, while one's own ethnic and racial groups are the most frequent reference group brought up during the interviews, the second most often mentioned reference group for these respondents is whites. When evaluating the afore-mentioned question of "how Asian or Latino am I?" it becomes evident that the respondents most often use the two poles of (1) what they consider to be the typical behavior for their racial-ethnic group and (2) what they consider to be "white" behavior as they evaluate where they are on the continuum of Latin-ness or Asian-ness.

Many of the respondents consider whites as the center or point of reference when they begin discussing other groups, probably because they are the people and faces with which they have the most contact, whether in the media, their educational experiences, or on a day-to-day basis. This usage by Latinos and Asians may originate from a hegemonic view of how whites perceive them; Latinos and Asians in turn are held by these white standards and form responses to such perceptions through a whitewashed lens. Some respondents start out by defining anyone outside their ethnic group as "non-___" (e.g., "non-Mexican"), and through their response, end up referring specifically to whites.

Almost all the respondents used the word American in a multicultural, all-encompassing, nationalistic way. For example, Peter, Joe, and Juanita, respectively, had very nationalistic and ideological claims of how

American they are: "One hundred percent American in my book," "True-blood USA American," "We're all technically Americans, whether North, Central, or South." Many refer to others outside their group in a very distinct manner, however, particularly referring to whites as "Americans." In fact, close to half of the respondents also denote "white" as "American," "America," or "North American."

For some respondents, the term "American" is synonymous with "white" seemingly because all other descriptors have already been taken to describe themselves or other groups—there are Asian Americans, African Americans, Mexican Americans, and then there are just Americans. So on the surface, it may seem that everyone is categorized by their race, and because whites come from a multiplicity of nations and make up the majority of American society, they adequately fill the "American" category. It is important to point out here, however, that respondents used ethnic labels like Puerto Rican American or Japanese consistently more than larger racial groupings like Hispanic or Asian, but not in ways or for reasons that one might think.

At first glance, it seems that this may be a generational phenomenon, that foreign born are more likely to use an ethnic label to describe themselves because of stronger ties to their native country. On the contrary, it is actually by breaking down the age groups that one is able to see the difference in usage of ethnic and racial labels. Those under thirty are only 1.5 times more likely to use an ethnic label to describe themselves or others, while respondents over the age of fifty are 4 times more likely to use an ethnic label rather than a racial label.

TABLE 2-2
*Frequency of Usage of Ethnic and Racial Labels to
Describe Oneself*

	Ethnic Label	Racial Label
Generation		
First (moved to U.S. as an adult)	13	6
1.5 (foreign born but raised in U.S.)	8	2
Second (born in U.S.)	13	5
Third	2	—
Fourth	—	1
Age		
Under 30	9	6
30–50	17	6
Over 50	8	2

TABLE 2-3
Respondents Who Equate "American" with "White" by Age

Age	American = White	% of Age Group Who Uses It	% of Total
Under 30	13	81% (13/16)	26% (13/50)
30–50	7	28% (7/25)	14% (7/50)
Over 50	3	33% (3/9)	6% (3/50)
Total	23	—	46% (23/50)

What does this have to do with Americans and whiteness? As older respondents are more likely to use ethnic labels to define themselves and others, younger respondents are not as likely to use ethnic labels and *more* likely to associate American with white. The younger respondents' focus is not on isolating individual ethnic groups, but does consider their American point of reference as being white. That is to say, younger respondents place less social distance between American-ness and whiteness *and* are more likely to use broader racial groupings (Asian American, Hispanic American) than are older respondents. In fact, most of the respondents who make such an association fall under the age of thirty, and nearly all (over 80 percent) of those under thirty in some way refer to American as being white. (See Table 2-3.) Such a phenomenon among younger respondents illustrates an alignment or acknowledgement of American-ness and whiteness that is not present in other age groups.

As Murguia and Forman note, the use of the word American in discussing one's own heritage or social environment indicates a less severe social distance between oneself and the majority society of whites.[5] Yet this is not exactly what the respondents are saying; rather, in their responses they place little social distance between being white and being American, and then decide how white they are to determine how American they are.

While it may be clear, the process of equating American-ness and whiteness is neither conscious nor overt. The respondents almost invariably connect the two ideas—being American and being white—in an inadvertent way, where they themselves do not realize the shift in context or subject (subject as in who the interviewer and respondent are actually talking about). While not directly asserting that Americans are white by nature, respondents would relate one's physical whiteness or ability to pass as white in the same breath that they discuss ideological concepts held by whites. As Juanita notes: "So we could pass, my mother and I, and a lot of us, could pass for white or at least mixed. And she to fit in somewhere, to fit with people, to fit with something she knew was definite and concrete, went with that white crowd and assimilated into it and identified herself with a patriotic American person."

Juanita later explains: "So they assimilated very quickly and are still very harsh on the fact that you are in white America, you are an American, you are, you know, practicing all the American traditions. You are not Mexican." To this twenty-year-old, patriotism, Americanism, and whiteness go hand in hand. But she does not subscribe to them entirely as her mother may have; rather, by being in white America, she cannot fully be herself. Interestingly, Juanita refers to herself as Mexican American throughout the interview, illustrating Murguia and Forman's point that she places little social distance between herself and white society while maintaining her own identity through her self-definition and responses.

Another respondent, Peter, can align with Americans in that he is "white on the inside, brown on the out." While he does have Latino friends, he and his friends relate mostly with whites and, as he claims, "most of them are Americanized" just like himself. Peter comes to the logical conclusion that his inner whiteness makes him Americanized, yet he refers to himself consistently as Mexican. Again, we see that while one may feel American or Americanized, their sense of their race or ethnicity still defines them in a way that keeps them in the middle ground. That is because one's placement on the racial-ethnic continuum is not static. Espiritu refers to this process as "ethnic switching," where a person decides whether he or she is Japanese American or Asian American depending on which ethnic identities are available.[6] The same is true here—the "Americanized" respondent is more "American" in the context of white society, but still associates with his nonwhite side in referring to his "fundamental" ethnic identity.

Often, respondents discussed their perception of whites or Americans while talking about stereotypes, ethnic background, or relating experiences they've had, but some instances came up during policy questions as well. Debie discusses the lack of bilingual education in America, she contends that "we are being white supremacist, going, 'we just need to learn American, it's not a big deal, we can get by.'" The strong words of sarcasm here are indicative of the animosity she feels toward hegemonic white culture. Debie relates America to a monolingual nation, which is further tied to white supremacy, which standing alone should have no bearing on one another. Manifested in the responses is a push and pull dialectic where Latinos and Asians relate to American practices but are clearly not full participants of white culture.

Several respondents noted that being American as their nationality can sometimes be confusing for others and disrupt their own sense of identity. On a basic level, Jon got confused when the interviewer posed a question about "American stereotypes" and needed to clarify if he should respond about Americans in general or specifically about whites. Another, Juanita, distinguished between "feeling American" and "feeling white American." These are just two simplistic examples, but there are many, most of which are more significant. Ricardo explained: "It comes back to the whole idea that American means white in their eyes, so, I'm not white, so I must not be American. I think this is an assumption that a lot of people make and it leads to a lot of misperceptions." Many have a hard time balancing the fact that they were born in America, and are therefore American, yet they are not perceived as such socially because they are not white.

But while some respondents are able to recognize in a calm manner the association between being American and being white, it is not so easy for others. One Cambodian respondent, Levan, mentioned above for her back-and-forth attitudes about African Americans, had an equally inter-esting take on what it is to be "American." In answering a question about Asians who change their names, the respondent said,

> There will be like those Asian pride girls and their Asian pride guys who stick to their only Asian groups and they hate on white people and they'll see me and [mutual Vietnamese friend], and they'll be like, "Oh look at those girls, they're so whitewashed," but we're not whitewashed, we're fucking normal. We're American, we're not whitewashed just because we don't like to stick with only our cute little girlfriends who are Asian with their platform shoes and dangling bells and our boyfriends in their little speedy cars does not mean we're whitewashed.

Here, Levan was trying to separate the association between being Ameri-canized and being "whitewashed," yet in other situations, she asserts her closeness with whites (and distance from African Americans) as being a positive attribute. Clearly, the link between white and American can cause an identity dilemma that may be unique to those in the racial middle.

I Am What I Am Not: Why Certain Groups Are "Not Like Us"

Of course, much of this identity-building work is shaped by racist ideology, to be covered in the next chapter. But we would be remiss if we did not at least address briefly in this chapter the striking pattern in table 2-1—that just as many (if not more) Latinos see Asians, or Asians see Latinos, as the group that they are the most distant from, as both groups see blacks as the group they are most unlike. Indeed, more than three times as many Latinos and Asians see that other racial middle group as distant than those who see them as familiar. Similarly, twice the number of respondents see blacks as the group they are most distant from than those who see them as a close or similar group. In contrast, sixteen respondents feel closest to whites while only two feel distant from them. We have already seen how primarily members of the second generation decide that they have been surrounded by whites and are used to them, sometimes more than their own group. So perhaps it is *lack* of contact with members of these other groups that makes respondents feel distant from them. Likewise, other respondents cite cultural practices of particular white ethnic groups with which they identify—such as religion, work ethic, and modes of expression/celebration (Jews, Italians, and other Mediterranean groups were identified in those cases). So it could also be such cultural practices—whether perceived or gained through actual contact with them—that make respondents feel distant from Latinos, Asians, and blacks.

Upon investigating whether such cultural factors or lack of contact are more influential on people's social distance perceptions of different groups, we find that lack of contact is more likely to be a reason given for not feeling closer to African Americans than it is for those in the racial middle. Also, most of the respondents who give the reasons that they have not had much contact with blacks are those who came to the United States as adults. For example, this Chinese-Taiwanese American respondent, Ly, who feels distant from both Latinos and blacks, says: "[They're] not harder to identify with, just there's not a whole lot of interaction with —the Latinos or the blacks. Or maybe it's the community we live in, where you just don't interface a lot." And Jim, another Chinese-Taiwanese American respondent, similarly states: "I will say usually the African American, I cannot say truly because I do not get to talk to them . . . so I cannot say hey, they are truly different than us. They may be the same, we just don't have enough exposure to them." Likewise, Elisa, an Argentinean respondent, observes:

> Yeah, I don't know Asians or blacks, so I could say, I would probably feel more comfortable around white people, because I don't know, I mean I would like to know more, but I just—I just don't. . . . The only races that I don't know anything about, or that I haven't been in contact much is the black and yellow. Yeah, I don't know Asians or blacks, so I could say, I would probably feel more comfortable around white people, because I don't know, I mean I would like to know more, but I just—I just don't.

Ly, Jim, and Elisa, due to lack of contact, leave open the question of a possible coming to awareness in the future, but for now, due to lack of contact, choose whites over other ethnic groups. These respondents are likely to combine more than one racial group together when they describe their lack of contact, making the spatial reasoning, as opposed to cultural, more overt.

Those respondents who choose the other racial middle group as that which they feel least comfortable with are much more likely to cite perceived cultural or behavioral differences than they are to cite lack of contact as the reason for their discomfort. Only three respondents cite lack of contact as their primary reason in this case, and all three are Latino respondents who are categorized as progressive (using criteria outlined in chapter 6). Because they will be quoted later on in the book, we will not quote from them here, but suffice it to say that, like the above respondents, they leave open the possibility to learning more in the future. In contrast, most of the others speak with some certainty about what they perceive to be cultural differences between them and the other racial middle group. One Brazilian respondent, Tomas, for example, who feels closest to white ethnic groups like Italians and other Mediterranean groups because of their perceived emotional expressiveness, says of Asians: "It's not a culture that [small pause] that I identify much with. I have to make an effort to engage, and to be with them." Juanita cites the perceived difference in religion he would have with both Asians and Arabs as reasons why he feels most distant from them. And Christopher, a Dominican-Honduran respondent, quoted at length in the next chapter for saying "an Asian is the opposite of a Latin," cites everything from "they bow, they don't embrace" to "they're detail oriented people" to the way he perceives them showing "honor" to their families.

Asian American respondents, like the above-cited Latinos, are also likely to draw on specific cultural details when describing their distance from the other racial middle group. For instance, this Bengali respondent, Reena, states:

> Probably the most distant, maybe like Hispanic maybe. Just because I feel like, I don't know. They're pretty liberal in terms of—I don't know why I just thought about this—but in terms of alcohol and stuff like that, we're very against drinking and stuff. But in a lot of—just because in Hispanic culture like it's common for children to have like a glass of wine at fancy occasions and stuff like that and there's like, I don't know, loud music and celebration and lively traditions that we don't have. Our culture, like the traditions and special ceremonies that we have tend to be more subdued and conservative.

Although occasionally some value judgments appear to enter into these statements, for the most part they appear to be accurate characterizations of both cultures as some of the practitioners experience them. For instance, the "loud music and celebration and lively traditions" that Reena perceives as lacking in her own culture are exactly what Tomas finds lacking in his experience with Asian cultures as well. While certainly there will be individual variations in whether or not members of these groups participate in these customs, in large part they characterize their differences as those of ethnic customs and practices that are not particularly racialized.

In contrast, when members of the racial middle discuss their differences from African Americans, there is much less likely to be any discussion of customs, celebrations, and the like. Rather, the framing of the differences is either in the above-mentioned lack of contact category, or in a category we will call different approaches to/experiences with discrimination. When asked if she feels close or distant from African Americans, relatively speaking, one Puerto Rican American respondent named Caitlin explains:

> I think we can identify with the racism part of it, and I think we can identify with the even some could possibly identify with the slavery piece since Cuba and Puerto Rico also have, and Brazil, and all of these groups have had slavery. But I think there's some distinct historical things that

sort of make it difficult sometimes to, I can't possibly understand what it was like to grow up in a country where things were *segregated*. I don't have, I don't even know what that means. I mean I can't imagine *that*. So I think that's different.

Some Puerto Rican American respondents in particular who could pass for white acknowledged that their experiences with discrimination could not approximate that of African Americans. A similar point is made by Alfonso, another Puerto Rican American respondent, who is a student of genealogy:

I think still African Americans have it a little worse, worse problem with discrimination. . . . I think I would have the hardest time identifying with African Americans. [Interviewer: Because of that differing experience with discrimination?] Right . . . I've learned in the studies of my family that on my father's side my great-great-great-grandmother was a slave in Puerto Rico, something that my parents didn't know . . . her grandmother was a free slave—free black—and her great-grandmother was a slave. . . . I think it's very different. I don't think I can claim to, you know, I don't think it would be fair for me to say, oh, I am black like you, my brother, because I haven't suffered discrimination like they have suffered. . . . My grandmother, my father, pass as white. . . . So we really haven't suffered the same way as other people have.

While there is some shared history of slavery and colonization, and even some "mixing" with blackness in the Puerto Rican American experience, lighter-skinned Puerto Rican Americans understand a difference between themselves and African Americans. This stands in stark contrast to Wanda, our black Puerto Rican American respondent, who feels equally comfortable with both Puerto Rican Americans and African Americans. The respondents are therefore clearly referring to a racial (and not ethnic) difference between them and African Americans.

One Filipino respondent, Jon, makes a similar point that, regardless of a shared history of exploitation, there are racial dynamics in the U.S. context that preclude Asian Americans in particular from identifying with black Americans:

Well, I identify with Africans, African Americans in the sense that we, Filipinos share the having been colonized and the aftereffects of colonization, not pretty, so I share that with Africans, but I always look at the African Americans have a stronger voice, I don't know why that is. Maybe because typically they've been here longer, so maybe they have more ownership over being a minority and we don't yet, but I think, I think that'd probably be a good answer. As an Asian, I don't identify with as much, even though I do, with Africans and Hispanics because Filipinos and Asians are viewed as the model minority. And I don't know why that is, why whites have modeled the Asians as the model minority. It's like that dumb kid in class, you always want to single somebody out as, you say, "Oh that person so-and-so, they can do it, why can't you?" Or when there's like another kid in class who's dumber than you or not on the same level as you, you try to be just a little bit smarter than that person so you don't look as bad. To be popular with the in crowd. And I identify with all the minorities, but as an Asian, as a model minority, you know, there is some sense of discontinuity between Asians and blacks or Asians and Hispanics. So, yeah. That was longer than it had to be, but got it out, got it out.

Jon clearly treads carefully around laying out his answer to this question, as manifested by the back-and-forth rhetoric of "I don't identify as much, even though I do. . . ." Interestingly, there are two main reasons he gives for not identifying with African Americans. The first one he identifies with a sense of envy and almost admiration, that blacks have a "stronger voice." Another Chinese-Taiwanese American respondent (quoted above for feeling "out of the box" of "Asian females") voices this same sentiment, of regret actually that Asian Americans are not more politically organized. Yet the second reason Jon identifies—for feeling "discontinuity" between blacks *and* Latinos—is this idea that he is a "model minority" and the other groups are not. Even though he distances himself a bit from this idea as juvenile, "kid in the class" logic, it has nonetheless affected his sense of solidarity with these groups.

Comparing these perceived ethnic and racial dividing lines among groups, it becomes evident that respondents take stock of both the racial and ethnic landscapes in the United States as they make assessments about which groups they identify and relate to most. Ethnic customs and practices, as well as racialized social structures, play a role not only in how closely respondents relate to "their own" categories, but how they relate to others as well. As we shall see more plainly in the next chapter, though, all groups are not equally "ethnicized" and "racialized" within

U.S. racist ideology, and respondents have internalized such messages to varying degrees. Racial and ethnic categories only take shape and meaning within such a racially structured system, which is held in place by such an ideology.[7]

Conclusion

While respondents do sometimes reference other racial groups to frame their own sense of racial/ethnic identity, by and large they look closer to "their own" ethnic and racial groups. As they do so, they are filtering through their own experience of ethnicity (often largely based on their own family experiences) along with their own sense of what members of "their own" groups (both ethnic and racial) expect from them, as well as what others outside of those groupings expect.

There is some sense that society expects them to be able to identify with their entire panethnic racial umbrella (either Latino or Asian American), and they tend to protest this form of sweeping generalization as neglectful of crucially important differences. There is also a sense, however, that, particularly in the context of predominantly white groupings, the panethnic label is able to capture a shared sense of experiences, particularly for later generations and those "one step removed" from their ethnic histories in other ways (e.g., adoptive parents or interethnic parents). Thus, it is important to study context to get to know whether ethnic or racial groupings are more salient for the particular individuals in question.

Further, stereotypical ideas of what members of both those ethnic and racial groups "should" look like and act like can constrain respondents' willingness to identify fully with those groups. Many respondents respond to this "boxing in" by identifying more with the whites with whom they are surrounded, others by identifying with other racial/ethnic groups, and still others by adopting a post-ethnic conception of themselves that transcends racial and ethnic categories altogether. Moreover, whichever of these options they choose, they consistently subvert the rigidity of these categories by relating to them as continuums (e.g., they are "more Asian" or "not as Latino") rather than as either-or questions. Clearly, such questions of which group (blacks, whites, others) Latinos and Asians are going to "become like" cannot be solved by simple quantitative survey questions. While qualitative work such as the present study may not be able to provide generalizable findings, it can suggest ways to better tailor surveys on this topic in the future. For instance, questions that ask respondents' racial and ethnic categories could be presented as a continuum (perhaps a scale of one to ten) that allows them to define for themselves how closely they identify with any particular group. Researchers must also dig deeper into *why* those in the racial middle choose to identify more with some groups than others by interrogating their racial ideologies, a topic to which we now turn.

3

Reshaping Racist Ideology
from the Middle

Some scholars contend that racial/ethnic groups in the middle can be seen as falling in step with the racial ideology that galvanizes whites and blacks. In other words, to the extent that U.S. racial ideology casts a negative light on blacks and portrays whites as the more meritorious and virtuous group, we would expect Latinos and Asians to either espouse similar thinking about blacks and whites themselves, or develop antiracist counter-ideologies as African Americans have done to critique white supremacy and advocate for the emancipation of full humanity for people of color. These two dichotomous expectations could be viewed as "whitening" and "browning" arguments respectively, and we will find some support for each in these data. Some of the most interesting aspects of these respondents' ideologies, however, occur at points that cannot be placed at either one of these dichotomous poles. Therefore, in this chapter I want to highlight most prominently the ways in which Asians and Latinos have crafted racialized thinking that have not appeared in any studies limited to black and white. Indeed, in some ways, being in the middle seems to allow these respondents more flexibility to use racial discourse even more explicitly than do either whites *or* blacks. Here I will explore some of the more unique strategies that they use to do so.

It would be impossible to enter into such a discussion without first clarifying what I mean by ideology. An *ideology* is belief system, rooted in the social structure, which serves to rationalize existing social arrangements.[1] Thus, racist ideology justifies why the dominant group is the most highly valued and materially privileged, even as it validates why various subordinate groups have less access to that power and prestige. To espouse racist ideology is not necessarily to assimilate or become like the dominant group. Although racist ideology serves dominant-group interests, they are hardly the only ones who subscribe to it. An ideology can only be effective to the extent that it is upheld by persons at all levels of the social-stratification system. It should not be surprising, however, that members of the dominant group tend to subscribe to racist ideology most wholeheartedly, while members of subordinate groups would be less likely to uphold all aspects of the ideology, and more likely to pick and choose some, or occasionally even none, of it.[2]

Research has identified "color-blind racism" as the dominant racial ideology of the late twentieth and early twenty-first centuries.[3] Through color-blind racism (or "color and power evasiveness"),[4] people discourage overt references to "color" as reasoning for why certain racial groups are "ahead" or "behind." Proclamations like "I don't care if you're black, white, green, or purple" and "I don't see color" are examples of typical phrases shaping this framework. Color-blindness as an ideology makes it taboo to draw attention to people's "race" in explicit ways, while racism continues through other more insidious means, such as racial "code words" (e.g., "at-risk" children, "welfare mothers," "ghetto") or culture of poverty arguments that "blame the victims" for their plight.

Studying U.S. blacks and whites, Eduardo Bonilla-Silva has identified four frames of color-blind racism, and various other rhetorical styles and storylines common to its discourse. The four frames are: abstract liberalism, naturalization, cultural racism, and minimization of racism. Abstract liberalism uses the language of equal opportunity and free choice for all as a basis for opposing many concrete policies of antidiscrimination. The assumption is that if we all just believe in these ideals, no particular policies or interventions will be necessary to combat the centuries of legal racial discrimination, disenfranchisement, and exclusion. A belief in the myth of meritocracy, which allows whites to deny any unjust enrichment from centuries of systemic racism, is an essential underpinning to this frame. Naturalization explains away patterns such as racial segregation in housing and endogamous social networks and marriages as "just the way things are," because people somehow automatically gravitate toward "their own kind." The assumption is that it is "just natural" (not socially prescribed or conditioned) that people avoid others who are racially unlike them. As with abstract liberalism, the resulting line of thinking is that nothing in particular needs to be done or should be done about something as "natural" as segregation, and the system of racism is thus overlooked as a cause of this separation.

A third frame of color-blind racism, cultural racism, discusses people of color not as genetically deficient, but instead as lacking in family values, discipline, work ethic, and morality. These traits are seen as learned in impoverished or unsuitable communities rather than as inborn. Also known as liberal racism, this ideology steers one away from supporting antiracist policy initiatives, because "values" are not seen as able to be changed through public policy. Minimization of racism is simply the outlook that racial discrimination is rare and occurs only in isolated, fluke incidents, if at all. What follows from this vein is that people of color are seen as whining, complaining, and overexaggerating discrimination.[5] Steinhorn and Diggs-Brown have demonstrated that this frame is a major source of a great "perception gap" between blacks and whites about the extent of contemporary discrimination, with whites largely underestimating it and thus unlikely to support policy initiatives to change it.[6]

Due to its focus on blacks and whites, the research on color-blind racism leaves open the question of how Latinos and Asians might make use of its ideological framework. Leslie Carr's survey of students found that 77 percent of students agreed with the statement "I am color-blind when it comes to race" while only 40 percent of black students agreed.[7] Bonilla-Silva's study reports that, on the four frames of color-blind racism analyzed, blacks used them 6 to 35 percent of the time, while whites used them 43 to 96 percent of the time.[8] Moreover, while a small minority (12 to 15 percent) of whites is racially progressive by Bonilla-Silva's criteria (they support intermarriage, affirmative action, and recognize the significance of contemporary racial discrimination), about three-quarters of blacks share these progressive (and non-color-blind) views. If Latinos and Asians are "browning" or joining the "collective black," they would use color-blind rhetoric sparingly; if they are indeed "whitening," they would use it more often.

It will be my contention that, rather than reproducing verbatim the dominant discourse of color-blind racism, some Latinos and Asians are indeed perpetuating the discourse of color-blind racism, but in ways that are not only unique to them, but arguably accessible only to them. I call this a "color-nuanced," rather than a color-blind, approach, to highlight the ways in which the racial middle draws on nuances of ethnic differences within racial categories more regularly than other research has found with whites or blacks. On the other hand, close to half of the sample (20/50)—to be analyzed further in chapter 6—would be considered racially progressive by Bonilla-Silva's definition. These respondents strive not to reproduce such color-blind or color-nuanced thinking. Clearly, the racialized space that Latinos and Asian Americans occupy is quite complex. Some are "browning" by refusing the accept the dominant racial ideology of color-blind racism, some are "whitening" by displaying usages of color-blind racism similar to whites, while still others are furthering the discourse of color-blind racism in the more sophisticated (color-nuanced) ways not accounted for by other works. It is these more creative strategies that I want to highlight most in this chapter.

Latinos, Asian Americans, and Color-Blind Racism

At first glance, counting up percentages of the sample's usage of the four frames of color-blind racism, Latinos and Asian Americans seem to fit mostly in between blacks' and whites' percentages, ranging from 42 to 66 percent, but closer to whites on most frames, as Yancey's whitening thesis might predict. In table 3-1, I use Bonilla-Silva's results for whites and blacks, and our own results for the Latino/Asian column.[9] Although these are not entirely comparable data sources, they serve as a good beginning point from which to progress to a more detailed analysis of our qualitative data.

For all frames, we can see that Latinos and Asian Americans seem to use color-blind racism more than blacks do. For three out of four frames, their usage is closer to whites than blacks (echoing Yancey's findings on other outcomes), and in the case of naturalization, their rate of usage is nearly identical to whites. It is important to note that on abstract liberalism, however, Latinos and Asians talk much more like blacks. Thus, even on this cursory glance, we can see that the whitening thesis is partially substantiated in Latinos and Asian Americans' racial attitudes, although not entirely. The browning thesis is more correct if only when it comes to abstract liberalism.

The picture gets even more complex once we take note of an important aspect that differentiates both Latinos and Asian Americans from the bipolar black/white comparison. When whites discuss the factors they perceive are responsible for racial differences, they typically are either referring mainly to blacks, or else they are lumping all people of color together. Likewise, when blacks use color-blind language, they are usually referring to their own group. When Latinos and Asians use the two frames of cultural racism, however, and minimization in particular, they are much more likely to either be talking about their own specific ethnic group or

TABLE 3-1
*Comparison of Usage of Color-Blind
Racism Frames, by Race*

	Whites	Latinos/Asians	Blacks
Abstract Liberalism	96%	50% (25/50)	35%
Cultural Racism	88%	66% (33/50)	24%
Antiblack		*30% (15/50)*	
Naturalization	43%	42% (21/50)	24%
Minimization	84%	52% (26/50)	6%
Antiblack		*18% (9/50)*	

another nonblack racial/ethnic group, rather than about blacks. If we re-strict our analysis of cultural racism to instances of *antiblack* color-blind racism, the percentage jumps down from 66 percent to only 30 percent of the respondents. Likewise, if we restrict our analysis of the minimi-zation frame to the times when our respondents are talking about how *blacks* overexaggerate discrimination (or, for instance, how blacks "use it as a crutch"), the percentage again jumps down, from 52 percent to just 18 percent of the respondents. For the other two frames (naturalization and abstract liberalism) it was not feasible to separate out antiblack discourse specifically, because usually the respondent was referring to a more global racial/ethnic mosaic (e.g., "Everyone should be judged on their own merit alone," or "Everyone just naturally wants to be with people like them-selves"). What is clear from this breakdown is that Latinos and Asians seem to be more willing to use color-blind racism when referring to their own and other "intermediate" racial groups, rather than toward blacks. A more detailed qualitative analysis, however, reveals that sometimes, even when blacks are not mentioned, they are the actual "unmentioned" tar-get of racism. Blacks end up being the unspoken reference point through which other groups are evaluated and compared.

Antiblack Racism: Veiled and Unveiled

Latino and Asian respondents do discuss antiblack racism explicitly at times, while at other times it is "veiled" through reference to another ra-cial or ethnic group. In a more overt style, Peter, a Mexican American man, is concerned that Hispanics might start acting more like blacks, in ways he believes would be negative:

Who do I think is more discriminator? I'd have to say blacks are more discriminat[ing] against whites than anything. I know it's hard to imagine that, but that's my true belief. Because the white culture is trying to appease everybody and do that politically correct thing. Where the blacks, that I've seen are more racist than the whites. [Interviewer: Can you give me any examples of what you've seen?] Oh, obvious where you have senators, black senators, calling other senators white boys where as opposed to if a white senator were to call a black senator a black boy, that'd be the most racist thing around. . . . I think blacks use the crutch too much. I don't think Hispanics have, but I think they're gonna start eventually using it. . . I hope to God they don't; it's bad for us to use a crutch. When you use a crutch, it'll ultimately hinder you just like affirmative action. [When asked which groups he identifies with most/least:] I think the harder one to identify with are blacks. . . . I just I don't like, like I said using crutches, and I know a lot of blacks do. And I know, you know, I don't like the double standard where they can use racial slurs opposed to other people can't use it because that's they'll say it's racism. I suppose they can do it and we can't. What I mean by we, I mean whites. And who can I identify more with? I'd have to say whites more than any other culture. More than Asian, more than Indian I guess I'd have to say.

Peter uses the metaphor of the "crutch" to activate the minimization frame of color-blind racism. He minimizes the significance of any racism that whites might perpetuate, concluding that blacks are the real culprits because they have a "double standard" by which "they can use racial slurs" but others "can't." Whites and other nonblack groups are characterized as fair-minded and holding everyone to the same standards, but blacks alone are characterized as allowing extra "crutches" for themselves. Blacks are seen not only as complaining and making too much of racism, but, in a step further, actually being the main culprits of "racism" themselves. This use of color-blind racism, incorporating a rhetorical style called "projection," was common of the whites in Bonilla-Silva's study.[10]

Yet there is an additional dynamic here not present with those whites. Peter is concerned that his own group, Hispanics, would begin to be viewed in the same way that blacks are viewed—using "crutches" that are typically associated with laziness, complaining, and other negative stereotypes from which he seeks to distance himself. Elsewhere in the interview he says he is sometimes referred to by others as a "coconut"—"brown on the outside, white on the inside." Although he identifies as 100 percent Mexican American because both his biological parents were Mexican, his mother remarried to a non-Hispanic white man who adopted him as his own. He is currently married to a woman who is "three-fourths Mexican, one-fourth German" and states he is glad his children ended up light skinned so they would hopefully not have to face some of the prejudices he did. He gets rather emotional when recalling this past: "If I get flushed when I talk it's because it does get emotional . . . when I was growing up a lot of the terms I heard were spic, wet back, things such as that." Peter's position is reminiscent of white ethnics who remember the days of "no Irish need apply" prejudice toward them, yet herald the "up by your bootstraps" mentality of "if I can do it, anyone can do it," discounting the significance of present-day systemic discrimination that is not at all warranted by those who currently face it. He wants to be associated with the positive image of whiteness, which is linked to hard work and no excuses, consistent with the dominant racial ideology of the United States. But he acknowledges that his access to that reputation is tenuous and will depend essentially on whether Hispanics as a collective become associated with blacks. Clearly, Peter hopes that association does not occur.

Antiblack racism also emerges when respondents discuss the topic of interracial relationships. Similar to Bonilla-Silva's white respondents, some of my respondents would couch their opposition (and that of their families) to interracial unions on the basis of nonracial characteristics. For example, Claudia, a Dominican American woman, recalls her daughter's relationship with an African American young man, which was unacceptable to her and other members of the family, although she insists it was not because of his "ethnicity":

> Well, one of my daughters, she had a relationship with an African American, and I didn't judge him because of his ethnicity, I judged him because of his actions, that's what I didn't like, his actions. . . . [Interviewer: How did the other people in the family react when your daughter was dating an African American? Did they have mixed feelings?] Yes, they did, they had mixed feelings. They had mixed feelings because he was older than her, and didn't have the same goals as she had. And but also I'm not going to lie. There was unkind, when they found out it was black. But that didn't come from me, it came from my mother. [Interviewer: She didn't really like it?] She didn't like it. [Interviewer: It's just because she

has a view of—] She has a view of—that African Americans—like she is scared. But it's something that me and my brother and sister have tried to teach her, that no it's not like that.

In this exchange, Claudia uses some discourse familiar to Bonilla-Silva's white respondents who express some back-and-forth resistance to interracial relationships. They may approve of them in the abstract, but once they are pressed to discuss details, and how it affects their own families, they discuss their resistance by valorizing a view that blacks are "just different" in terms of values, and in this case "goals" and "actions." Claudia also uses a common storyline that Bonilla-Silva identifies when she distances herself from a racist family member to prove her own non-racism.

The unique "intermediate" dimension to Claudia's negative view of African Americans comes out later in the interview, however, when she is asked which racial or ethnic group she identifies with most and the least. She states she feels furthest away from Ecuadorians because "I don't know, because maybe how they also have relationship with black community. Well not all of them, some of them. I don't know I don't know maybe I'm wrong." Claudia uses some of the rhetorical styles Bonilla-Silva identifies to distance herself from her own views by using the "I don't know, maybe I'm wrong" maneuver. Yet Claudia never goes as far as to say that she herself feels negatively toward the black community; rather she says she cannot identify with another Hispanic group because of their perceived ties to the "black community." Ecuadorians serve as the "veil" through which this respondent feels comfortable enough to express her disdain for African Americans without having to do it more explicitly. There is a sense that, in the unwritten rules of racial discourse, it is within the realm of nonracist acceptability for her to be able to make negative judgments about Ecuadorians without seeming racist, because she is somewhat of an insider by being Latino just like them.

This quote from a different Dominican American woman, Dolores, demonstrates a similar pattern to whites in terms of couching her racial preferences in nonracial language, like "good," "clean," and "safe," to refer to the predominantly white neighborhoods she prefers:

If I had to move someplace else, it wouldn't matter who lived in the neighborhood as long as it's a good residential area where it's just clean, and people cared for where they lived, and they were just generally good people, it doesn't matter if they're Dominican or not Dominican. My mom lives on the Lower East Side just to keep us away from [the local Dominican neighborhood]. . . . I like not living close to that, but it doesn't matter . . . I just want to be where it's mixed . . . and the location is good. You know, those kind of things, like I want to walk in my neighborhood at night and not worry, you know, that I'm safe. I want to be able to be in a district where the school district is a good one. [Interviewer: Right.] Because it tends that, if you live in a neighborhood, basically in [city name] here if it's a Latino or black neighborhood, unfortunately, the schools are really bad. So, I always look for a good education, clean area. That doesn't have to be like a race thing, that's just people.

Here she includes her own specific ethnic group (Dominicans) in with blacks as she explains her residential preferences. Dolores uses a more overt "veil" because she explicitly includes blacks by the end of her explanation of why she would not want a predominantly Dominican neighborhood. Consistent with color-blind racism, she insists her preferences are not "a race thing," but uses the vague color-blind explanation of "just people," rather than a more progressive analysis that structural racism and the lack of funds and services available in communities of color are responsible for these outcomes, not the "people" inside them.

Similarly, Debie, a Filipino American respondent, separates herself out from others in her own group, especially those whom she characterizes as more like blacks. Unlike Dolores, however, she never mentions blacks explicitly. Instead, she divides her own ethnic group into categories that are either more or less like blacks, as indicated by the racial code words of "hip-hop" and "ghetto." She does actually describe as "more white" the subgroup of Filipinos that she considers to be more like whites:

Most Asians in terms of economics they just tend to be more affluent because it's like you know they're just hardworking. . . . So they tend to have better jobs, live out in the suburbs, and live well-off, and those communities tend to be mainly white. So I know a lot of Asians that don't even really consider themselves Asian or even if they do, they just act—they don't have a connection with their Asian heritage, they're much more white. And at the same time I know a lot of like Filipinos and Koreans that are really like ghetto, I mean really like into the hip-hop culture. So I think it all depends on like the environment you grew up in. . . . In terms of all the minorities, Asians tend to be like, they're often more well-off than the other minorities, just because of like their hardworking nature, their parents are always doctors and were like in the financial fields. So . . . they don't struggle with their standard of living, they don't necessarily need to identify with their cultural group in order to like feel secure on where they are because most of the time they're already pretty well-off. That might be different for Filipinos though, because with Filipinos it's sort of different . . . Filipinos are either really white or really ghetto, [laughs] it's weird.

Elsewhere in this interview, Debie points out that she was unlike most Filipinos at her school growing up in that she did not identify with "hip-hop" and "ghetto" culture. In the above quote, though, she characterizes Asians on the whole as "more white" because of their "hardworking nature." The adjectives she chooses like "secure" and "well-off" cast a more positive light on this group. For Debie, veiled antiblack racism operates by essentially saying "I look down on/distance myself from X group because they are too much like blacks." Being culturally "like blacks" is cast as a negative, but other ethnic groups (here, one's own ethnic group) get substituted as a proxy for blacks. This veiled antiblack racism dynamic demonstrates how the racial middle reproduces color-blind racism in color-nuanced ways.

I'm OK, You're Not OK: Selective Deconstruction of Stereotypes

As indicated by the above quote, several of the interviews touched on stereotypical generalizations about particular racial and/or ethnic groups—whether they were groups in which the respondent claimed membership or not. Sometimes respondents reflected on stereotypes that *others* held about their own group, while other times they admitted to holding stereotypes of their own. Within the same interview, they would use progressive racial ideology to deconstruct a particular stereotype, yet elsewhere throw these analytical skills out the window by agreeing with other stereotypes. The selectivity of this pattern further demonstrates how the racial middle can often hold color-nuanced positions that combine both color-blind and color-conscious (or, more aptly, culturally conscious) discourses.

The Filipino American student Debie quoted above, who separates her own ethnic group into "really white" and "really ghetto" subgroups, displays an interesting moment of critique of white supremacist discourse when considering her parents' attitude toward interracial dating:

The thing about Filipinos in general is they're a little racist towards like African Americans, but it's sort of like, it's just how it is. I don't agree with it. But I've never dated someone who's black, but I know people, I'm friends with people who have and their parents were like really upset about it. Some parents are more OK with it than others it really depends on the family. But I do know families that take it really hard if you're Filipino and dating a black person. Now, if you're dating a white person, it's a whole other story, because you'll learn that Filipinos are really like . . . they really look up to Americans. I resent that too, but it's a whole 'nother issue. [laughs] But like they really look up to white Americans. So if their kid dates like a white American, they sort of look at it as a really good thing. . . . Like I dated someone who was Polish, and like my family doesn't care either way I guess—well no that's not true I take that back. I think they would care if I dated a black guy, but like I've never tried that, so I don't know. But they were cool with it, they were like "wow, he's tall, and he's pale, and that's cool."

Here Debie uses the naturalization frame of color-blind racism when she states, of antiblack prejudice among Filipinos, "It's just how it is." On the matter of Filipinos "really look[ing] up to white Americans," however, she states, "I resent that." Thus, although she indicates an acceptance of negative prejudice against blacks, she is more outspoken in her disapproval of positive valuation of whiteness. Indeed, she resents the idea of white superiority when it is voiced by members of her own ethnicity and poses herself as its voice of critique. Yet she is not able to extend that critique to antiblack prejudices, and her discourse is typical of color-blind racism for most of the rest of the interview. In the opening lines of this quote, Debie uses the diminutive phrase "a little" to minimize the impact of the next word, "racist." She also assures us that "I don't agree with it" to distance herself from the racism. She does indeed soon reveal prejudices in her interview. Two times during this quote she assures us she's never dated anyone black, including another common distancing rhetorical strategy of color-blindness: "I've never tried that, so I don't know." Debie does seem quite knowledgeable, however, about whether whites or blacks are valued more as dating partners among Filipinos, although she does add the clarification that "it really depends on the family."

Another area where we have already seen Debie rely on stereotypical thinking is when she valorizes the "model minority" stereotype about Asians. Recall that she characterizes Asians as "well-off" due to their "hardworking nature." One could actually present a more progressive critique of this model minority generalization, as indeed another Asian respondent named Kali, a statistician originally from India, does in the following quote:

> They think that, the perception now, because Indians do so well is that they are really smart and that they are all educated and they are very successful and that's not true because there are a lot of dumb Indians in India. It's just that the ones that come here, the smart ones come here to go to school. Those that are not career oriented, not very smart stay in India. So you got the crème of the crop, and you know that [the stereotype]'s not necessarily true.

As it turns out, however, her sophisticated analysis of the structural factors that operate to create a certain group's experience do not extend much past Indians. She uses a stereotypical cultural-racism frame to interpret the experience of her Chinese coworker and contrasts it with her own experience as an Indian:

> We are so diverse within India because each state is so different . . . not like China were everyone is Chinese and speaks the same language and stuff like that. . . . Most Indians will integrate, you know, they have white friends, they, you know first of all with the language, everyone speaks English so that makes a difference. You know the Chinese don't. I know this girl at work . . . she's been here since she was two years old . . . can you believe is living in the heart of New York and she can't even speak English?! . . . Everything is in Chinatown—Chinese hospitals, Chinese food . . . Chinese libraries . . . Chinese friends . . . you will never find that with Indians. . . . It's bizarre. I'm shocked.

While she leaves at least some wiggle room at times in her interview for Indians to be less than monolithic ("*most* Indians . . . ," "*some* Indians . . . ," although by the end she states, "You will *never* find that with Indians"), she speaks with sweeping generalizations about "the Chinese" ("*Everyone* is Chinese . . . ," "The Chinese *don't* . . ."). Instead of exploring the structural factors that account for why Indians already speak English upon arrival to the United States (colonization by the British, higher education, etc.), she poses it as her Chinese coworker's own lack of effort, interest, or motivation that she does not speak English as well as herself. Her argument is similar to one used by whites about blacks "segregating themselves," especially when she contrasts with Indians who "integrate" and "have white friends." Elsewhere in Kali's interview, she continues extolling the virtues of the great diversity of Indian culture, and this time contrasts it with Hispanic culture: "The Hispanic culture has a very strong culture and representation. Indians are very divided even among themselves in terms of culture." While we might give her some benefit of the doubt in characterizing India as more diverse than China, nation to nation, clearly, her overgeneralization about dozens of Latin American cultures shows that she is more willing to challenge white supremacist notions about her own group, while she uncritically accepts them about other groups.

In contrast to Kali's glossing over ethnic differences among Latinos, Joe, a white-Cuban biracial American, who is well traveled in many Latin American countries due to his occupation, makes sharp distinctions among them. In particular, he singles out his own ethnic group as more deserving of the model minority stereotype than many of the others:

> I say this not because I'm Cuban, but as my observation, and I think the statistics bear it out as well, but—Cubans are seen in higher status than most Latins that have come to the United States, compared to let's say Puerto Ricans, Dominicans, and Central Americans for the most part. And even to an extent maybe even Venezuelans and Columbians—though maybe it starts to blur there. Cubans are very industrious. They've done extremely well for themselves compared to the other Latin American populations . . . doing especially better than the Nicaraguans, or Salvadorians. . . . Cubans are very crafty, they're very industrious, they'll think outside the box. I mean who else would take a 1960 Chevrolet something or other and turn it into a boat in order to cross the Florida straits. I mean really!? You know a boat! And it worked, but that's how they are.

The phrase "that's how they are" sounds familiar as stereotypical language whites tend to use to generalize about blacks and/or other minorities, but here it is being used by someone who identifies as white-Cuban, so theoretically he is speaking about "his own" group (using the third-person pronoun "they"). Perhaps he uses this voice to position himself as an objective observer, since he begins by saying that he is not just saying it because he is Cuban. The kind of structural analysis that the Indian respondent quoted above used to critique the model minority stereotype (analyzing human capital factors, economic conditions of each country and its migrants, government/refugee assistance unique to Cubans, etc.) could certainly have be applied to the various Latino groups listed in the above quote. Joe instead relies on a combination of naturalization and cultural racism to explain the differences in these various Latino groups' socioeconomic positions. The hardworking/"industrious" generalization that Debie used to describe Asians comes up again here, this time posited as an essential trait of Cubans.

Joe understands at the abstract level, however, that generalizations about an entire group only go so far. At one point in the interview, when describing the racial/ethnic makeup of his ideal neighborhood, he begins with a typical color-blind statement: "I could care less if who lives next door to me . . . is black, Hispanic, Asian, Muslim, as long as they're good people." And his rationale for his position is one that actually deconstructs racial stereotypes of who are "good people." He states: "Because you know, I could live next door to a Cuban guy and he could be a jackass . . . and there's plenty of them too, plenty of Cuban jackasses." More to the point, he can recall personal family experiences attesting to how painful it can be to be the victim of unjustly applied stereotypes. He remembers how difficult it was for their family to leave Miami and relocate to a Midwestern state where it was constantly assumed that his Cuban father was a drug dealer. Even though at some level he critiques the unfairness of such stereotypes, ultimately he finds them as inevitable and even justified:

> So if you got a lot of Cubans in the drug trade, and you're Cuban then unfortunately you may be associated with that. Is it fair? Maybe not, probably not. . . . Mexican groups are seen as kinda being lazy. I don't think that's necessarily fair. I mean they work . . . backbreaking work. But Mexico is seen generally in terms of government as being corrupt. . . . That's a fact. . . . Is it fair for that to reflect on all Mexicans? No. But when you have something that's going on . . . until you get it cleaned up that's kinda what you're gonna have to be prepared to live with. . . . Are all people of the Islamic faith terrorists? Of course not, no. But right now they've got a small minority of people . . . doing heinous crimes in the name of the Islamic religion. Well, until they get that cleaned up, they're going to have to live with the repercussions of that.

The usage of the pronoun "they" is interesting here, because while Joe acknowledges that stereotypes are true of only a "small minority" of any given group, "they" have to "live with the repercussions" because "they" have not "cleaned up." Here the "they" is one and the same—it is as if those who do not live out the stereotype are still at fault, guilty by association. Those who erroneously apply a stereotype to all members of a group are somehow not at all at fault in this equation.

Roxanne, a Mexican American respondent, has a similar recollection about her father's emotionally charged rejection of unfair stereotypes being applied to him.

> I remember one time when my dad had a restaurant—there's the typical Mexican that was leaning against a sombrero, with the sombrero down taking the afternoon siesta, that laziness . . . that was the logo for the franchise restaurant, and him not liking it, and him saying "we just work too hard for this to really be, um, the way it is." And I guess in some respects I understand what he was saying, no, I don't think we're a lazy people, I think we're people. And I understand if you really study that culture you understand why they have those noontime naps, when the temperature's up over a hundred degrees, you don't work, [laughs] you know? And it's easier to wait until a cooler time of the day, it really made a lot of sense so in that respect I was . . . pretty insulated I guess to a large degree my family pretty much insulated me, I went to school, I came home, [pause] I never felt like I couldn't do anything that I wanted to do, and I never felt like I shouldn't go someplace because I was Mexican, Hispanic, I never, it never stopped me, I just never ever thought about it.

Although she cannot recall facing any racial prejudice or discrimination herself, Roxanne nonetheless has a sophisticated understanding of why her father recoiled at anti-Mexican stereotypes. She breaks down the "grain of truth" in the stereotype by showing how perceived "laziness" is not some essential cultural trait, but rather a situational adaptation to structural conditions. Using the abstract liberalism typical of many whites, she concludes that she "never even thought about" her race or ethnicity—"we're people." She presents herself as sympathetic to her father's outrage about the franchise logo ("in some respects I understand what he was saying"), but there is a detached distance from his passionate position on the issue.

Even though above Roxanne is astutely able to deconstruct stereotypes about her own group, she consistently minimizes the significance of racial/ethnic discrimination and prejudice in everyday life. This minimization is perhaps most evident in the anecdote she relates about her fourteen-year-old son's use of ethnic slurs with his friends:

He goes to school with white children, black children, Jewish children, and then right now they're really heavy into throwing the slurs. . . . it's kind of their way of identifying themselves. In other words, he's identifying himself as Mexican, or Hispanic, spic. And the Italian kid is identifying himself as wop. And I don't even know what the Vietnamese boy is [laughs] . . . they're exchanging these horrible ethnic jokes, I mean things that, that, I just—no way! But yet, it's like they've got to get it out of their system. . . . I don't think it's malicious as much as this is part of what I am. . . . I've told him a number of times, and he never hears it from us, we don't exchange jokes like that at all. . . . All I can do is teach my kids that it's not an acceptable way, I don't think they're being malicious about it I think they're just experimenting with the language.

She has a laissez-faire attitude toward her son's joke telling even though she gives lip service to the idea that it is "unacceptable." Indeed, she repeatedly justifies it as not malicious, and by the end of the excerpt, it has been reduced to mere linguistic experimentation. Immediately after this discussion, she adds that she has not faced much in the way of racial slurs that she can recall, and that in her male-dominated line of work (mortgage banking), she has faced more gender-related taunting than anything else. Thus, although Roxanne is capable of deconstructing an anti-Mexican stereotype in a progressive manner, ultimately she is not able to deconstruct the significance of the stereotyping that her teenage son and his friends perpetuate.

Cultural Racism within the Middle: "Asians Are the Opposite of a Latin"

The sample for this study includes Rebecca, a Macanese American young woman with a Dominican boyfriend who she thinks she will eventually marry. Heather, a white-Filipino biracial American, has a close Mexican friend and chooses Mexicans as the group she feels is most similar to being Filipino/Asian. A third respondent, April, is a Korean American high school teacher who has recently married a Mexican immigrant, making him a U.S. citizen. Through this marriage, she inherited three Mexican stepchildren, two of whom just arrived to her home weeks before the interview. These three respondents with close Latino-Asian ties are actually the anomalies in the sample. (Heather and April have both lived in

California, and Rebecca lives in New York, probably the only two U.S. regions where these two groups can come into the most frequent contact with each other in large numbers.) The much more common pattern was for Latinos and Asian Americans to view each other as greatly distant from each other, more so than every other racial/ethnic group in the United States. Indeed, about a quarter of the sample (13/50) listed Latinos if they were Asian American, and Asian Americans if they were Latino, as the group they felt they had the least in common with, or felt the greatest social distance from. (California and New York residences were prominent in this portion of the sample as well, so let us not view them as racial utopias by any means!) Examining racial ideology is an important part of understanding how this perceived gulf between groups emerges.

Respondents often used cultural racism to make sense of why they felt this gulf between them and the "other middle" racial group. For instance, Joe had this to say:

> Is there an ethnic group that I feel is hard to identify with? Probably I would just have to say the Asians, because it's just such a different culture. It's just a very different culture, different way of thinking. That's not being critical, I just think it's an observation. It's just, I've got Asian friends, I appreciate them—I like them a lot, love 'em to death. But don't expect me to like completely understand, or fall in line with the Asian way of thinking or the Asian way of doing some things or beliefs. It's just different. And that's just—there's nothing wrong with that. I may not identify with it as well.

Joe uses the phrase "I've got Asian friends" in much the same way whites have been observed using "I have black friends" in studies of color-blind racist ideology. It seems that those in the racial middle ideologically hover in that middle, not just to "veil" antiblack racism, but also to make use of essentializing strategies that pose certain groups as "just different" culturally, in much the same way whites have been found to do with blacks. Christopher, a Honduran-Dominican American, gets more specific about some of the cultural practices that he senses are the source of these differences:

> Asians would be the ones I have a hard time identifying with. They're very different. They're the actual opposite of a Latin. Honor to them is a lot more involved. There's the mannerisms are very different. They bow

and they don't embrace. They're very, [pause] oh gosh, how do you say it? Detail-oriented people. It's like everything they do is on the line and everything they do is such a greater reflection towards them and their family. I don't think the Latins do in that degree; some do, some do to some degree. . . . I think it's the way they go about doing things. It's just the way they go about it. We're very open and loud; they're not. We're very inclusive; they're not. . . . A Dominican can hang out with, dare I say it, a Puerto Rican or a Cuban or a Panamanian. But you check, I had a friend of mine who just recently got married; he's Japanese-German, married a Korean girl. Imagine how that went. It was like, there were two in-laws; one was on one end of the room and one was on the other end of the room. One had their garb on and their Korean garb and the other had their Japanese garb. Both ceremonies were recognized and represented for the ritual of the rite of marriage, but it was like, OK, we're over there and they're over there. And it was like, whoa! Whereas if it were a Latin wedding, if they were Panamanian and Nicaraguan, move out to the middle. Everybody gets to it. It's just different. So for me, I've always had a hard time trying to identify with Asians, me personally.

Some of the language here sounds like the familiar stereotypical generalizations seen in the previous section, where an Indian respondent uses "we" language to contrast her group with "they," the Chinese, with no room for exceptions noted. As he contrasts "Latins" with Asians, Christopher says "we're" this and "they're not." Interestingly, he not only asserts that Latinos are louder, but also more inclusive of ethnic differences than are Asians. He seems to have somewhat of a glorified picture of Latinos' eternal willingness to overlook such differences, particularly given the comments of other Latino respondents we have quoted above that note a clear distinction among some Caribbean and some Central and South American groups.

But Latinos are not alone in using cultural racism to interpret the distance they feel from their "opposite." Even though Filipinos are the one Asian group that is often paralleled with Latino culture because of its shared colonization by Spain, Spanish language, and Catholic religion, Debie, a Filipino American respondent, makes plain her distaste for Latinos:

I totally have a hard time identifying with Hispanics. [Interviewer: OK, why do you think that would be?] Because there were a lot of Hispanics at my high school and I just never really got along with them. [laughs] It was just my experience. [Interviewer: Yeah.] And it wasn't like we got in fights but it was just like we had nothing to relate with so we had no conversation. I don't know what it is, that's just with me personally.

This overgeneralization is striking, that a young person at a high school would feel that she had absolutely no common ground for even a conversation topic with any Latinos at her school. Debie feels she has the most in common with other Asian Americans and the least in common with Latinos.

In choosing their most distant group, these respondents sidestep the common white/black dichotomy of what is considered to be one's racial "opposite." Rather then aligning themselves with whites to choose blacks as their most distant group ("whitening"), or aligning with people of color to choose whites ("browning"), they traverse a color-nuanced landscape that is more varied than many whites and blacks acknowledge.

One final point on this contention that Latinos and Asians are "opposite" concerns the difference between how those inside and outside the "racial middle" would view this potential schism. One interview question asked of the respondents concerned what were they most often "misperceived" as by others, because this misperception is a typical experience of those in the racial middle. As reported in chapter 2, the most common pattern in the sample is for Asian American respondents to get mistaken for Latinos, and Latino respondents getting mistaken for Asian Americans. This was reported even more frequently than being mistaken for another ethnicity within one's own racial group (although this was by far the type of group respondents themselves felt closest to). While many "insiders" to these two groups may see themselves as "opposites," outsiders (particularly whites) are nevertheless sometimes lumping the two together in their minds. Because the most powerful group controls the dominant ideology, it would stand to reason that this "opposites" idea is a more uniquely "middle" component to U.S. racial ideology, which stands in contrast to what many whites generally believe. Those in the racial middle could nevertheless still be conscious of dominant ideology and understand "the other" racial middle group as their most serious "competitor" in a "race toward whiteness"; thus, they would strive to rhetorically distance themselves from their "opposite" for more structural, rather than cultural, reasons.[11]

Affirmative Action Views from the Racial Middle

While many whites may perceive Latinos and Asians in a homogenous racial middle, creating many similar experiences in a racist society for both groups, in their *own* minds the two groups feel they could not be further apart. One of the areas where this difference between the two groups seems most pronounced in the interview data is when the respondents discuss affirmative action. While Bonilla-Silva's work shows that a majority of whites oppose affirmative action, this is not true of those in the racial middle. A majority of the respondents actually support affirmative action programs (29/50) and at times articulate eloquent and even unique justifications for why it is still necessary. (These responses will be covered in chapter 6, on progressivism.) Many take a "mend it but don't end it" type of position that corresponded with the official platform of the U.S. Democratic Party at the time of the interviews. A sizeable part of the sample (12/50) is ambivalent about affirmative action. Their responses are not definitive in either direction, and sometimes respondents even decline to answer, feeling not informed enough to do so. Only a small minority of the sample (9/50) comes out unequivocally opposing affirmative action. As evident in table 3-2, for those that either support affirmative action or are ambivalent about it, there does not seem to be any major difference between Latinos and Asians. For the minority of the sample that opposes affirmative action, the vast majority (7/9) are Asian Americans.

Whether ambivalent or clearly opposed, Latino and Asian respondents sound much like whites in the ways that they downplay "color" as they discuss the drawbacks of affirmative action programs in theory. They often use the abstract liberalism frame of color-blind racism in ways most identical to whites in Bonilla-Silva's study. Whites' framing of the affirmative action question can tend to be adversarial, as in, "If I can't benefit from this, why should *they* be able to?" Although the (7) Asian Americans who oppose affirmative action are usually not quite as angry, some sound similar to such whites in that they perceive themselves as losing out due to the policy. Both Latinos and Asians who are ambivalent or opposed to affirmative action cast it as unfair and paying undue attention to race. Yet some Latino respondents, typically those who use color-blindness most frequently, critique affirmative action policies in an abstract liberalism manner yet still want to "use" the policy to their own benefit. Latinos, whether ambivalent or opposed, hold the opinion more consistently than Asian Americans that affirmative action may give them a "leg up" on the

TABLE 3-2
Views of Affirmative Action

	Support	Ambivalent	Oppose
Latino	14	6	2
Asian	15	6	7
Total	29	12	9
	(58%)	(24%)	(18%)

competition, and if so, they will in practice take advantage of that despite disagreeing in theory with the concept.

Such an oppose-it-but-use-it position may also be influenced by the relatively high socioeconomic status common to the sample for this study. When some respondents reflect on their relative successes in life to conclude that they did not really "need" programs like affirmative action to get where they are, the idea of needing such programs in order to obtain gainful employment seems little more than a theoretical abstraction. Furthermore, if everyone in their family is relatively successful, it becomes more difficult for them to imagine people of their own background facing barriers that they did not somehow "bring on themselves." So to the extent to which the respondents' discourse on affirmative action sounds typical of whites, we can see their socioeconomic status talking, whereas when they defend their right to still take advantage of the program when it may benefit them, we can see the color-nuanced position of the racial middle coming more to the forefront. In effect, they have adapted the majority ideology to benefit their own specific group.

One Mexican American respondent, Roxanne, who was quoted above selectively deconstructing a stereotype about lazy Mexicans but taking a laissez-faire attitude toward her teenage son's ethnic jokes, uses all four frames of color-blind racism in her interview. She repeatedly resists framing her own experiences ethnically or racially, and insists "that was just home" or "that was just family" when describing cultural practices that emanate from her Mexican traditions. In one of the most illustrative examples of abstract liberalism in her interview, she states: "I don't go out and I don't think about I'm brown and white and what have you. You know I'm earning a living and I'm making the most of what I've been offered in this country and I'm living the American dream. I think that's pretty true of all of us." Roxanne follows a common pattern in that she minimizes the extent of racial discrimination that she believes herself and others like her have faced (see chapter 5 for more on this point). She suspects that "foreign nationals" face the most discrimination today, and she points out that she goes out of her way to help translate or provide bilingual assistance to clients facing language-barrier situations, such as Asian Americans. She does not acknowledge, however, much structural discrimination that might be affecting folks' life chances, and instead she attributes people's lack of economic success to individual shortcomings, particularly lack of work ethic. In fact, when discussing welfare policy, she states: "My family's experiences have always been one of striving to get ahead, [so] it's hard for me to understand why someone wouldn't want to do that especially when so much opportunity is available in this country." This links economic troubles primarily to individual desire and motivation. These sentiments taken together suggest that she would be resistant to race-based affirmative action policies.

Even though Roxanne does not think any of the traditional reasons for affirmative action programs have much bearing on her own and other Mexican Americans' lives, however, she sees affirmative action as something that, if there, she might as well take advantage of it:

> I like to identify myself as Hispanic and I believe to a certain extent it's helped me, believe it or not, get work. I think this position here, this job with the bank fills a quota. And if it gave me the edge to get in here then so be it, I have no problem with that. [laughs] I know for a fact that I'm educated enough to hold the position, so it's not a big deal, but I think that there is a certain advantage to that.

Although banks are not allowed to use "quotas" according to Supreme Court precedent, Roxanne shares that she chose to keep her Spanish surname upon marriage so she could reap these perceived benefits of it in the workplace. Further, she urges her children to do the same, even though she expresses some cognitive dissonance about this position because it seems to conflict with her "self-made man" philosophy on most everything else:

> It sounds terrible, but in competition for a slot or something, if I can use it, I will. And I, I honestly believe that in the banking industry it is used as a marker of—they need so many loan officers than are female and so many that are ethnic—it helps. My children, I told them the same thing in education, when it comes to scholarships and that if checking that box means that that gives you an eighth of a point, then check the box.

[laughs] There's not a lot of gimmes in this world, take the ones you can get! [laughs] It doesn't mean that you don't work hard, it doesn't mean that you know you're not qualified for what you do, but if it gives you a gimme, take it!

Roxanne has framed her "in my backyard" affirmative action position as within her individualistic philosophy by saying, in effect, if there is something that can boost your chances to succeed, grab it, no matter what it is. Whereas most blacks frame their support for affirmative action in terms of either past discrimination or current likelihood of employers still discriminating,[12] Roxanne uses a clear self-interest interpretation. While other research has found that "self-interest" arguments lead to a rejection of affirmative action policies on the part of whites,[13] clearly for those in the racial middle a self-interest individualistic argument actually can lead to qualified support for affirmative action as a policy.

Joe, a white-Cuban biracial American, quoted above using selective deconstruction of stereotypes, is one of the few respondents who is unequivocally opposed to race-based affirmative action. His opposition is clearly framed using abstract liberalism:

I don't want race, creed, color to be any part of any kind of affirmative action. I don't want people getting jobs over other people because of the color of their skin, or their heritage—irregardless of if they're white, black, or Hispanic, Asian, or whatever. I just don't think it should matter. . . . I don't agree with that; I want it to go away. You know, if we didn't have to put that down I think we'd be more fair for everybody. Because then it's based on more on merit then the color of my skin or the fact that you know, I have Cuban blood in me.

Joe's views emerge from his views of the United States as an equal playing field. Above we have seen that he views any prejudices existing about certain groups such as Cubans, Mexicans, and Muslims as somewhat deserved due to isolated actions of certain members of the groups. Further, he believes that any group in the United States that seems to be "lagging" socioeconomically is due more to their not "taking advantage of the opportunities that are presented to them" rather than to any structural barriers. When discussing an African American parent at his son's school, he seems to conceptually separate the parent out from an implicit stereotypical assumption about blacks' work ethic when he confers his approval upon him and his family: "They've busted their butt and done what they had to do and they're succeeding, you know, and not making excuses for anybody or any of that." The implication here is that most blacks are "making excuses" when they pinpoint racism as an obstacle to success, rather than describing the reality of American racism as it affects their daily lives. This position echoes that of another respondent quoted above (who also opposes affirmative action), saying that blacks use their race "as a crutch."

Yet even though Joe is staunchly opposed to affirmative action, he himself is willing to "use" his race even as he critiques others who he perceives as doing so:

> However, I can tell you that normally whenever I'm asked, like on other applications or what have you, I always answer Hispanic. I have to admit that part of it is because there are currently still in place, though I may not necessarily agree with them, there seems to be some amount of opportunity by saying that I'm Hispanic opposed to just say Caucasian. You understand what I mean? Yeah. So, though I may not necessarily agree with that—technically I really don't—but it's kind of a, hey dog eat dog world and if that's an advantage for me right now then I'll sure capitalize and take advantage of it.

Consistent with his individualist worldview, Joe believes people should take whatever opportunities present themselves, regardless of what other group of people it may theoretically affect.

Because affirmative action in this case is one such opportunity, however, they are in an ideologically precarious position. This abstract liberal frame of opposition to affirmative action emerges out of white Americans' experience, and it is therefore easier for whites to say they oppose it because they do not have to make a choice whether or not they will partake of race-based affirmative action benefits. Nonwhites, however, are not in the same position. If they follow the theory behind individualistic, laissez-faire Republicanism, it should lead them to oppose affirmative action, but if they follow the practice of individualistic, laissez-faire Republicanism, they should be seizing the opportunity to take advantage of it anyhow. Thus, one white privilege, particularly within the U.S. Republican and Libertarian parties, is to be able to take a consistently principled position regarding race-based affirmative action (they oppose it and they will not —and actually cannot—take advantage of it). Those who are nonwhite are backed into an ideological quandary surrounding this issue, which is perhaps why many respondents are unclear in their positions on affirmative action, even when they are ideologically color-blind in most other topics of conversation.[14] In these few cases, some might even say that these respondents are trying to "mimic" white racist ideology by opposing affirmative action on these grounds, but then become stuck by following its logic into a corner that actually does not benefit them.

Similar to the purpose behind veiled antiblack racism, these respondents are using color-blind ideology to separate themselves from a negative image they perceive to be associated with African Americans. That negative rubric, in the case of affirmative action, includes the notion that blacks "use" the serious claim of discrimination "as a crutch," to make "excuses" for their own shortcomings or lack of motivation, and to "take advantage" of institutions in an illicit and deceitful manner. These Latino respondents do not want to be associated with these negative racial stereotypes, so they join the abstract liberalism bandwagon with which to oppose affirmative action. They want to make clear that if they do take advantage of affirmative action programs at times, they do it without the supposedly suspicious intentions generally attributed to blacks. Their comments seem to say: "I may be a racial minority, but not *that kind* of racial minority."

Levan, a Cambodian American respondent, in discussing her opposition to affirmative action, is most critical of African Americans (and Asian Americans) for the above-discussed reasons. In chapter 5 we shall see that even though she is passionate about the prejudices she faces from whites, she consistently uses minimization devices to downplay the extent to which racism has affected her life—another "veiled" way to distance oneself from blacks into a separate "racial middle" group. When asked about her position on antidiscrimination policies, she references her job at clothing retailer Abercrombie & Fitch, and a class action suit some employees filed alleging racial discrimination to make her case:

> I honestly think it's annoying. I honestly hate the race thing because people gotta pull the race card, and it's for stupid stuff like, "Oh oh is it because I'm Asian?" or "Oh, is it because I'm black?" . . . People use the excuse to bring it in because they can't figure out that what they're doing wrong is what they are doing wrong specifically and not because of what their background is. I think it's just a big excuse and it gets really annoying. . . . Everybody at Abercrombie, not everybody, but a lot of people

like to do the whole racist thing with Abercrombie and they actually sent me a letter saying if you want in this, then you can get something out of it, so what they'll do is they'll track you down if you're an employee, they'll send you this and if you sign it, you'll be part of the suing thing against Abercrombie and you'll get something out of it, but it's stupid because it's like they'll always be like, "Do you think Abercrombie has kept you from being promoted because of your race?" and I could just make that shit up and be like, "Yeah yesterday, they made me clean the toilet" and I don't think, it's people being so picky about it. And I'm sure the reason that we get sued is because of some store in Ohio or something stupid like that, but I'm not affected by it because our store is diverse, so I mean it doesn't bother me, but it's just people want to be greedy about it. They want an excuse. It [antidiscrimination law] is necessary, but some people take advantage of it.

While most of this quote is similar to the ideological positions that whites typically take to oppose affirmative action, one aspect stands out. Levan points out that she "could" say she has experienced racial discrimination but she chooses not to do so, because she does not believe it has happened to her. Because she does not believe she has experienced racial discrimination at her own workplace, she generally assumes that others have not and thus are being dishonest about it if they say they have. As we shall see in chapter 5, often people in the racial middle *do* experience racial discrimination regularly, but either do not notice it or have chosen to minimize it in various ways, seeing such experiences as isolated incidents, not bothersome, and so on. In choosing to frame their experiences with discrimination as not race-related or significant, some respondents clearly also seek to distance themselves from those minorities (particularly blacks) who are looked down on by whites for admitting their experiences with racism.

While not directly minimizing racism or criticizing blacks and other groups for "tak[ing] advantage of" affirmative action, other Asian American respondents joined the above Cambodian American respondent in distancing themselves from any perceived benefits of the policy for them and their group. Scott explains why he feels that Chinese in general do not look to the government for assistance:

Because Chinese, China is such a longstanding culture and tradition, people think of things on a longer term basis, and yes there are lots of

—for example, we recognize always that there's discrimination . . . but it was always with an eye towards, well, we're doing this to better our children, and their children, does that make sense? So, again, we've always viewed that as outside of governmental policy, and more that, if you want it, if you want to see things bettered for your family or for your people, it was up to you now to make the sacrifices to improve yourself so that your children will have a better place and the their children will have an even better place. . . . If I think that there are not enough say lawyers— Chinese lawyers, say. Then I would study hard and be a lawyer, and help my children to be lawyers, and then soon enough [there would be more]. . . . as opposed to if only the government could change this policy then it might affect these people and give them a better life, the thinking is much more along, how will it help our people generations down the line, not just these specific people.

Scott is careful to contrast this position on nongovernment intervention with the typical American "up by your bootstraps," individualistic, self-made man position, insisting that the unit of analysis here is the extended family, not the individual. Elsewhere he discusses how, when letting his family know that he and his wife were buying a restaurant, the entire family got together and pooled their money to help him so he would not have to turn to the bank for a loan. Although they ended up going with a bank loan anyhow, this respondent acknowledges that he might feel such sense of familial obligation "kick in" as becomes an elder in the family. While this is Scott's framing of his opposition to affirmative action, it is not the case that all Chinese respondents unilaterally rejected government social programs (like welfare and affirmative action). In fact, another Chinese-Taiwanese American respondent was quite vocally critical of the U.S. government for being so far behind the rest of the industrialized world in not offering any kind of national health care plan. Nevertheless, it is important to point out that this cultural ethic is a significant factor in framing some Asians' opinions about affirmative action. The above passage also demonstrates why qualitative, in-depth interview research methodology is crucial in exploring the question of whether Latinos and Asians are "like blacks" or "like whites" on particular issues. While a quantitative study might simply group this respondent together with whites who oppose affirmative action, it is clear that the rationale he uses to oppose the policy is qualitatively different than that used by most whites.

The common white narrative of "losing out" because of affirmative action,[15] however, also makes an appearance in this sample, particularly among Chinese American respondents like Jim: "Actually we should not have that [affirmative action] . . . because we are not a minority group, and we get hurt [laughs] so we can see it's not fair, [laughs] my opinion is that." Some Asian American respondents have experienced that at some schools, Asian Americans are no longer considered an underrepresented group toward which affirmative action efforts are directed. Indeed, one Filipino American respondent related a story about his sister receiving a scholarship that they extended to her because of her Spanish surname, and when she arrived at the campus and revealed that she was Asian American, they explained that technically they did not normally extend the benefit to Asian Americans. (She was able to keep the scholarship, however, so it is unclear whether this was an official criterion for the award.) Nevertheless, whether real or imagined, the perception that they may be losing out is certainly a factor in framing the resistance of Asian Americans toward affirmative action.

Whenever these conversations about unfairness come up in the interviews, the critiques are always directed toward affirmative action policies in college admission and never toward occupational employment. (Indeed, several Asian American respondents share anecdotes about discrimination in the workplace, as we shall see in chapter 5.) Yet in discussing college admission, particularly for parents of children who were about to or had recently gone through the process, a sense of perceived unfairness is evident for the affirmative action opposers. As another Taiwanese-Chinese American respondent, Ly, explains:

> Actually I don't think anything other than any—like I said, I've never been discriminated against—I do think that when the kids were going through college applications though, that I don't think it was beneficial to be Asian, because the consensus is that it's much harder, everything else equal, much harder for kids to go into the same school, because there are a lot more accomplished Asians who are competing for the same slot, so I think when it comes to college stuff, I found it was a disadvantage for the kids. But I don't know that for sure, it's just my impression from everybody saying that. And the facts are that there are a lot of very strong Asian kids that are applying. Other than that, I don't really see any—I think it's how much effort you put it how much results you get.

Although the general mood of this quote seems much like the typical white storyline of "we lose out because of our race," in reality Ly's position carries a different meaning than that. When "angry white men" complain about the "unfairness" of affirmative action that they perceive themselves to be victims of, their racial scapegoat becomes blacks and occasionally other people of color. Ly does not at all feel his children have to compete with "unqualified minorities"—rather, he identifies the source of racial competition as other highly qualified Asians. Even then, he still acknowledges that he cannot confirm his perception, that it is just based on what "everybody" says.

Later on in Ly's interview, however, the same respondent combines the "Asians are disadvantaged by affirmative action" argument with the characteristically white color-blind racism frames of minimization (using the storyline "the past is the past") and abstract liberalism ("it's just not fair"), along with cultural racism when he suggests that affirmative action encourages laziness on the part of black Americans:

> I think we've had affirmative action for *so* many years. And I realize when you go back to slavery and all that, that black people were badly discriminated. That has been *so* many years ago now. . . . I don't think whites should be discriminated against, just because he's white, and that the black person should get it, because hundred years ago, their grandfather or their ancestors were discriminated. So I don't think affirmative action should be in place anymore. I just think it encourages—whenever you give one group a break, it just encourages that group to go take it easy, and say, well, I'm gonna get in—in terms of like college acceptance, I don't need good grade point average, because I'm gonna get in because I've got a certain ethnic background. Those kids don't deserve the grades, [said angrily] because they didn't exactly get discriminated—so no different than the affirmative action. I can understand fifty years ago that people discriminate, they needed to get extra incentive. That's not the case anymore. So therefore to answer your question, I don't believe affirmative action should be in place anymore . . . not to mention affirmative action is really a negative thing for Asians anyway [said angrily] but that's not the reason that I, I just think that it's not fair. Set aside the Asian negative benefit for the Asians, but more importantly is that it's just like raising kids—you don't give the incentive to work, you're not going to work. If you make it low standard, then that's all you're going to get is low standard, because that's what affirmative action does, for certain groups.

Latinos and Asian Americans perpetuate racist ideology in ways that are quite similar to whites—there is no denying it, especially when confronted with quotes such as this one. Survey research on Latino and Asian Americans attitudes that assume they are merely parroting white ideology, however, masks the ways in which they have uniquely adapted the discourse of racism to their own circumstances. Unlike whites who oppose affirmative action, some Latinos have to work at negotiating how they will both espouse the dominant discourse of equal opportunity and "cash in on" a potential benefit. Likewise, some Asian Americans oppose affirmative action in ways unique to their own racial group by stressing self-help over government and even seeing members of their own group as their foremost competitors. They typically do not draw on feelings of being entitled to slots that have now been "taken away" by unqualified others, a common component of white racist ideology. Yet as we see, they are not immune to internalizing the antiblack stereotypes that permeate the culture.

Antiblack Racism in Theory and in Practice

I am not suggesting that survey research on the racial attitudes of Latinos and Asians does not tell the truth about the particular racial statements with which members of these groups may or may not agree. Rather, it does not tell the whole story or give the full context within which such attitudes and beliefs are held. I find this not only with these in-depth interview data on affirmative action, but also when respondents discuss the messages that their parents gave them growing up about racial others. Other research tells us that Latinos and Asians have been affected by antiblack attitudes in their framing of interracial intimacy and marriage. They are much more likely to intermarry with whites than with blacks.[16] Respondents report that their parents made it clear that whites were more desirable partners than members of other racial groups, especially blacks. This pattern will be explored in more detail in the next chapter on interracial intimacy. Bonilla-Silva's research finds that whites are often likely to, in theory, say interracial marriage is OK with them, but once it gets closer to home, such as with their own children's dating and marriage choices, they are more resistant.[17] In this sample, however, particularly with some Asian respondents, the reverse relationship between parents' theory and practice emerges. That is, some respondents experienced their parents espousing cultural racism when discussing African Americans in the abstract, but when individual members of this culturally stigmatized group came closer to home, Asian American parents embraced them with open arms.

As chapter 6 will reveal in more detail, it seems that Latinos and Asians who come from parents of mixed ethnicities are already poised to question racial dividing lines a bit more than their mono-racial-household counterparts. Charlene, a Filipino-Thai American respondent, regularly pokes holes in the arbitrariness of racial ideology and practice, beginning with her own parents and extending outward into the broader social arena:

> My parents never said anything about "oh don't be friends with these types of people," or "you can't trust these types of people," although they, especially my mother expresses very racist opinions about Hispanics and blacks and whites. But she never applies them to specific people that I was friends with, so I don't know, it's almost like all the white people I knew, they were the "good" white people, all the black kids I knew, they were the "good" black kids, but in general, you know, you can't . . . "they're lazy, you can't trust them, they don't value work," that sort of thing. [laughter] [Interviewer: So it never translated into telling you you couldn't play with, be with certain people because once they had a face on them, they were OK?] Right, exactly, exactly. But then there's also things like not wanting, so whenever they thought about moving, not wanting to move to a neighborhood where there was too many blacks or too many Hispanics or going to, or us going to a public school where there were too many blacks or too many Hispanics. You know, always worrying when a house came up for sale, "Oh, is another black family going to move in?" but then if a black family did move in and we became friends, that was fine.

Here the conflicting racial messages of childhood culminate in a happy ending—"we became friends, that was fine." Yet reports from whites in other research often tell of the reverse, sadder ending, as in, "my parents told me we are all the same" but the resulting experience in practice is resistance when actually socializing or dating interracially.

Another ethnically mixed Asian American respondent, Rebecca, with Chinese, Macanese, and Portuguese origins, also observes a more positive response from her parents to the actual blacks she brings home than the imagined blacks they denounce sight unseen:

> It's weird, in theory they'll say, "The black boy's no good for you," whatever, but in practice I'll have black male friends and they'll be like, "Oh my gosh he's so nice, and he's so smart!" But, I think it's the reverse for white males—if I were to date a white male, I think they wouldn't— I think they would be like, "Well . . . our grandchildren are gonna be pretty," and then in practice they'll be like, "Well, what does he know about your culture, what does he know about struggle," and they wouldn't say that about a black person. They would say like, "If you wanna move up, then marry a white person" or something, but "don't expect them to understand you."

We could conceive of these Asian parents answering survey questions that confirm negative stereotypes about African Americans, simply because a survey asks them to consider abstract hypothetical individuals as opposed to actual blacks in their lives. Such results would perhaps overstate the extent to which those in the racial middle subscribe wholesale to racist ideology. As we have also seen in the earlier section on selective deconstruction of stereotypes, members of the racial middle tend to be more complex in how they espouse stereotypical thinking, embracing some components of it while rejecting others—a color-nuanced approach. In this particular case of Asian parents and antiblack racism, the complexity of this negotiation of stereotypes results in an ultimately positive outcome —the deconstruction of racial dividing lines, and the embrace of a multiracial social circle. Thus, while social scientists tend to interpret white racial attitude surveys as conservative estimates, acknowledging that whites can sometimes understate the extent of their prejudices, perhaps for those in the racial middle, such results may indeed overstate the case of just how "white" they really are.

Conclusion

Occupying an intermediate position in the U.S. racial hierarchy does not simply mean that one is somewhat like whites and somewhat like blacks. While certainly the above quotes demonstrate that several Latino and Asian American respondents use color-blind ideology in ways similar to that which has been documented in research on whites, they additionally make use of color-blind racism in ways unique to them. Indeed, whites particularly have been reported to be a bit more simplistic in their usage of color-blindness than these respondents are. They typically use blacks as their nonwhite group of comparison, and when addressing the "intermediate" groups, they are often lumped together with all people of color. If whites do separate out intermediate groups in their discussions, they tend to be singled out for more "positive" stereotyping than blacks. For instance, some elite white men in one study praised the work ethic of Mexicans and Asian Americans as a whole while viewing negatively that of blacks.[18] They are held up as "model minorities" if only to cast a negative comparison with African Americans. From a white perspective, a distinct hierarchy seems to emerge on a scale of valued to devalued: whites, Asian Americans/Latinos, blacks. Indeed, some analysts have used a "middleman" minority framework to analyze the experiences of these groups.[19] In contrast, from the viewpoint of Latinos and Asians themselves, the situation is more complex. Latinos and Asians seem to resist racialized generalizations about their own groups, stressing the *ethnic* distinctions among them that are sometimes lost on other whites, and even on members of other "outsider" nonwhite groups. In the process of stressing these ethnic distinctions, they use them both to deconstruct racist ideology for some groups (especially their own) and to reify it for others.

Racist ideology has been constructed for the benefit of the dominant group (whites) in order to make it work toward their advantage; Latinos and Asian Americans must therefore be much more sophisticated about how they use it, because in its most commonly used forms it does not address them directly. While the fact that racist ideology has been constructed for the benefit of whites might suggest that there is less flexibility in its usage for Latinos and Asian Americans, actually in some ways there is more flexibility for them to make use of it. Specifically, they have room to exercise antiblack racism in ways even more camouflaged than whites do by using these ethnic distinctions among themselves and other racially-similar groups through which to "veil" their negative sentiments about blacks. We saw a Dominican respondent "veil" her antiblack racism through Ecuadorians, and a Filipino respondent "veil" her antiblack racism through Filipinos who are "ghetto" or like hip-hop. Two other Latino respondents made fewer ethnic distinctions, but rather felt freer to discuss blacks explicitly once they lumped their own racial category of Hispanic together with blacks (at the same time distancing themselves as individuals from that collective). This veiling dynamic demonstrates that as "insiders," Latinos and Asians can exercise an ideological option that makes them more comfortable casting negative light on African Americans if they combine their own racial group along with it.

Further, their selective deconstruction of stereotypes shows that those in the racial middle often have the conceptual tools to unpack the kinds of reasoning behind cultural racism, but at times choose not to do so and instead fall in step with dominant racial discourse. Many may tiptoe around generalized assumptions about African Americans but feel more comfortable relying on stereotypes both for other ethnic groups within their own racial category and for other categories in the racial middle of which they are not members. A Cuban respondent who mentions Muslims and Mexicans as somewhat deserving of racial profiling, an Indian respondent who generalizes about all Chinese, and a Honduran-Dominican respondent who posits Asian Americans as the "opposite of a Latin" are just some examples. Perhaps because at any time outsiders may lump them together with these other "middle" groups, these respondents want to take great pains to distinguish themselves from each other. As we shall see in chapter 6, however, there are plenty of other more progressive respondents who point out the shared discrimination and historic struggle against white supremacy that they share with others in the racial middle and with African Americans.

If color-blind racism has been characterized as a more sophisticated and savvy form of racism than the more overt racism that preceded it historically, then clearly Latinos and Asian Americans, as intermediate groups, have taken this sophistication to an even more elevated level with their color-nuanced positions. Bonilla-Silva and Embrick discuss this more complex manifestation of color-blind racism as they compare Latin American race relations to those of the United States.[20] My research suggests that both Latinos and Asian Americans, as intermediate racial groups in the U.S. racial hierarchy, may indeed contribute to these new dimensions of racism.

4

Interracial Border Crossing

Commonalities and Diversions in the Racial Middle

Every group tends to express a certain degree of ethnocentrism toward their own culture. While the prospect of "blending into" the majority may be trumpeted as an overwhelmingly positive experience—the ultimate in citizenship, toward which all should aspire—every group that has experienced it historically has also gone through some fear about losing what is unique about them in the process. For instance, many white ethnic groups still pride themselves on the aspects of their culture that are distinct from the larger American majority, and participate in largely symbolic celebrations of that cultural distinction from time to time. Such events include the Irish American parade on St. Patrick's Day, and Scottish/Celtic festivals.[1] Members of every group seem to cling to the aspects that make them unique, and hope that those aspects that they pride themselves on would not die out or be lost to succeeding generations who would forget "their roots" or "where they came from."

Still, as Mary Waters's work points out, white ethnics certainly have the choice of hanging on to these unique European cultural artifacts.[2] There is no penalty for them doing so in the larger society, in the same way that Latinos and Asian Americans are looked down on for allegedly "not speaking English." As we shall see particularly in the next chapter on prejudice and discrimination, negative stigma is still attached in the dominant culture to those in the racial middle who appear to be attempting to retain aspects of their "brown" cultures instead of leaving it all behind and assimilating completely into American culture. Nevertheless, a very clear narrative runs through many of these interviews of those in the racial middle, expressing that very desire to retain aspects of their culture, and a poignant fear of the possibility that those aspects would be lost. Language is the most significant of those cultural aspects, repeatedly discussed by respondents in their discussions of the presence (real or hypothetical) of racial/ethnic "others" in their families. They express a hopeful desire (although not usually a rigidly exclusive one) that their family members would at least consider other family formations that would help them retain their own cultural traditions and keep them from being forever "lost." Several respondents even use the same phrase: "it would be nice" for them and/or their children to end up with someone who shared similar linguistic and cultural practices. This kind of in-group preference is cultural, rather than racial, because it often exists without any accompanying sense of superiority or inferiority about other groups, and includes an ultimate resigned acceptance of most others as potential mates.

In saying that they display an acceptance of *most* others, however, I am referring to white Americans more so than African Americans. As we have seen in the previous chapter, those in the racial middle have also internalized the racism of the dominant culture to varying degrees. Latinos and Asian Americans have received clear messages about the ideal of whiteness in American culture, and the corresponding disdain for blackness. Thus, it should come as no surprise that, when embracing racial "others" into their families, Latinos and Asian Americans are much more likely to have families that approve of non-Hispanic white intermarriages than they are to approve of intermarriages with blacks. Indeed, while several of our respondents are out-married to white spouses, only one respondent has a black (Jamaican) spouse, and she too is black (Puerto Rican American). While one other Korean American respondent was bold enough to marry a Mexican (noncitizen), she was not facing the same pressures to retain cultural traditions as discussed above; she was raised by white American parents who did not attempt to learn about Korean culture or transmit it to their daughter. Nevertheless, it is telling that whether their parents are white, Asian, or Latino, a good portion of the sample got clear racial (not just cultural) messages that out-marriage to whites is more acceptable than out-marriage to blacks, and their own dating and marital choices have largely reflected that.

It is important to note that there certainly is a numerical explanation for the pattern of out-marriage to whites more than other groups, so there is a demographic aspect partially affecting these choices—there are more whites available for the taking. On examining respondent testimony, however, it is clear that these numbers do not operate in a vacuum. Beyond whites being more readily available, many families communicate specific understandings about who is and is not an acceptable dating/marriage partner to their children, and whites consistently rank higher on the hierarchy of acceptability than do blacks. While there may be some cultural underpinnings to this ethnocentrism as well, it is more clearly racialized, because in both cases the families assume a monolingual English speaker, whether they are white or black. Theoretically, if neither whites nor blacks speak the home language of the respondents, then they should be considered at an equal position on the hierarchy of acceptability (if indeed culture were the only issue). So it is evident that more than just in-group ethnocentrism is fueling the rejection of blacks.

While the above patterns were common in both Latino and Asian respondents, there were also important ways in which some members of the two groups differed from one another. First, it was only Asian American respondents who noted actual rejection of whites as potential partners—no Latino respondents indicated complete rejection of white interracial intimacy. Some Asian American respondents actually expressed a disdain for certain American cultural values that, in their view, would de-emphasize education and reduce respect for their elders. This was a more "severe" ethnocentrism than that expressed by the majority of the total sample. Most of the sample did have a fear of cultural loss, but the fear of language loss, for example, was not typically accompanied by a rejection of the English language or any negative judgment of the English language. In contrast, when some Asian American respondents lament potential cultural loss, it sometimes coexists with a disdain for "degenerate American values" that they do not want adopted by their children. They may worry that they will become disrespected and that racism will be internalized to the point of damaging their own "Asian-ness," as exemplified by actions like the popular eye fold surgery that some Asian American women undergo to escape the negative "slanty-eye" stereotype.[3] At times, this is not as much an expression of disdain for whiteness in general as it is distaste for the decadence, individualism, and superiority that has come with the affluence of the United States. Many Asian American parents try to do everything they can to avoid having their children become as disrespectful to them as they fear white Americans have become towards their own parents. One does not sense that Asian Americans' rejection of whiteness here is biological or even cultural, but rather is a reaction to U.S. dominance on the global scene, to the neglect of the important contributions of Asians.

On the flip side, the second area where Asian Americans and Latinos diverge is on the matter of whiteness as a positive—as an actual step-up from their own group. Only Latinos express this view. Clara Rodriguez has used the term "pigmentocracies" to refer to the "colorism" predominant in Latin American communities, and she traces its history back to slavery.[4] While there were some key differences in how slavery in the United States and slavery in Latin America operated, in both cases the experience of being colonized by European powers led to a higher value on lighter skin. Thus, still today, research on both Latinos and African Americans in the United States shows that the lighter-skinned members of each group receive more privileges, both in terms of prestige and status as well as material benefits like jobs and housing. Lighter-skinned Latinos tend to hold higher positions and be less spatially segregated than their darker-skinned counterparts.[5] All this history and its contemporary vestiges have apparently resulted in a shared narrative that prizes lighter skin and whiteness. Indeed, as a minority group that is already defined as partially European (Hispanic), they stand to reap the greatest gain through an emphasis on phenotypic features (relative to Asian Americans). Thus, some Latino families will more than settle for an out-marriage to a white —in some cases, they would even prefer it to members of their own group. While the dominant pattern for both groups in the racial middle was to have at least some fear of cultural loss and devaluation, in the case of Latinos in particular, the value placed on "whitening up" was so strong that it trumped all concerns about cultural loss.

Patterns of Preferences Expressed by Family Members

There were two different interview questions where respondents were asked to reflect on views on interracial dating and marriage. The first question read as follows: "How did your family feel about you dating outside your ethnic group? How did you feel about it? Did you ever do it? What was the reaction? [Probe for racial/ethnic groups not mentioned.] What about outside your religion? Did any members of your family do so? What was the reaction?" A second question that occurred later on in the interview asked the following: "Do your children (and grandchildren) see themselves as _____? Is it less important to them than it is to you, or about the same? What would you hope they learn about being _____? Would you prefer they choose someone _____ to spend their lives with, or does it matter? Are certain groups more preferable than others?" The interviewer was expected to fill in the blanks with the racial/ethnic label

TABLE 4-1
Family's Preferences for Dating and Marriage Partners by Race

	Latinos (n = 23)	Asians (n = 27)	Total (n = 50)
Preference for same ethnicity	5	6	11
Preference for same religion	4	2	6
Preference for same race	2	5	7
Rejection of whites	0	3	3
Acceptance of whites	11	6	17
Rejection of blacks	5	4	9
Fine with all	3	8	11

the respondent used most frequently to refer to him- or herself. Certain parts of these questions received more input from some respondents than others, depending on their level of experience with each part of the question. When counting up patterns, I count a mention of a particular theme as one occurrence of it. So if a respondent discusses disapproval of blacks and acceptance of whites, he or she is counted two times, once in each of those categories. Alternatively, if they mention neither of these, they may not be counted at all, particularly if they do not want to address the question or are not sure about it.

Examining table 4-1, clearly the most frequent pattern, even more than a preference for one's own ethnic group as intimate partners, is an acceptance of whites as partners. Certainly this means that those within the group are also accepted, but usually that went without saying for most respondents. It is only when members of their own group were actually discussed as preferred over others ("it would be nice . . .") that they were counted in that first category.

Religion seemed to be less important to families than ethnicity and race overall, but Latinos were twice as likely to mention family's strong religious preferences. While this sometimes went so far as to request Catholics only, sometimes it was more important to families to have a Christian of any denomination, so long as their initial marriage was in the Catholic Church. Indeed, there were some restrictions on religion placed by some family members that seemed to be both religious and ethnic. A few Latino and East Asian families showed resistance to Hindu and Muslim cultures, sometimes using what they perceived to be a restrictive view on the status of women as their major reason.

While Latinos were more likely to mention religion, Asian Americans were more likely to discuss preferences along the lines of the panethnic

umbrella of an "Asian" race. Few Latinos describe their parents as preferring someone "Latino"—they sometimes request someone who speaks
Spanish, but as we will see from the quotes presented in this chapter, this
request is not racially bound. When Latino families speak of in-group
preferences, they almost always are within a specific ethnicity (another
Mexican, another Puerto Rican American, and so on). Because such countries are closer to the United States, it becomes easier to be able to refer
to these specific ethnicities, and also to expect other Americans to be familiar with them (as part of the greater "Americas"). Asian families, as it
turns out, are not just looking to retain their particular language through
in-group marriage, but they are also looking to ward off certain Westernized values of which they disapprove. These cultural differences include
respect for one's elders, conservative styles of dress, and extreme value on
education. Because they perceive several Asian cultures to be similar to
them in that respect, Asian families seem to allow room for other Asian
ethnicities to be preferable to even white partners, regardless of whether
they speak the same language or not. These values differences did not
seem to come up as much for Latino families, who were more likely to
describe marriage with whites as a positive. While both Latinos and Asian
Americans prefer whites more than they prefer blacks, there is no sense
that Asian Americans feel whites "uplift" their race. Indeed, Asian American families were the only ones to actually reject white partners; no Latino families did so. While these differences between Latinos and Asian
Americans will be explored in depth later on in the chapter, I begin with
an examination of the most common pattern across both groups—the
hopeful desire that same-ethnicity mating would occur as the seemingly
"easiest" way to preserve cultural traditions, particularly language.

"It Would Be Nice . . .": Fear of Cultural/Language Loss

Discussions about why a romantic partner within one's own ethnic group
would be preferable focus on mainly cultural aspects: ability to speak one's
language of origin, to observe certain special holidays, to be able to cook
certain staple foods for special occasions, and so on. Respondents believe
it would be easier to pass such traditions onto the next generation when
both partners share them. Many observe that even in situations of group
in-marriage, however, cultural traditions such as speaking one's language
of origin are not necessarily passed onto the next generation. Thus, while

families will often say that within-group marriage "would be nice," they would not stand in the way of marriage to other groups, especially not to whites. We might conceive of this in-group ethnocentrism as a gentle prodding toward in-marriage, but not often a position of rigid inflexibility based on any notions of superiority or inferiority (as occurs with antiblack racism). Rather, it is a narrative punctuated by a sadness about impending cultural loss—one that may indeed occur with or without a same-ethnicity romantic partner. But the prospect of a same-ethnicity partner is one hope among many that families hold onto as a small reassurance that perhaps some traditions may be more likely to be passed down the generations, despite every pressure to the contrary in the wider society.

Scott, a Chinese-Taiwanese American respondent who is foreign born but grew up since childhood in the United States, now has a white wife and two biracial children. Although he describes his extended family as completely accepting of his white wife, a clear preference for Chinese in-marriage was indicated to him while in his dating years:

> Now there was of course though a fair bit of pressure, not from my parents but from kind of my greater family, to date a Chinese girl. . . . It's harder to find, there are fewer of them. . . . But you know when I was in college, every time I visited my uncle in Georgia, you know they would have set up three dates for me. [Interviewer laughs] I'm serious [Interviewer: Three different girls?] Yeah, yeah. Not every time, but you know, but there would at least be one. You know, here's a hundred dollars, here's the key to the sports car, go have a good time. [laughter] . . . All of my family is very accepting of [white wife] and I don't think that that's an issue—she was, of course, worried about that—but if they had their wishes and desires they would have preferred that I married a Chinese girl.

Respondents often experienced their family's gentle prodding toward dating and marriage within their own ethnicity as kind-spirited efforts that were not meant to exclude or be unkind to other groups. In other words, preferences for one's own ethnicity were seen sympathetically and not resented as heavy-handed or restrictive intervention. As one Mexican American male respondent, Ricardo, relates:

> I don't know, it's a tricky question, because when I was little my mom definitely wanted me to date a Latina and I did go out with the occasional Latina girl but I didn't restrict myself, I don't think. I dated different

kinds of girls. So my mom kind of changed her opinion, and, was telling me just as long as she speaks Spanish. Just 'cause, she says, whoever you are going out with has to be able to communicate with the family. And I can understand that and I felt comfortable with that, like, my mom was pretty understanding as far as girls of other races are concerned. And yes, I have, I've dated a black girl, I've dated a white girl, and actually my current girlfriend is white. She does speak Spanish so my parents like that. She visited me one time in California and spoke to my grandparents in Spanish and the reaction was good, they really liked the fact that she spoke Spanish. I think that's all that they really cared about.

Ricardo makes a recurring point that within-ethnicity preferences often have a basis in concerns about transmitting culture (particularly language) to the next generation, and are not necessarily about groups being superior or inferior to each other. In this case, clearly the potential mate's ability to speak the extended family's language was more important than whether or not she was Latina. This ability to speak the language, and willingness to learn the language, could also communicate a level of cultural respect to the parents—a reassurance that their culture is not looked down on by the "outsider." Again, as with the first example, both exceptions were made for whites. We do not have enough information here on the mother's reaction to the "black girl" to know whether this language exception would have been extended to nonwhite others.

This Mexican American female respondent, Edita, similarly explores how families' concerns about language are connected to their desires for their culture to be respected by potential new family members from "outside" the group:

Yes. I have [dated interracially] several times, but my parents aren't very comfortable with it just because they want Spanish-speaking grandchildren and they're nervous about the fact that if I marry outside of our culture, I'm gonna end up with someone who just speaks English, and they're not happy about that. And, I don't know, I've always thought that I'm going to teach my kids Spanish, but then I wonder if that's really going to happen and how realistic that is. Because with my close friends, I speak English to most of them, so it would just be awkward speaking to my children in Spanish. . . . I think, for some reason, my mom seems to like white people over blacks or Asians, basically anything if they're not Hispanic to begin with. I'm not really sure why, but she says they're the ones who seem the most interested to learn our culture. Like you're more likely to run into a white man who spent fifty years studying Spanish, I don't know, this is something she thinks. [laughs] I don't really agree with her, but whatever, I don't care, that's her.

Edita's mother's primary concern is also language—that is, her daughter's ability to pass on the Spanish language to the next generation, and how her choice of a romantic partner might affect that ability. But the second part of the quote shows that language is only one aspect of culture, and that her mother seems to respect anyone, regardless of race/ethnicity, who would be "the most interested to learn our culture." This type of person would communicate respect for her own "minority" culture and alleviate fears that she and her family would be looked down on by cultural "others." The mother acknowledges that potentially this cultural respect could be embodied by someone outside of their culture, such as a "white man." This concern about not speaking the language, however, might also sometimes be used to "veil" antiblack racism, when whites are deemed acceptable out-marriage partners, but blacks are not. When her mother is simply concerned about cultural loss and lack of respect, she can empathize, but when she uses this concern as a smokescreen for antiblack racism, she becomes critical. Edita does not believe African Americans would be any less likely to spend "fifty years studying Spanish" than any other group.

Parental pressures are sometimes tough to negotiate, particularly for the younger adults in the sample. Rebecca, a Chinese-Macanese-Portuguese respondent, agrees with several other Asian American young adults in the sample that dating *in general* is frowned on by one's elders, regardless of ethnicity. Thus, she feels that no matter *who* she brought home, if the person appeared to be more than a friend and perhaps a more serious distraction from her studies, this would be problematic. Several young respondents concealed their dating activities from their parents entirely. Rebecca, however, was able to get her parents' permission to go on a platonic lunch with a young man (who is actually her current boyfriend) by letting both sets of parents talk to each other on the phone. In an interesting twist, the boyfriend is actually Dominican, but his stepfather speaks Cantonese. In this way, Rebecca observes that the language piece is an important component of her parents' preferences:

Well, my boyfriend is Dominican . . . but it's weird 'cause his stepfather is Asian and so his little sister is half Asian, half Dominican . . . so I tried to call my mom one time and I was like, "Hey Mom, I'm gonna go out to dinner with [name]'s family" and she's like, "What, what?" because they met him once and they thought he was white cause he's a really light Dominican, and they didn't like him because he seemed too much of a manly man or something, I don't know what it was, 'cause Asian guys are very gentle, and they're very mannerly and stuff like that. . . . But when I mentioned his name, they get like really upset and so I tried to put his stepfather on the phone cause they speak the same language and so they just got confused, so they never really clarified what ethnicity he was, so . . . [Interviewer: So his stepfather speaks Cantonese also?] Mm-hm, and he spoke to my mom and was like, "Hey, could [respondent name] come over for dinner Monday" and then my mom's like, "Oh okay!" . . . Of course like when—she has some inkling that maybe he might be Asian . . . "you can go out to eat."

Of course, this young woman is utilizing a common youthful tactic with her parents, giving them as little information as possible so they can hopefully assume whatever they need to assume in the appropriate direction and she will not have to be officially dishonest. But the anecdote also raises some interesting recurring points about ethnicity preferences. In this case, when her parents thought the boyfriend was white and not Asian, they "didn't like him" (showing distaste for whites, which is more typical of Asian Americans than of Latinos in the sample). These inferences were based more on phenotype alone, however, so once her parents got more information about her boyfriend's family background, and recognized that there was some aspect of appreciation of their own culture in his experience, they were more willing to accept him into their daughter's social circle, even though he appears non-Asian. Yet again, we do not know whether if he had appeared as a darker-skinned or black Dominican her parents would have made a similar exception. But clearly, language is an important "swing factor," particularly in the case of whites or those perceived to be white.

Caitlin, a Puerto Rican American mother of two adult children—one who married another Puerto Rican American and one who did not—is now a grandmother to children of mixed cultural backgrounds. Her disapproval for the way some of her grandchildren are being raised clearly has more to do with language than with the racial identity of the children's mother. This seems believable also because Caitlin was herself adopted by white parents and has a white spouse now herself (not the father of her children though). So it does not seem to be whiteness itself that she is disdainful of, but rather the lack of effort to pass down the Spanish language, and to a lesser extent other cultural traditions:

> Who they [my children] spend their lives with doesn't matter to me, but my oldest son is married to a Puerto Rican and he lives in Puerto Rico and his children are growing up in Puerto Rico. And that is very important to me. My youngest son is married to a North American woman who is—she's fine, they're separated but I still love her, and he has a new girlfriend and she's North American, but I think there's a very distinct piece of him that's very clear that he's Puerto Rican. I think I worry about his daughter though because she's growing up in the United States and she's not speaking the language and so I'm trying to convince him to, since he's the primary caregiver, that he needs to socialize and be the socialization in the way that she can speak Spanish, he should talk to her in Spanish. . . . He lives in Orlando so he has access to Spanish, you know, just put the Spanish on and let her figure it out, she will. So I'm a little worried there. . . . Yeah, because the other two [who live in Puerto Rico] are both bilingual and, I mean, one's four, how bilingual is he? But he speaks and understands it . . . he speaks Spanish every day of his life, so its important for me for them to be bilingual, and bicultural. And I think that [granddaughter]'s not going to be bicultural, and that, I'm sorry for that.

Interestingly, Caitlin's disapproval is actually more targeted at the choices her own Puerto Rican American son is making in not speaking Spanish with his daughter than with the identity of either his ex-wife or his current girlfriend (both "North American"). There is, however, a connection being made here. More of an effort must be made to teach a child a language when she cannot hear two adults speaking it back and forth to each other in the home. There is a sense that this cultural transmission is "easier" when both partners share the same language and ethnicity.

The Taiwanese-Chinese American respondent, Scott, whose uncles always set him up on blind dates with "Chinese girls," is currently married to a white woman with whom he shares two children. He also admits it would be "easier" for him to teach his children Cantonese if his wife spoke it also. Even though he is perfectly happy with his own out-marriage choice, he would still prefer his children consider marrying someone Chinese, possibly because he now understands through everyday lived experience how difficult it is to transmit one's culture without a partner who is equally equipped to do so. When asked if he would like for his children to choose someone Chinese with whom to spend their lives, he responds:

> I would say that it would be a positive. I would even encourage it if I could. . . . I would certainly like it if they dated a Chinese girl, and probably I would be more involved in the Chinese community than my parents were . . . because I just recently passed the stage where like I think in English, [so] I will have to work harder to be Chinese than they will, and my children would even have to work even harder.

When there is only one parent that speaks the language and the parents do not communicate with each other in that language, it requires much more of a conscious effort to instill bilingualism. This is a task that is likely to fall by the wayside given the myriad tasks assigned to a parent, particularly a male parent whose spouse spends more of the time with the children than he does. Scott points out, earlier in his interview, when asked whether his children speak Chinese:

> I would love to teach them but the reality is it's [wife] that spends the most time [with them]. I mean, they are interested in Chinese, and I teach them words all the time, and they have a little book like a little learner thing, and they are interested in Chinese and know probably twenty words, say, but it's hard to embark on a dedicated curricula [*sic*] without investing a lot of time. I don't want to force it on them so hard that they're like, oh, gosh, dad, Chinese, you know, what about baseball? [laughs] So it's part of who they are and part of what they learn—they know that they're Chinese as well and they're interested in that—but as interested as they are in football or writing, or Clifford the big red dog. [laughs]

When the language is not spoken regularly in the home, it becomes an endeavor of a "dedicated curricula." Thus, perhaps foreseeing this pattern and fearing that their grandchildren or future grandchildren might not be able to speak to them in their native language, parents advocate for a same-ethnicity partner to make that job easier, and thus more likely to occur.

This in-marriage preference, however, does not seem to be a rigid proscription, perhaps because many families realize it is hardly the potential "outsider" mate alone that would keep the language from being continually taught. Several respondents idealistically want to raise their future children to be bilingual and/or bicultural but do not feel that they are fluent enough to be able to do so. So it would not even be a potential "outsider" spouse but their *own* lack of cultural/linguistic knowledge that would be the break in that chain of cultural transmission. As Neva, a Mexican American respondent, states of her future children:

> I don't know if they'll as strongly identify as Mexican American as I do, but I'm concerned about who will teach them that. Because I, myself wasn't taught that, and I talk about that with my mom like, "Mom, why didn't you teach me to be more tied to my culture," and one of the things that she said was "how can I teach you, when I wasn't taught myself?" And that's very true. So, I hope they'll speak Spanish, but I don't know how they'll learn it because my Spanish consists of one college semester of it.

Desperately wanting to fit in, some parents of the first and second generations often deemphasize the native language, stressing only English in the home. This sometimes is a source of collective regret in the subsequent generations that they do not have more cultural knowledge. Waters's study of white ethnics revealed similar regrets and nostalgia for an era in which respondents imagined their families to be more culturally connected. Some would even "revive" symbolic aspects of the culture—not usually fluent language, but certain customs and special occasions—in order to alleviate their sense of loss.[6]

Crystal, another biracial white-Asian respondent, when reflecting on future children, similarly reflects: "I just hope that they're proud of it [their ethnicity] and learn some of the holidays and cultural aspects, like the food. And hopefully my grandma will still be around." Here the grandmother is seen as the only one who can really pass on such cultural traditions. Another Vietnamese respondent, Lisa, also looks backward generationally (to her parents) as she considers who will transmit cultural knowledge to her future children: "I hope they learn like from my parents. Since they're growing up here, I probably won't be able to speak Vietnamese to them everyday like my parents did with me, but I just want them to get along with my parents, know the tradition, know about New Year's, know the holidays, know some of the language, that's really important to me." It is this collective sense that, even with a spouse who shares their same ethnicity, it may be difficult to reach back far enough for cultural

knowledge, that perhaps allows respondents to ease up on any rigid re-
quirements of in-group marriage as a means of cultural transmission. If
they cannot solely transmit it (without the help of the older generation),
why should they then presume that a spouse who shares their ethnicity
would be of any greater help than they themselves would? There emerges
from the interviews a sense of resigned acknowledgment that, while it
may "be nice" for cultural transmission to continue, the reality is that it
may not, with or without in-group marriage.

This kind of acknowledgment and acceptance emerges clearly in the
following quote from Rohit, an Indian respondent, who sees greater acceptance of out-marriage even with the succeeding generations of siblings
in her own family:

> The first time it [out-marriage] happened in the family, they were almost
> like really upset and outraged about it, that was my second sister that
> did it, and then my third sister did it, they were OK, they accepted it.
> And now I see things have changed a lot, because you know obviously I
> got married sixteen years ago, my sisters got married six years ago, and
> within that ten years, things have changed a lot. . . . There is a lot of mod-
> ernization of India that's happening, and so overall the parents are be-
> coming more open [and] . . . more flexible now. . . . You know I would
> say that since we decided to stay in this country, I would be very open
> for my children to marry anyone. I've seen both kinds of marriages work
> and fail, so Indians marrying Indians have failed, and Indians married
> non-Indians have worked tremendously, and vice versa. So I just wish
> them that they find the partner in life that they are mutually compatible
> with, and they—what I would instill in my kids is the value that marriage
> is not just a disposable item and that you make every effort to make it
> work. And it's OK whoever they choose to be their life partner. I think
> just because of the fact that I'm more comfortable with Indians, that is
> something that yes, I would ask them to keep in their minds, but again,
> like you know I have so many American friends and non-Indian friends
> that I'm so comfortable with on a one-to-one basis that I would be open
> to that as well. As long as they're happy and have the right match, and
> they make the right decision, I would support it.

Taking note of the fact that Indian culture has become progressively
more Westernized, Rohit feels less of an imperative to see her children
in-marry as a means of preserving culture. Although she still wants her

children to keep Indian mates "in mind" (or "give them a chance," as another Asian American respondent says), she is open to this sense of inevitable progression toward greater acceptance of intermarriage through the years, even in her own family. Their word choices reveal that the racial/ ethnic identity of the mate is certainly correlated with their more pressing concern: that their children would actually become so embedded in the dominant culture that they would no longer even regard members of their own group with the same esteem they give to "Americans." Internalized racism is a major issue faced by those in the racial middle.[7] Parents fear this kind of demoralizing self-regard happening to their children, with or without an interracial marriage. If their children made the choice to date or marry outside their group, they would just hope that this choice did not emanate from this kind of self-loathing they fear. Moreover, they would hope that such a partner would also join them in nurturing the self-respect of their child and their culture of origin and not detract from it.

Thus, while dating and marriage within one's own ethnicity "would be nice," for non-racialized reasons, many respondents and their families also are open to other mating possibilities, particularly with the white Americans with whom they are familiar. White Americans are not only more visible and in greater numbers, but are assumed to be more likely to be respectful of "others" than other nonwhite groups outside of their own. Already concerned that their group will not be respected in the wider society, some respondents would not want to further jeopardize that status by associating with a group they know to be held in even lower regard in the United States: African Americans.

Antiblack Racism: Concerns about Status, Color, and Compatibility

Although described by a much smaller proportion of the sample, there is another cluster of views on interracial border crossing that is common to both groups in the racial middle: the specific prohibition of dating or marrying blacks. This is discussed by ten respondents, spread evenly across Latinos and Asian Americans in the sample (five Latinos and five Asians). The sentiments expressed by these respondents sound familiar to those that most other research on this topic has found to be present in white Americans.[8] These concerns are heightened, however, by the ever-present knowledge that members of the racial middle occupy a tenuous status and cannot afford to be "brought down" by someone ranked lower than themselves in the U.S. racial hierarchy. A marital choice of a black partner has greater chance of jeopardizing the "honorary white" potential of someone in the racial middle.[9] Some of these viewpoints have already been discussed in the previous chapter on racial ideology. Recall the young Filipino American respondent who admits that, in her experience, Filipinos are "a little racist toward African Americans," but they would be open and accepting of a white partner. Heather, another Filipino American respondent whose father is white and mother is Filipino, observes that her parents had a preference for Asian Americans and whites over blacks and Hispanics:

> There was a time when I was in high school that a black guy came over just as a friend, I invited him to have dinner, and my mother asked me to ask him to leave. . . . I have dated outside of my race. I have dated black men, but I've never told my parents about it. Yeah because I don't, I absolutely don't think they would approve of their daughter dating a black man. . . . They put less potential on Hispanic and black people than they do on white people and Asian people. And that's the way they've always spoke about it.

Although at one point Heather perceives that her parents would disapprove of both blacks and Latinos as dating partners for her, her concrete and vivid experiences have only been ones that included African American men. Interestingly, she has a considerably younger brother who shows a strong preference for African American women, of which she has noticed her parents becoming more accepting over the years. Although Heather attributes this to mainly a generational change, one cannot help but wonder if gender also plays a role in the family's greater lenience toward their son's dating choices.

Likewise, Rosa, another biracial respondent who has one white parent, experienced greater openness in her family toward whites than other races, particularly blacks. She now is also married to a white man herself. Rosa reflects on the differences between her white (Russian) mother and Mexican father in how they might respond to her dating someone black:

> I never dated anyone who was African American or Asian. I don't know how my parents would have reacted. I think my mom would probably

have been more okay with it too. My dad probably would have taken him a little while to get over it. And I think it is just because growing up in Mexico you have the diversity—in terms of white, or you are indigenous, but there aren't really that color sections off [race is on a more fluid continuum]. In Mexico, you don't have that many Africans, so I think just because it is different, my dad would have been a little shocked—just because he didn't grow up around people that are black.

This quote is interesting because, like Heather did, Rosa combines the other racial middle group in her response only once, and then the rest of the discussion largely focuses on blacks alone. Several other respondents experienced this "anything but blacks" attitude from their families. For instance, Alfonso, a white–Puerto Rican American respondent, also married to a European white woman, recalls:

I guess when I dated girls at that time and later women who were American, it was OK as long as they weren't black. A couple of times there, I was dating people who were black, and [she said,] "why are you doing this to us? What have we done wrong to you?" Why—you know [laughs] . . . it was more from my mother. My father, my father was always, much more welcoming anybody that I was interested in, but not my mother.

Interestingly, some respondents make distinctions between parents as they single out the one that would voice the loudest disapproval over their interracial dating choices. Rosa focuses on her father, while Alfonso focuses on his mother. Although this pattern might lead one to believe that it is the opposite-sex parent that raises the most opposition, I found that the pattern overall was mothers voicing more preference for in-group marriage, regardless of the sex of the respondent. Mothers perhaps see themselves as guardians of the cultural traditions like language, food, and holidays, and thus may feel more of a vested interest in making sure such practices get passed down to the future grandchildren. Recall many mothers who were concerned about their grandchildren being able to speak Spanish quoted in the previous section. In the case of this Puerto Rican American mother, we see that choosing a black partner is even interpreted as doing injury or harm to the parent, a deep disgrace. This kind of emotional reaction is seldom present in the cases of out-marriage to whites, particularly in Latino communities where the clearly communicated "pigmentocracy" values white over black.[10] We will explore this more in a later section, as we see how there is a Latino notion of raising the family's status by marrying lighter and bringing it down by marrying darker.

This is not to say that some initial discomfort may not be present in some cases when members of the racial middle date or marry whites. But it is seldom accompanied by the visceral emotions described in the cases of interracial intimacy with blacks. One Mexican American respondent, Neva, captures this difference between out-marriage to whites and out-marriage to blacks in the following quote:

> Most of my family is not only Hispanic, but married to other Mexicans. Recently, my cousin married a white man, but there really isn't a lot of that. [Interviewer: What was the reaction to that?] Well, my cousin [name], my cousin was—a couple of years after his marriage, we definitely do joke about him being the white guy in the family like he doesn't like spicy food, and we'll be like, "Oh, Mexican style," and put chipotle stuff on it, but it wasn't like, it was that kind of like teasing, joking, but it wasn't anything that caused any harm. [Interviewer: Do you think it would be the same for all races?] Oh, definitely not. My cousin is currently dating a black person, and those jokes aren't so funny. And they definitely are giving her a hard time for it. . . . They're prejudiced against black people, definitely. . . . Not so much my mom, I don't know what she thinks about that, but my other family members, if they were white, they'd joke about me dating a white guy, but if they were black, no.

Clearly, when family members bring home a white intimate partner, the joking is more lighthearted. At most it may be directed to something like eating preferences, which are not tied to any particularly deep-seated emotions. Indeed, there is no fear of the family losing status. In contrast, in the case of a cousin who is dating an African American, "those jokes aren't so funny." Neva eloquently captures the difference between the "it would be nice" kind of focus on cultural differences like food and language (that here are assumed to exist with a white partner) and the more rigid racial categorization of the viewed-as-inferior African American partner.

Another biracial Cuban American respondent named Monica, who is married to a white man, acknowledges a similar hierarchy of preference in her Cuban father's desires for her:

Yes, I will tell you my father was always real open to me dating Latino men. He never had a problem with me dating Latino men. He would encourage me to. My mother on the other hand, didn't really care I don't think. She never really pushed one way or the other. And my father didn't really either—he jokes about my husband being a *gringo*, and in the very beginning he used to tease all the time. But it was just a way of—he was just a white man. But now it's—they're very close and he has a very strong respect for him. . . . [Interviewer: So did they have any views as far as African Americans, or Asians?] They would not have wanted—my father would not have been happy if I had dated and African American, at all. There's a significant amount of racism from my grandmother, which I think might've been passed down to my dad. That's funny, I shouldn't say that—that's not true. My father was always very good about respecting people of different cultural backgrounds and different races. *But* he would not have been crazy about me dating a black man. My mother would have been concerned, would not have been opposed to it, but would have been more concerned about the stress of the relationship, because she knows the personal stress of marrying someone that's from a different country. So, I think she would have expected that there be some difficulties with me dating an African American.

Again we have a distinction being made between a father who is more rigid in his racial/ethnic preferences for his daughter's marriage and a mother who is a bit less restrictive, but this is also due to the fact that Monica's father is her only Latino parent. As with parents discussed in the previous section, this father certainly feels that it would have been nice for his daughter to marry another Latino, but he has grown to have "very strong respect" for her white husband, despite the occasional light-hearted teasing. If the husband had been African American, on the other hand, this respondent feels her father would not have warmed up to him as well.

Interestingly, she characterizes her mother as being perhaps more supportive, relatively speaking, of such a situation, yet uses the explanation of being "from a different country" to justify any resistance her mother might have had, despite the fact that most African Americans would not be "from another country" in as close a sense as her dad was from Cuba. To characterize African Americans (but not white Americans) as being "from another country" highlights the concept of blacks as both cultural and racial "others." Although a majority of white and black Americans share the experience of fluent English and are steeped in various other American traditions, here they are characterized as on the same par with a first-generation immigrant who grew up in "another country." Thus, cultural concerns are used as a "veil" for racial ones, because they are not being applied wholesale to all persons in the United States. In a sense, both parents display antiblack racism, but the mother does so in a more color-blind way than the father, who is more overt.

Other respondents and/or their families also use color-blind racism— often the cultural-racism frame—with which to disguise or justify their disdain for intermarriage with blacks. Usually they do this through using an economic or socioeconomic explanation that erroneously assumes that all blacks are lower class. For instance, Luis, a Brazilian American respondent whose parents are still in Brazil, describes the general mentality on intermarriage in this way: "There are a lot of blacks in Brazil —well, they're much more integrated than they are here—we have lots of cities struggling between all variations. And there was perhaps a hidden or background idea of—not that it's wrong to date a black person, but, it was more economical [socioeconomic] and stuff. It was never spoken, but it was sort of in the background. So we all knew."

With the phrase "not that it's wrong to date a black person," Luis makes a definitive effort to distance himself from overt racism, in favor of a more color-blind approach that stresses the "economical" [*sic*] code words that place race "in the background." Bonilla-Silva's work shows how a key aspect of cultural racism is to rely on "anything but race" smoke screens, often socioeconomic, as code words for fundamentally racialized arguments.[11]

Scott, quoted at length above for his family's gentle prodding to marry a "Chinese girl" (which he did not), similarly prefers to couch his family's resistance to intermarriage with blacks in socioeconomic terms:

> So there was this current of probably that other than whites might not have been acceptable, but I never explored that, but I was never curious and I never liked anybody like that. I always—my feeling of that was though that it wasn't necessarily ethnically based as socioeconomically based, I mean, stereotypically blacks and Hispanics are less well off, and so I think that it was important, not that I marry into means or marry into money, that was not necessarily, but that you married somebody that had a good family. It was always like "a good family," that kind of thing,

but what that meant—other than proper upbringing and morals and whatnot but just—weren't going to be a drag on the greater [last name] family. . . . Well, if you bring them in, hopefully they're not just gonna be bums [laughs] and so it was more that kind of thinking. . . . The only prejudice that I feel like my parents had was towards blacks, but I felt like that was much more economically based than the fact that they didn't like blacks, because I saw them welcome blacks openly when they were our own neighbors. There was never a "oh you're black." [laughs] But there was a little bit of "they don't work hard, they're lazy," I'm not saying that that's true. . . . They wouldn't like whites [laughs] who were not hardworking, lazy, didn't try to make something of themselves. And at the time we were still relatively poor, so the black person that lived next to us, our black neighbors, not like they were rich, but just that they had jobs, we all lived in two-bedroom apartments, it wasn't like it was great or anything [laughs] but the fact that they weren't on welfare [meant my parents accepted them]. So like I said that's the main prejudice that I felt like my parents have, and it bothered me a little at the time, but upon reflection, I could see that it was not rooted in race but in economics.

This passage begins with a recurring theme, where respondents who clearly have not dated blacks say they "guess" their parents would not be too accepting if they did so themselves, but because they have not had the experience it is not an issue of great concern to them. In other words, their tastes have matched their parents' exclusive preferences, for the most part. For instance, Levan, another Cambodian respondent, states: "I guess if you think about it, it's like, white people would be more acceptable, and there aren't many races after that, but it would always be the black ones last." And similarly, a respondent with an Indian father and white mother, Raj, reflects: "I guess, if I think about it, the Indian side of my family would much rather prefer that I dated a white lady before dating like a black or Hispanic woman. I don't know why, but they would, I guess." At times, these views of "blacks last" are so matter-of-fact that they barely warrant explanation. Scott does visit a bit more explanation on this antiblack ideology, however, and concludes for himself that it is really not racial at all. Because he is able to pick out a black family (their neighbors) that defied his family's stereotypes, and to vaguely assume that his family would also apply this disdain to whites who were not hardworking, he concludes that his family's general disapproving posture toward blacks was really more of a socioeconomic concern. Interestingly, he thought of this as a racial prejudice earlier in his life but now excuses it as a more "rational" conclusion.

Whether concerns about intermarrying with blacks were related to socioeconomic status, racial status, cultural difference, or all of the above, this plurality of respondents is clear in the messages they received about blacks being undesirable partners. But perhaps more indicative of anti-black racism than these explicitly voiced concerns are the behavioral patterns of the respondents themselves: the only respondent who married a black American was someone who was already deemed black herself, a black Puerto Rican American. All other respondents either married within their own group or married white. Thus, whether explicit or subtle, the antiblack messages were effective in influencing actual behaviors to a large degree.

Asian American Variance on Everyday Ethnocentrism: Fending Off Degenerate American Values

Although those in the racial middle have much in common regarding the messages they receive about interracial border crossing, there are some differences between Latinos and Asian Americans on these matters. A distinctly Asian American dynamic was the actual discouragement of marrying whites. No Latinos actually expressed disapproval of whites wholesale. This Asian American ethnocentrism was connected to a specific rejection of certain American cultural values, so it did not merely single out whites —it was really directed at any non-Asian, whites included. Parents who seemed resistant to out-marriage to whites cited certain cultural values, such as respect for elders and high emphasis placed on education, that they feared their children would lose through their process of becoming "more American." These fears seemed to go a step beyond those who simply wanted to retain language and certain celebrations, customs, and foods. They contained an element of cultural superiority and a fear that their children would be infected with a more disrespectful posture.

As discussed in chapter 2, there exists a distinct, additional hierarchy in the minds of some Asian Americans about the superiority of certain Asian nations over others. The history of Japan's colonization of other nations renders them somewhat of an Eastern superpower—respected, feared, and resented for what is sometimes perceived as its sense of entitlement over others. Although China seems to rank a bit lower than Japan, due to its history of communism and isolation from Western cultural influences for some time, both Chinese and Japanese Americans have dominated the pan-Asian movement in the United States, having the longest histories of migration and largest Asian American populations up until the 1960s. There has been some resentment expressed historically by members of other Asian ethnic groups—such as Filipinos, Koreans, and Vietnamese —that the Chinese and Japanese have taken precedence over other groups in pan-Asian organizations.[12] Further, some tension exists between South Asians and the rest of the Asian panethnic category, particularly due to the British influence over India (which has spilled over into Pakistan and Bangladesh to some extent) and the greater significance of religious culture (Hindu and Muslim) in that region than in the Far East. Indians were not even included in the census's Asian racial category until 1980, and in the earlier part of the century they had sometimes enjoyed a status similar to whites.[13] Thus, these divergent experiences have led to definite notions of superiority and inferiority between and among various Asian ethnicities, which were sometimes expressed in respondents' discussions of the most and least preferable mates.

This preference for one's own ethnicity is often even more limited than just someone from the same country. Several Asian cultures observe rigid designations within their own particular nation as well. For instance, Paul Spickard's work outlines a distinct hierarchy among the Japanese, where whites are preferred before blacks and Latinos, but also Japanese from one's own village or immediate surroundings are preferred before the Okinawans or the eta—in fact, for the Issei (the first generation), Chinese and Korean partners would even be preferred before these Japanese "outcast" groups.[14] Chinese and Indian respondents discuss similar within-country hierarchies, particularly held by parents who did not live in the United States. Some Asian countries were even structured by rigid caste systems, which were connected directly to skin color, religion, socioeconomic status, and geographic region. One Indian respondent, Rohit, cited earlier noting an increase in openness toward intermarriage with succeeding generations, describes her own parents' outlook on the issue:

Forget about dating outside of my ethnicity, my parents wouldn't want me to date anyone outside of my religious group, so as I said, it had to be a Hindu boy. And I ended up marrying a Hindu boy, so they were happy. But even within India, there is almost like a lot of differentiation between the north, south, east, west, each state has its own culture and religion, and so I grew up in New Delhi, the capital of the country, and there were people from all kinds of, all states of India there, but my parents, they really wanted me to stick to Hindu boys, yeah.

Rohit explains that caste hierarchies in India are correlated with particular religions, so even an Indian young man outside of her religion would still represent, in her parents' eyes, an unacceptable diversion from her own group. Similarly, Bruce, a Chinese-Taiwanese American respondent, conveys his parents' own resistance to his marriage to another Chinese woman who is not from Taiwan: "I think they would prefer like Taiwanese, they would prefer that. But my wife not Taiwanese. She is Mandarin, Chinese [and] . . . actually they are not happy."

In these cases, it is certainly not enough to be "Asian"—one's marital partner must be within one's own specific ethnic group, which is defined within a particular nation-state. While some respondents reflect back on their parents' rigidity and contrast it with their own more flexible attitudes, others do want to continue the in-marriage pattern with their own offspring. Says Victor, a Korean respondent:

> My daughter is, a coming-up junior [in college]. . . . And we are very concerned—we want her to meet another Korean man, rather than anybody else. . . . Yes, I would rather, yes, see them choose Korean over other nationalities. [Interviewer: OK, and are there any other groups that you feel are preferable to others, other than Korean, such as any other Asian ethnicities, or any types of white ethnicities, or anything like that?] I guess not, not that much. Except just Korean [laughs] and that's what matters.

In these cases, there are no secondary exceptions for whites over blacks, as were made in many other respondents' families. There is often not much explanation given for why, in these cases, perhaps because interviewers were either white or not of the same nationality of the respondents, and the respondents did not want to say anything about whites that might have offended them. In one case, however, a younger Bengali respondent, Reena, did elaborate a bit more on why her parents would prefer her to marry another Bengali and not a white person or anyone else:

> My family is opposed to the idea of me dating outside of my ethnic group. . . . [Interviewer asks if anyone in her family has done so.] One of my mom's cousins who she was very close to in Bangladesh moved to

America, went to college here and ended up [laughs] marrying a white man. [laughs] And initially, people were not thrilled about it, but they were OK with it. But every Christmas and on holidays she would send us postcards and Christmas cards that would show her wearing clothes that people didn't think were appropriate or like, other aspects of her lifestyle that people in our family did not consider appropriate. So, they just in general have a very negative outlook on people marrying outside of our religion and outside of our culture because they believe that people will be just like her. [They fear] that if I would marry outside of my religion and culture, that I would completely abandon any Bengali values and traditions and completely assimilate into American culture.

Reena's family goes far beyond the "it would be nice" recommendation of marrying within one's own ethnicity to holding a "very negative" view toward those who do not in-marry. This negative outlook includes a disdain for Westernized styles of dress and other "lifestyle" choices that are considered to reflect more deeply held values and morals held by white Americans, as opposed to simply the amount of spice one prefers on one's food that can become the fodder for lighthearted joking. The family reaction to this cousin's marriage to a white man as not "appropriate" is clearly a more grave matter here than for those in the "it would be nice" camp. Those from Bangladesh are considered as indeed having a more superior value system than that of white (and other) Americans. Other Asian American respondents, though not as restrictive about intermarriage issues, similarly discuss aspects of American society that they perceive negatively, such as putting elders in nursing homes and lack of pressure on children to pursue higher education. Accompanying these shifts in value systems may be the ultimate in disrespect—that their own children would begin to view their own cultures as somehow "backward," thus internalizing anti-Asian racism for themselves.

Are Whites the Ideal Partners? Latinos and Whitening Up

In contrast to the above, predominantly Asian American pattern of disdain for intermarriage with whites, there were several Latinos who describe their families as being highly supportive of intermarriage, to the point of it being an actual improvement over marriage within one's own ethnic group. While many respondents already quoted here have families that prefer marriage within one's own ethnicity, followed by marriage to whites at a close second, some (mainly Latinos) would even actually position whites at first place. Most respondents who bring up this attitude are fairly critical of it, as an unfortunate outcome of self-loathing, but they see it as worth nothing nonetheless. This is a pattern in the data that quite clearly demonstrates that the larger racist ideology of greater society can be more powerful than even social-psychological in-group preferences.

One Latino male respondent, Christopher, whose father is Honduran and mother is Dominican, observes:

> I've gotten a whole plethora of reactions which have left me with question marks over my head. For example, when I first started dating a beautiful Southern girl many years ago . . . blond haired, blue eyes, South Carolina. And people would look at—friends of mine or my mother's family and what not—they'd look at the picture and they'd go, "Wow," and they'd say in Spanish, "Abanzando la raza," which is a joke. What does that mean? What does "abanzando la raza" mean? Literally, it means "to help along, or speed up, or make better the race." And at last, what does that say about how they look on themselves? You know, if we're getting a blond-haired, blue-eyed girl that means we're ugly looking, and they're better looking? . . . It was something that stuck to me. What did they mean when they said that? They never seemed to mind it [dating whites] at all. You know, I've dated in and outside of the Latin American culture and I like them both. And it's because of my assimilation to both ends of the spectrum that I have no problem with it. But that always stuck to me because it made my wonder how the Latinos, I'll be specific, how my side, the Dominicans look on themselves. It kind of says something about their self-esteem as a culture here in the city, maybe in the country.

Although he finds it a telling symptom of perhaps low self-esteem—or what some racial/ethnic sociologists would call internalized racism—Christopher finds he has reaped the benefits of these relatively positive attitudes of his family toward his dating outside of his own ethnic group, because for him, dating interracially has meant dating within the socially approved group of whites. As opposed to some Asian American characterizations of whiteness that focus on values and morals, these Latino assessments focus more on the European physical features that have been correlated with high status in most North and South American societies.

A black Puerto Rican American female respondent, Wanda, makes a similar observation to the above respondent when she answers the question of whether she has dated any others outside of her own ethnic group:

I did all of them. The reaction was mixed but there weren't that many people to react, it was only my mother really. [Interviewer: Did she give you any messages about who was preferable? Was she open to whoever, or—] I know my mother preferred white. My mother, I think, you know, she wouldn't say it, but—[Interviewer: Was that the whole "furthering the race" thing?] I think so. . . . Not so long ago I said to her, I said, "Mom, I just keep wondering, you're always talking about how"—you know, she doesn't say anything that's racist. That's the funny thing about it. But it's how she reacts to the whites as opposed to somebody else—by "white," is "white American." She will react more positive to white American [than] to Spanish, or to a black or something.

Interestingly, Wanda does not characterize her mother's views as "racist," though perhaps she means overt prejudice here. She makes the astute point that racism often is not communicated through overt disdainful comments about "undesirable" groups but rather through more positive evaluation of the most valued groups. Thus, although her mother "doesn't say anything that's racist," she clearly gets more excited and encouraging about white people than other groups, even the "Spanish" that she would consider her own.

This seemingly greater acceptance of intermarriage with whites on the part of Latinos (more so than Asian Americans) in the sample has deep historical roots. In the United States, antimiscegenation laws were never aimed at Latinos, while such legislation often restricted Asian Americans (and of course blacks) from marrying whites. Furthermore, in both the North and South American context, with its history of European colonization and slavery of darker-skinned peoples, there exists a historical devaluation of darker skin and a favoring of lighter skin, even within same-ethnicity groups, as we have seen in chapter 2. Although the explicit language of this positive valuation of whiteness focuses mainly on beauty and appearance, studies show consistently that people attach meanings about the intelligence and competence of others according to these skin-color expectations and norms, with the lighter skinned getting the material rewards of highest status, even today.[15] Latin American cultures in particular have a long history of observing these steps up in status occurring in their midst. Even within families, lighter-skinned siblings have received higher esteem, prestige, and attention, and more opportunities, than their darker-skinned siblings, resulting in great pain and emotional strain for both. Thus, there is a sense on the part of Latinos especially that "honorary whiteness" will be one step closer for the family if intermarriage with whites occurs within it.

Views on Interracial Intimacy: Important Indicators of White Supremacist Ideology

Intermarriage has often been seen as one of the ultimate indicators of the total assimilation of various racial/ethnic groups in society. That is, to the extent that members of groups begin marrying outside their own group, particularly to whites (historically the largest outside group), the more they are seen as part of the majority, fully "American," perhaps no longer even an ethnic group. Alternatively, for those of us interested in racist discourse and ideology, it is often an area where the persistence of racism can be detected most explicitly. Intimate connections are often the last great barrier to be erected between "us" and "them."

In the southeast small city where I grew up, where the dividing line erected was primarily between whites and blacks, the small numbers of Asian Americans (no Latinos that I can recall) seemed to slip through the cracks of strict prohibitions. They accompanied whites to proms and other dances with no great attraction of attention—after all, they shared advanced-placement courses, bus rides, and neighborhoods with whites with a frequency that blacks in the school did not. But if I think more deeply, the "long-term" relationships of the high school order, which went beyond a dance date or dinner, did not really include these "racial others." They were fit for largely platonic associations but not more intimate connections in the eyes of most whites. Parents and students never made this explicitly known—there were no major scandals or parental disapproval dramas like there were with black-white dating—but looking back now, clearly, those more-intimate contacts just were not happening for the "middle" groups. Whites, thus, seem to have given a conditional acceptance to members of the racial middle in ways that are not all encompassing or life threatening, in the form of courtesies not extended to blacks. This, however, hardly makes them white: just maybe, perhaps, a bit more acceptable than blacks, the "honorary white" status that Bonilla-Silva describes.

When we look at this racial hierarchy from the vantage point of Latinos and Asian Americans themselves, we see that they are highly complicit in its maintenance. Leeway is given for white partners that is not given for blacks. Often antiblack prohibitions are not explicitly stated, and are seen as taken for granted or matter-of-fact. While some concern is expressed for cultural customs to be maintained through in-group marriage, it is recognized that there are other reasons why such customs would get passed on, or alternatively would not get passed on, which would not have anything to do with intermarriage. Thus, in-group preferences are more often cultural than racial, and not usually without some wiggle room for exceptional cases, as many of our sample's intermarried respondents (nearly all married to whites) can certainly attest. While for some it "would be nice" to do without intermarriage, for most it is just as nice to be incorporated into the white majority. But the fact that intermarriage with black Americans is not equally seen as making one "American" means we are not looking at an indicator of "assimilation" here, but rather an indicator of successful maintenance of a white supremacist/antiblack racist ideology, one which only a minority of the sample, who I characterize as racial progressives, are currently poised to undo.

5

"No racism, only that one time . . ."
Clinging to the American Dream, Despite Exclusion

These interviews with Latinos and Asian Americans are replete with tales of stereotypical assumptions, feelings of exclusion and marginalization, outright hostile slurs, and the institutional discrimination that comes with being "not white" in a racist society. Such accounts were disturbing to me, but unfortunately not surprising. What struck me most was the extent to which a majority of respondents did not find their various experiences with discrimination problematic. On the whole, they did not use the words "discrimination," "prejudice," or "stereotyping" in their accounts. The most critical assessment levied against the perpetrators of this racism came when respondents used the term "ignorance," which often excused the perpetrator and instead blamed schools and/or media for this societal level of knowledge about Latino and Asian American peoples. Respondents largely characterized their experiences in U.S. society, however, as those of inclusion, acceptance, and unfettered access to the American dream. Indeed, *more than half* of the respondents who reported some kind of stereotype, prejudice, or incident of discrimination minimized its significance and impact on their lives. Although they engaged in various strategies of minimization that I will analyze here, the most common (used by a third of the respondents) was the "only that one time" rhetorical strategy. Respondents repeatedly said there was "only one time" that they faced dehumanizing treatment, even when more than one time was discussed during the interview. This "sunny" reframing of a racialized America clearly indicates that the self-reporting of incidents of prejudice and discrimination included in these interviews can only be a conservative estimate of the totality of such incidents that Latinos and Asian Americans must encounter on a daily basis as they go about their lives.

One psychological interpretation of this recurring pattern in the data might simply be that these respondents are "in denial" about the extent of racism they face. Sociologically, however, an understanding of the ideology of white racism is needed in order to fully grasp how these Latino and Asian Americans have been incorporated into it. Historically, a crucial component of racist ideology has been to pit various nonwhite groups against one another to prevent potential solidarity and alliances among them—the "divide-and-conquer" tactic. The creation of the "model minority" stereotype has been an important tool of this divisive ideology. The model minority stereotype has historically been applied to many different members of nonblack racial minority groups, including Russian Jews, Cuban Americans, and Asian Americans, among others. Even successful African Americans can be held up as "tokens" to accomplish the ideological function of the model minority stereotype. This device singles out nonwhite persons who have become successful in order to discount the significance of continued prejudice and discrimination routinely directed at members of these groups. When white Americans observe those designated as model minorities, they come to believe either that racism should not be an obstacle to socioeconomic success unless individual victims of it "decide" that it will be (thus "bringing it on themselves"), or that racism simply no longer exists as an obstacle at all. As a divide-and-conquer strategy, the model minority idea frames blacks who have historically been most vocal in opposition to racism as essentially "different" from the "other" minorities and may avert them from bonding together to realize and organize against the common oppression they face.

Some Latinos, and particularly many Asian Americans, have been extended admission into this model minority club. While we can see from the previous chapter that many are savvy enough to understand that this stereotype is hardly true of any one ethnic or racial group en masse, white racism makes it difficult for them not to subscribe to the model minority idea at some level, because it functions as a double bind. It essentially presents nonwhites with two options: (1) become a model minority by professing that racism either does not exist or is not serious enough to affect one's life chances, or (2) highlight the significance of racism and be characterized by dominant society as someone who whines, complains, and has not successfully taken advantage of the supposedly ample opportunities there for the taking for anyone who truly desires them. Already vilified by racist ideology for being "foreign" and "not American," Latinos and Asian Americans would be seen as even more "un-American" by being one of those "complainers" if they actually testified to the persistence of racism in their lives. Thus, far from engaging in a delusional denial dynamic, these respondents are making a prudent choice to attest to the validity of the American dream and refuse to be further characterized as un-American in the eyes of whites.

Prudent survival strategies notwithstanding, it is still possible to distill from these interviews ample evidence of contemporary racism directed at Americans of Latino and Asian descent. Some of the experiences these interviewees report are similar to what other research has found that black Americans face. These include facing stereotypes that they are drug dealers or criminals, that they are untidy or undesirable neighbors, that they are ignorant or lazy, that they only work certain jobs or eat certain foods, or that they are undeserving or unqualified for their academic or career position. And although the particular terms and slurs themselves may be different linguistically from those leveled at African Americans, Latino and Asian Americans share with blacks the painful experiences of being called hateful slurs and being the butt of jokes about their nonwhite appearance or features. The most recurring experiences of discrimination, however, actually fall into categories more unique to nonblack minorities in U.S. society. That is, when reflecting on negative experiences associated with their racial/ethnic background, respondents most often discussed standing out because of the way they look (being asked "where are you from?" or worse yet "what are you?") and facing assumptions of foreignness, particularly having their immigration status or their ability to speak English questioned.[1]

While such stories are often told with clear annoyance, often they are also told in a way that indicates amusement, even pity, for the "ignorant"

TABLE 5-1
Types of Prejudice and Discrimination Faced (n = 50)

"What are you?"/"Where are you from?" (questioners)	34
Stereotypes that we tend to only work in certain fields/jobs	16
Job/workplace discrimination	15
Standing out because of the way I look	11
Assuming I cannot speak English/not smart/foreigner	10
Assumptions of criminality/threatening/deadbeat	9
School/education discrimination and curricula	7
Dehumanizing slurs and jabs	6
Stereotypes about being undesirable neighbors/tenants	4
Assuming "we all look alike"	3
Stereotypes specific to Asian Americans as passive/weak	3

TABLE 5-2
Minimization Strategies Used (n = 50)

Only that one time, only in the past, other than that one time	12
Supplanted race/ethnicity (gender, weight, local geography is more the issue)	10
It doesn't bother me	8
Standing out actually helps people remember me, works in my favor	7
Other groups have it worse	4
I surround myself with people who accept me	2

perpetrator. Many respondents report these kinds of prejudices happening so many times that they have lost count. The multiple minimization strategies that respondents develop to arrive at a place where they report things like "it doesn't bother me," "other groups have it worse," "it doesn't happen much anymore," or even "I enjoy having the chance to educate people" are instructive, because they indicate indeed just how often these folks have had to encounter such assaults on their individuality and humanity (to the point where they have devised such buffering/distancing mechanisms to neutralize the effects of it all). Indeed, sometimes the very respondents who report that this almost dull and distant hum of stereotypes in their lives is hardly detectable to them are the ones who have lost jobs, slots in educational programs, and other institutional privileges because of such racism.

Methodologically and theoretically, then, it is important *not* to conclude that these respondents are unreliable informants about their own experiences because they both discuss the racism they face (without using the "r word" of course) and characterize their lives as racism free. Indeed, in doing so they are informing us about an important social reality, in the ways that society constrains them to interpret incidents of incomplete access to the American dream. To take respondents' words at face value that the constant barrage of questioning whether they are "really American" does not bother them at all, and to then assume that Latinos and Asian Americans thus do not face racism, is faulty logic, for it locates these actors in an individualistic framework where they are the sole receptors of their own actions. Philomena Essed challenges the idea that those who do not use the words "racism" or "discrimination" to describe their experiences are employing a psychological strategy to reduce cognitive dissonance.[2] Far from being isolated actors, these respondents are situated in a larger "color-blind racist" society where clear penalties apply to those who dare to admit that race matters.[3] Thus, in framing their race-related experiences as benign and nonracial, they are not merely expressing their own interpretation of the events they face, but they are relying on a socially created definition of what racism is (and is not). That is, if someone is not overtly coming out and telling you they do not serve or hire "your kind," then it must not be racism, as society defines it. Indeed, Essed likewise analyzes how socially created frameworks that serve dominant interests constrain the tools available for targets of racism to "diagnose" their own experiences. These findings should also alert us to how effectively color-blind racism constrains the perceptions of those who live in between the poles of black and white.

Moreover, to accept at face value respondents' declarations that their lives are characterized by "no racism at all" assumes that they would even be aware of the times when discrimination and prejudice befall them. In a color-blind racist society where racism and its white privileges are often far from blatant, sometimes racism can fall below the radar of its victims. For instance, in a pioneering study comparing black and white graduates from a technical high school and their experiences in the blue-collar job market, Deirdre Royster discovered that black students unanimously described their teachers as positive and supportive, while those same teachers were giving all kinds of boosts and job opportunities to their white students, unbeknownst to their black peers.[4] If one experiences racialized exclusion from certain benefits with a "friendly face," then unless one compares notes with a white peer, there is no way of knowing that the seemingly positive treatment is not even half of the privileges that others experience. To apply this lesson to the present study, for the numerous examples where Latinos and Asian Americans are asked "where are you from?" and "what are you?" and they good-naturedly reply to this seemingly friendly query, they have no way of knowing that this "friendly" person has never asked folks that appear white this same question. The racist hoop they are being asked to jump through is a "friendly" obstacle reserved only for them and those who share their not-black-but-not-white appearance. This undetectable friendly-faced racism, coupled with the color-blind racist ideology that constrains individuals from acknowledging racism at all, work together to produce this "no racism . . . except for that one time" pattern.

In the sections that follow, it will become evident that all these "one times" clearly add up to a multitude of incidents where Latinos and Asian Americans are denied full access to the American dream. Some are more aware of the injustice inherent in their own anecdotes than others. For the majority that deemphasizes that injustice, I will also examine the most typical minimization strategies employed in the process. Thus, multiple dimensions of racism are revealed through these accounts. They expose not only the ways in which people stereotype and discriminate against Latinos and Asian Americans, but also the ways in which contemporary racism disguises its own severity in the eyes of its victims.

The *"Where Are You From? No, Where Are You From?"* Dance

Although the largest groups within Latino and Asian communities (Mexicans, Chinese, Japanese) often have generational histories in the United States that either equal or predate that of many non-Hispanic whites, stereotypical assumptions about their "foreignness" linger. My collective sense from these interviews is that my respondents are surrounded by a constant cloud of "curiosity" about where they are from or "what are you?" that I as a white person never experience. For instance, Jay states: "OK, well any given day I would say between one and four times I get asked about my ethnicity or some comment made about the fact that I'm Asian." Another respondent, Heather reflects: "People ask me all the time, 'what are you?' All the time. I mean it probably happens within a week of meeting somebody new, and I meet somebody new all the time. So it happens all the time." In fact, eight additional respondents used this exact phrase, "all the time," to describe how often someone asks or comments about their ethnic background. Other interviewees chose different words that conveyed the same sense of this constant barrage of questioning they experience, reflecting that it happens "a lot" or it is very "common." Some respondents say it happens so often they have "lost count" or "stopped keeping track."

Given the recurring nature of this type of "othering" behavior that my respondents have experienced, they not only have vivid recreations of how such conversations usually go, but they have also developed strategies they tend to rely on for coping with the questioning. Several respondents described what I call the "where are you from? No, where are you from?" dance. This back-and-forth conversation between the Latino or Asian American respondent and his or her questioner reveals that the questioner is so attached to his or her own prejudgment of the respondent's foreign-ness, that s/he is unable to let go of it once it is challenged.

The questioner persists in insisting that the respondent fits into his or her "foreign" box. Charlene, a Thai-Filipino American respondent, describes the dance:

> Usually either people [ask,] "Where are you from?" or, and I'll say I'm from Memphis, and they'll say, "Where were you born?" And I'll say I was born in Augusta, Georgia. And they'll say, "Now, where are your parents from?" And then, or then it'll be something where they'll try to guess where I'm from. "Oh, are you Japanese? Are you Korean, are you Vietnamese . . ." and they'll go through the whole list, which I know they'll never going to get. And then you just sit there and let them go through, and just go, "No, no, no, no." [laughter] That's usually the way that it works.

This kind of questioning is so common among the respondents that a variety of assessments of it exist. Some find it amusing, and some find it annoying. But regardless of the feelings it evokes, almost unanimously the respondents who describe this dance do not readily volunteer the information that the questioner seems to desire. Their descriptions of how these conversations "usually" go clearly indicate that they sense the questioner's prejudgment and refuse to be boxed in by it. This is an important point to keep in mind, because several respondents go on to say that the questioning is not annoying and they do not mind it. In the above case, Charlene is laughing. Even when a seemingly "sunny" acceptance of this type of questioning is verbalized during the interviews, however, there is also a clear sense of unwillingness to play along with this prejudicial "curiosity."

This defiance usually involves answering the question truthfully even though eventually the respondent discovers that this is not the racial/ethnic information that the questioner really wants. Occasionally, however, respondents even refuse to give up the racial/ethnic information the questioner desires by answering dishonestly, in a way that shuts down the conversation. This strategy is described by Michael, a Puerto Rican American respondent, who often "passes" for white in the United States, with his last name being the biggest ethnic marker for him. Thus, the questioners are most often focusing on his Spanish surname, asking about the "origin" of his last name. He says he can usually sense whether people are asking out of genuine interest (usually if they are also Latino) or whether their question stems more from what he calls "social status." He feels they want to demote his social status in their minds if they find out he is Latino, so rather than fall into this trap, he prefers to say that he cannot remember or has lost track of the origin of his last name. He reports this technique is effective in shutting down what he feels is an offensive line of questioning. Another coping strategy then is to refuse to even enter into the choreography of the dance at all.

This Korean American respondent named Sarah, who grew up in what she calls a "Caucasian" household with white adoptive parents, also regularly experiences "the dance": "I'm asked a lot by white people, 'where are you from?' I get that all the time, 'Where are you from?' And sometimes I'm confused, and I'm like, 'Well, I grew up in Atlanta,' and they're like, 'Oh, before that.' And I'm like, 'Ohio' [laughs], and they're like, 'Oh, before that?' And then I get what they're trying to do." For a majority of the respondents, they have never known life in any country other than the United States, or at least they cannot recall it, in the case of those who moved as babies or as very young children. They have to step outside of their own experiences and understand the racist thinking of Americans that includes the idea that a "real American" appears physically "white." They must inhabit in what W. E. B. Du Bois calls a double-consciousness experience.[5] Sarah actually describes a cognitive shift between those two dominant and subordinated viewpoints within this account. She moves from naively inhabiting a world without racism for a brief moment to resigned acceptance that everyone is not going to be as open-minded to her own experience as she would hope.

In contrast, Edita, a Guatemalan American respondent, says she knows right away that the questioner is expecting a "foreigner" profile, but she still responds in a way similar to the other respondents by not immediately volunteering racial/ethnic information about herself:

> I do get asked where I'm from a lot and I like to be smart with people and tell them Falls Church, Virginia. Even though I know what they're asking, they're getting at something else. But sometimes people will ask like, "Oh are you fill in whatever country" and it's weird. I've even been asked if I'm, like what are the countries? I get asked if I'm Mexican or El Salvadorian all the time, Puerto Rican. And then one time someone asked me if I was Filipino, which I don't understand. And then someone else asked me if I was Middle Eastern, I don't remember the country. But

yeah, I get asked that kind of thing all the time. [Interviewer: And so your reaction to it is?] I just answer it or do the Falls Church thing, it's kind of frustrating.

Both Edita's and Sarah's quotes underscore the point that this dance happens "all the time." Further, another crucial aspect of this quote demonstrates how whites often interchange their perceptions of Asian Americans and Latinos into one box. Notice Edita does not discuss being asked if she is white or African American. While most of the ethnicities she lists would indicate that the questioner has in mind a Latino background (Mexican, Puerto Rican American, Salvadorian), others (Filipino, Middle Eastern) demonstrate that whites may often be operating from a "not black, not white" cognitive box that lumps not only all Latinos, but all Asian Americans and Middle Easterners (and in other respondents' experiences, even all Muslims) into one common racial grouping.

After Edita makes the above statement, the interviewer then asks her, "Do you get mad when people ask you, is it a bother?" Her response is instructive of the kind of minimization that I will explore further in this chapter: "Not really, no. It's *only* a bother for me when people are like, 'what are you?' Because I'm a lot of things." [emphasis added] The word "only," often included in the phrase "the only time" or "only when," is an important qualifying phrase used heavily in these interviews. It is used so often by many of the respondents that it conveys the overwhelming desire on the part of the respondents to *want* to say that the United States includes them without hesitation, and to thus minimize these assaults to one's humanity even when they happen "all the time." A question like "what are you" is especially dehumanizing, even more so than "where are you from?" as this respondent points out, but is unfortunately recounted by many respondents.

Rebecca who identifies as Chinese, Portuguese, and Macanese, discusses encountering the "what are you?" question and how she typically responds. Keep in mind that respondents are rarely discussing one specific time this happened to them; because it happens so regularly, they indeed are describing in general a typical account:

When they're like, "What are you?" I always say Macanese just because, I know they won't know what that is. . . . People think like it's a joke, it's like a Macanese is a Mack daddy in Chinese, and so they're like, "Ha ha ha!" . . . And then, I gotta tell them the history of it, like the Portuguese took over . . . and so, I guess that, like I always have to clarify, but it's not, it's *not like troublesome* for me to clarify, I like for people to know who I am, I like them to know that there's not just Chinese, not just Japanese. [emphasis added]

Because the panethnic racial categories of Asian Pacific Islander and Latino/Hispanic include so many different ethnicities, elsewhere Rebecca points out that it is both white and black Americans that tend to lose sight of the smaller and lesser-known countries of origin included in these racial groupings. Respondents with generational connections to these lesser-represented Latino and Asian ethnicities express frustration with the lack of historical and geographical knowledge in the United States. There is a typical rhetorical strategy, however, that many of the respondents use here when she states that it is not "troublesome" to her and that she "likes" having to educate the questioners. Interviews often indicate clear passionate emotions about this questioning even as they include the "it doesn't bother me" or "I don't mind it" disclaimers.

Several Filipino American respondents discussed the confusion they often faced because of the ignorance of the history of the colonization of the Philippines by Spain. Those who had Spanish surnames especially confronted this on a regular basis. Respondents experiencing these (and other, non-Filipino related) confusions often forgave the questioner for their ignorance, placing the blame on the educational system instead. In the case of Jon, he had decided that it is easier on him if he corrects the questioner with a nice, rather than hostile, disposition:

Usually, I have a pretty good attitude about it. I go, "Hey, I'm Filipino." There's nobody—you know, you attract more flies with honey than with vinegar, and it's an honest mistake. You know, what it boils down to is that people just don't know any better sometimes, I don't want to say they're ignorant because that makes me seem condescending, but if someone, if they honestly just don't know what you are, then you can't get mad at them because it's not their fault for not having that experience or knowledge. So you have to be kind about it, you don't want to be condescending. Just be cool about it and get them on the same page as you. So, if somebody doesn't know what I am, say, "Hey, I'm Filipino." Um, but I usually try to break that misconception right away, I say, "Hey, I'm [Jon]. My last name means [states meaning] in Spanish, but I'm Filipino," and a lot of times they say, "Oh yeah, I didn't know that." But then they know, they learn something new and they're more conscious of it and don't make that mistake in the future. . . . I would say most Filipinos are very hospitable, you know, and very nice about it. So, I don't want to speak for everybody, but that seems to be the general trend with us. For me, you know, try to be nice to everybody. If somebody asks me, *I don't get mad at them.* It's not their fault. It's an honest question. [emphasis added]

Jon, though, is more forgiving than the next respondent. While both respondents absolve the questioner of blame and instead fault a general societal lack of knowledge, this Cambodian American respondent, Levan, is quite willing to apply the term "ignorant" to the questioner in a way the above respondent resists. Further, even though she uses the rhetorical device of minimization when she states that it "doesn't annoy" her and that it is at best "entertaining," her language clearly suggests annoyance and even anger about this recurring "ignorance" she experiences. This portion of the interview was so passionate and eloquent, and covers so many recurring issues that other respondents also experience, that I quote her here at length:

They'll always ask me where I'm from . . . some Asian people [get asked], "Oh are you Vietnamese, oh are you Chinese?" but with me I always get "are you Asian or are you Spanish or are you mixed?" . . . *It doesn't annoy me*, it's actually entertaining. . . . Something annoying [would be] like, "Oh you speak English really well." No shit, stupid, you know what I mean? [laughs] That's probably *the only* annoying thing that I get offended about, and it's not like I get it often, but I have. . . . So I can't, *I won't let myself be irritated* because some people just don't know. Or, I get annoyed if some people are like, "Where's Cambodia?" . . . Some people just aren't aware. . . . And that's probably another thing that bothers me, like if I say I'm Asian, "Chinese." It's like, "Do you know any other place?" I don't look Chinese, but not everybody knows. . . . *I'm not going to get offended* if somebody that doesn't know is going to call me Chinese, but at the same time it also irritates me . . . Like in school, world history, what do you learn in world history? . . . It's the same shit every year. . . . And it pisses me off . . . you can't get mad for people not knowing, but it's just how the stupid country works. . . . You have to go out of your own fucking way to learn a little more besides the little stupid shit you learn in school. . . . [Interviewer: So how do you respond to it when people ask you about what your race is, do you just answer it or—] Well, I always tell them to guess. I give them like five guesses and most of the time they won't get it, and then I'll tell them and sometimes they're like, "Oh wow, you don't look like it," of course I get that a lot or sometimes they'll be like, "Where is that?" or "is that Asian?" And then I'll be like, "You know where Thailand is? Do you know where Vietnam is?" "Oh, yeah, yeah, yeah!" "What? Yeah, it's right in between that, fucker!" It's like, even one country over, people aren't fucking aware of. . . . *I'm not mad* because I don't know every single country in Africa. . . . But it's like one country, they'll know where Thailand is and they'll know where Vietnam is and Cambodia is right in fucking between them, but they won't fucking know where that is. In a way, I'm just kind of like, [rolls eyes] you roll your eyes at them, but how can you not fucking know? [emphasis added]

In the first few lines of this quote, Levan uses the common phrase "the only [thing]" to describe the prejudiced assumptions she confronts about her ability to speak English. The negative assumptions Latinos and Asian Americans get assaulted with about their English-speaking skills will be a topic covered more in-depth in the next section. Not only does she attempt to use words like "only" to minimize these clearly hurtful experiences, but she also occasionally states things like "I'm not going to get offended," "I'm not mad," "I won't let myself be irritated," and "it doesn't annoy me." Hopefully, however, the reader is struck by just how annoyed Levan clearly is. This same discussion also includes phrases that would seem to "contradict" those above, including "it pisses me off" (stated two different times), "bothers me," "irritates me," and is "stupid." And the profanity scattered throughout also indicates a passionate level of frustration about this constant barrage of "ignorance" about her ethnic background and experiences.

Cambodians (Asian) and Cubans (Latinos) share the common U.S.-issued label of "refugee." Both groups arrived here under quite different circumstances, however, receiving different levels of assistance from the federal government and having experienced different socioeconomic backgrounds in their native countries. While Cubans were fleeing a communist governmental structure that was not amenable to the socioeconomic growth to which many more democratic-minded people felt entitled, Cambodians were quite simply running for their lives from a genocidal despotic regime. While many of the immigrant narratives for members of the larger Latino and Asian American groups mirror those of some European groups (leaving freely and voluntarily for the United

States in search of greater economic prosperity), Cambodians cannot lay claim to the same type of narrative. Understandably, it is frustrating to be lumped together with the more "normative" Asian immigration experiences as a Cambodian American. And to have to make a special effort to learn about one's own group in the educational system of a country that chose to incorporate you must be highly frustrating, at best. While the focus on European history discussed here certainly alienates all nonwhite groups, there appears to be an added level of frustration that even a cursory study of the "big nations" in Asia omits. Levan is excluded from the American dream not only as an Asian who, surprising to many whites, "speaks good English," but also as a Cambodian who is assumed to be "Chinese." Thus, the "what are you?" or "where are you from?" dance can often reveal multiple layers of ignorance and prejudice on the part of its perpetrators. Moreover, the phrases that respondents choose to recount their experiences with the dance also indicate just how penalized they would feel if they actually admitted unequivocally how much it hurt.

For one Mexican American respondent named Roberto, who is more cognizant of that hurt, seemingly every interaction is a painful reminder that his appearance and his name scream "foreigner" to others, no matter how much he feels his experiences and behaviors are nothing but "American":

> When you shake people's hands and you introduce yourself with your name, you wonder what goes through people's minds, because they always say, "Oh I know this family who's Mexican American," or they try to relate —they go out of their way to say that they know somebody who's Mexican, to make me feel comfortable. I don't need that to feel comfortable. I shake their hand and say, "Where do you work, what are your interests," you know? But I always have to hear people say that they—if I'm related to the Mendezes that are here, or do I know them, or how often do I go to Mexico? No, I don't know the Mendezes, I'm sorry, I don't go to Mexico. I guess the worst thing is that people need to feel comfortable a lot.

He just wants to have the same kinds of conversations that he perceives that other Americans have with each other, yet people continue to focus on his otherness rather than what he might have in common with them. Roberto shares with another Latino male respondent, Michael (a white Puerto Rican American), the experience of actually having changed his name for some periods of his life to a non-Hispanic-sounding name and subsequently getting a taste of how conversations, and even job interviews, would go if people did not automatically perceive his Latin-ness right away. Those who have not been through such actual live sociological experiments may be more habituated to the questioners as an inevitable part of life. Having experienced "how the other half lives" seems to make it harder to minimize the "where are you from?" stigmatization— they have experienced firsthand that those perceived as white/American are not subjected to this line of questioning. Contrasting such treatment from others with what he considers to be his own actual Americanized life, Roberto reflects: "I can become white, but they will not allow me to."

"You Speak Such Good English": The Complimenter

In some of the above quotes, a respondent may first approach an encounter with prejudices with some degree of naivete, not filtering perceptions through the lens of how a white American might be viewing him or her. This naivete may be experienced as "she just wants to know what U.S. state I am from" or "he just wants to commend any American child on good grammar." Eventually, however, the respondent begins to use her double-consciousness filter to realize that the questioner (or in the case of the English-language insults, the complimenter) is actually assuming her foreignness, indeed, her un-Americanness. The above Cambodian American respondent recalls painfully being duped into thinking the complimenter was genuinely commenting on her grammar rather than assuming she could not speak English at all. It is her older sister, more well schooled in U.S. racism, who had to fill her in on the unfortunate reality of this prejudice. The prejudice is based on the assumption that anyone who appears to fit in the not-black-not-white box cannot speak English well. It stems from the notion that Latinos and Asian Americans must be foreigners, even when some have a longer generational history of U.S. citizenship than some whites.

Several of the respondent narratives about people's assumptions that they do not speak English are also layered with minimization strategies. We have already seen the "only one time" and "it doesn't bother me" strategies, but another important minimization strategy is the "but I don't have it as bad as other minority groups" strategy. That strategy gets employed at the end of this vivid example of hurtful stereotyping recounted by Charlene, a Thai-Filipino American respondent:

> When I went to a Christmas party this Saturday night . . . and one of the [party guests] . . . had a daughter-in-law who was from Japan and had married their son, and so they start talking to me and the husband says, "You know, you really speak very good English." I said, "Well, I ought to; it's my native language. I grew up here." And he says, "Really? But you don't have an accent at all! Amazing." "Did you not hear me? I said, I grew up here!" And then of course, he wanted to talk to me about Japan and what it was like, which I know nothing about. I've never, you know, other than flying and stopping off at the airport, I have never been to Japan, and it's not like I share this sort of common knowledge about all Asian countries, so that was sort of awkward because I kept trying to impress upon him that I don't speak the language, I'm not from there, I'm not even Japanese, but it didn't seem to register in his head. So I think that that sort of stereotype that "you're Asian, you must," you know, "Wow, you speak English really well," you know that sort of thing. I think that that's still out there, but on the other hand, it's not, they're not necessarily negative stereotypes in the way that you have stereotypes about blacks. "Oh, they're lazy, untrustworthy, violent," like, Asians don't have that. If there are stereotypes out there, it's like, "Oh, they're hardworking, they're smart, they're submissive and quiet," that's about as bad as it gets. Or they're foreign. So it's different. And I think, you know, is it better? Well, it's *better than being black*, if you want to be frank about it. Is it better than it was in the past? I don't know. [emphasis added]

What is offensive to Charlene is not only that it was assumed that English was not her native language, but that the complimenter in this case lumps all Asian ethnicities together into the one he seems to know best (Japanese), without regard for the fact that this may not be her experience and that there are many other Asian ethnicities out there that she could be. Furthermore, even if he did happen to "get right" the nation or nations that correspond to her ethnicity, she impresses on the complimenter that "I was born here!" so she many have little to no experience with life in the actual Asian country being discussed.

This lack of historical and geographic knowledge comes as a repeated annoyance for our respondents, because of the way it is used to discount their individuality and humanity. For instance, another Korean American respondent, Jessica, vividly recalls when a high school friend she had for years caught wind of a reference to her being "Korean" and exclaimed with surprise, "But wait, [Jessica], I thought you were Asian!" There is a sense of Americans lumping individual Asian nations and the entire continent or the panethnic label of Asian all into one cognitive rubric and having difficulty maintaining distinctions between the two. While these may on the one hand seem like benign geographical knowledge errors, they clearly have the collective effect on respondents of making them feel singled out as different, foreign, and un-American. These complimenters are often, at least at first glance, unable to recognize the potential of shared experiences they have with second-, third-, and fourth-generation Latino and Asian Americans who were born in the United States and see the world through the English language and an American cultural lens, just like they do.

At the end of the quote about the complimenter at the Christmas party, Charlene makes use of the "others have it worse" minimization device, by pointing out that this assumption of being foreign is "better than being black." The model minority, divide-and-conquer ideological wedge has worked well in this case. Because the respondent perceives so many positive stereotypes about Asians, she decides that she would rather be cast as exotic and foreign than criminal and dangerous. Knowing that these negative antiblack stereotypes exist, she concludes that many of these everyday hassles are preferable to those that African Americans face. The fact remains, however, that white Americans can expect to face neither cluster of prejudices and the discriminatory treatment that often results from them.

Asian Americans are certainly not the only respondents that face this language-based/"foreigner" form of prejudice and discrimination. Latino respondents confront it regularly as well. Like their Asian American counterparts, Latinos are also likely to use minimization strategies to discuss it. For example, when asked about any stereotypes she notices that Americans have about her group, Maria, a Puerto Rican American respondent, replies:

Probably that people don't accept you, or that people don't think that like I'm American or that I know English, or anything like, [they say:] "oh you don't have an accent," like, I was born here, and I don't have an accent, and I know English as good as the next person. So it's like having a last name, or looking a certain way, people judge you sometimes on first impressions but I don't really have that problem anymore. [emphasis added]

Some respondents tried to describe discrimination and prejudice as something that they faced in the past, often limiting it to childhood. In fact, other respondents described hateful epithets such as "chink" and "spic" being applied to them and consistently remarked that these were cases of school-aged "bullies" that no longer besieged them. Although this "it was in the past" dynamic is not explored further in the interviews, it could mean that the adult respondent has developed a coping mechanism where such epithets no longer bother him or her, or it could actually indicate a move toward more covert forms of racism, which the respondent no longer detects.

Several other respondents indicate that the assumption that they don't speak English well has cost them institutional privileges, particularly in the educational realm—both K–12 and college. Ricardo, a Mexican American respondent, recalls:

> I was never really in an ESL [English as a second language] program, it was actually weird because after I learned English then they started to say maybe he doesn't know English and they started putting me in ESL classes but I was already familiar with English and I could already speak English, so it was kind of a waste of my time and their time, but hey that's what happens when you are Latino, they assume you don't know English. [Interviewer: So do you think you were put in the wrong classes?] Oh, so many times. I remember for many years I wondered why I was in the lowest reading group, even though I knew perfectly well that I was never really tested. And around fifth grade or so they actually did test me on reading and they found that I was in the completely wrong reading group. And they were like confused 'cause they didn't understand how I could get so advanced being in the lowest reading group. But I mean I would say that they made a mistake from the beginning.

Another Dominican American, respondent, Claudia reflects on how even these bilingual education programs, which were supposed to be for the benefit of Latino people in particular, have been implemented by people operating from these same prejudices. Rather then using these programs as a temporary bridge to assist first-generation immigrants to transition into English, those in charge seem to be operating from an assumption that these children *cannot* learn English. She points out:

My children were in bilingual education. And I remember my second daughter complaining about that all subjects were teaching [*sic*] in Spanish, and she was there for like five years. And not only that, but also they place a child because of their last name, or because they don't speak English, keep a child five, six, seven, eight years—it is possible—just because it's economic, and when you call and complain as a parent—few parents complain because they don't know their rights—and they say, "No your child didn't pass this test." If you push and push they say, "Yes, oh I'm sorry, we're going to do it, we're going to do it," and they did it.

When individual teachers carry their prejudicial assumptions into the classroom, these biases quickly become institutionalized. It is this respondent's belief that many more are negatively affected, because they are not able to negotiate the bureaucracy as successfully as she was able to do by being persistent. Another Guatemalan American respondent observes that the bilingual children were "lumped together" with the learning-disabled children at her school, thus clearly stigmatizing them, as opposed to recognizing their superior ability to retain two languages. U.S. whites can often confuse ability to speak English with intellectual ability, as if those who speak languages other than their own are not intelligent.

As Claudia also points out, many Latinos and Asian Americans face prejudice and discrimination (sometimes even sight unseen) simply due to the linguistic origin of their last names. Reacting to a last name is quite a faulty substitute for getting accurate information about an individual person. Many of the respondents had Anglo-sounding last names due to marriage, parents' or adoptive parents' names, or parents' choice to Anglicize a last name once in the United States. Further, there are certainly people who have Spanish last names or last names in various Asian languages who have acquired them through marriage or other means not related to their ethnicity. Nonetheless, respondents still experience people using their Spanish surnames to extrapolate all kinds of assumptions about them, their experiences, and their ability levels. Monica, a white-Cuban biracial respondent, recalls:

I was a National Honors Society student, very, you know, in advanced classes. They [university] accepted me on full scholarship on the condition that I would go to summer school and meet with a mentor every day because they wanted to make sure my English was good. When my father came to visit the campus with me, and we both sat down with the advisors, they were telling me about this scholarship opportunity and they were talking about that all that was required was that I meet with a tutor on an everyday basis and that I had to go to summer school. And if I didn't meet with the tutor, they would come and find me. And my scholarship was contingent upon this. I looked at my dad, and I'm like you gotta be kidding me. You know what my grades are like, you know how I perform academically and these people are telling me I have to go to summer school because they think I'm gonna need help getting ready for college because of my background. And at that point he didn't think it mattered because it was a full scholarship, he wasn't gonna have to pay for it. I actually turned the scholarship down, because of my principles. I worked too hard in school and I'm not gonna let someone tell me I have to acculturate to campus because I have a Cuban name. And this was very disconcerting, in some ways it didn't help me, to have my background. . . . Otherwise I haven't been affected by it; *I haven't had any negative experiences other than that one time.* Otherwise it's been fine, more positive than negative I'd say. [emphasis added]

Even after encountering her and her good English skills (indeed, English is the *only* language she speaks fluently), this institution would not budge from its stereotype of Latinos who cannot speak good English, and it barred access to resources unless she complied with its demands. Notice the "only that one time" minimization strategy that frames this serious institutional discrimination as an isolated incident, although there are numerous other times during the interview that she addresses assumptions made about her based on her last name. This is probably the most serious one she can recall, because it involved an institution—it was clear and blatant. Often respondents think that if an incident is not as blatant as this then it must not "count" as discrimination and so they downplay it.

Interestingly, Monica's brother Joe (also interviewed for this project) who is worlds apart from his sister politically and ideologically nevertheless had a similar incident, also seen as isolated, with a college-recruitment process:

The only time that I can think when it ever became an issue was when I was in high school, I was a high school senior playing football and I was, I was pretty decent and I was trying to get a scholarship to play college football at a smaller school. And my coach was attempting to say to a college recruiter "you ought to take a look at this kid, his name is [Spanish name]," and so he automatically thought I was a typical Latin kid. The Latin kids get homesick, and so he said, "Nah I don't wanna talk to Latin kids. Cause they get homesick and they end up leaving after a year." And he goes "no, no, you don't understand just meet the kid." So that's the only time I've ever heard anything semi-negative or whatever. [emphasis added]

Now the assumptions attached to a last name have extended beyond language-speaking abilities and to an entire profile of typical behaviors, sight unseen. Where the criterion for the position should have been football-playing ability, Joe's abilities were not even considered because of his last name. The assumptions attached to this last name, however, although not about language directly, still hinge on notions of academic ability, because the recruiter assumed that he would not be academically successful because he was Latino. It is important to note that the coach must have actually shared this information with him. How many more times have applications not even been considered, whether for jobs or academic positions, because of an Asian- or Spanish-sounding last name?

Job-Related Stereotypes and Discrimination

As we have already seen, racialized stereotypes are often related to an individual's abilities, whether intellectual, emotional, or physical, to accomplish certain tasks. Several respondents, when asked to think of any stereotypes about their groups, often mention those that are work related. Although some Asian Americans reference the "good at math" dimension of the model minority stereotype, others point to stereotypes that confine them to low-wage, dead-end jobs. For instance, two Indian American respondents discuss the "Apu" stereotype popularized by the popular cartoon series *The Simpsons*, which they believe leads people to conclude that Indians cannot speak good English and work only at 7-Eleven stores or gas stations. Another Cambodian respondent talks about her annoyance with a friend who always asked a Vietnamese American friend, "When is your mom going to do my nails?" Interestingly, she also minimizes her resistance to this taunting by using color-blind logic. She says her objection to the joke is not that it is race based, but that it is a sign of an unimaginative

comedian to always go to the issue of race for the joke—thus she objects
to it on the grounds that it is boring, not racially offensive. Whether they
minimize their objections to them or not, obviously the stereotypes are
pervasive enough to be mentioned by multiple respondents. Indeed, several respondents question why the higher socioeconomic-status members
of their groups seem altogether absent from stereotypers' minds. Says an
Indian American respondent known as Raj: "it's slightly negative in that
it just shows you in more of a poor, impoverished situation, but people
know it's not true. A lot of people have Indian doctors." In my sample, it
seems that while East Asian respondents may be confronted by a model
minority stereotype, South Asians and Southeast Asians still face stereotypes similar to those applied to Latinos en masse regarding low-wage
service-sector work, even as the specific job titles may differ.

When it comes to Latinos, the most frequent job-related stereotypes
mentioned were maids and "lawn mowers" (landscape workers). As with
the above Asian stereotypes (male convenience store worker or gas station
attendant, female manicurist), these stereotypes are clearly gendered as
well. It is important to note that there is a difference between describing
the occupational segregation of Latinos or Asian Americans as they are
concentrated in certain jobs and expecting that members of these groups
are *best-suited* to or can work *only* these jobs. For instance, one Dominican-Honduran respondent reports how offensive it was to be at a party
and overhear a Latino friend being asked if he knew of any good maids.
Another Salvadorian American respondent relates the offensive joke:
"what do you call a Hispanic without a lawn mower? Unemployed." These
kinds of prejudices completely neglect the fact that the occupational segregation patterns from which they derive have more to do with openings
and availabilities in the U.S. economy than with the abilities and interests
of Latino peoples. As with all of the prejudices discussed here, they are
dehumanizing because they do not allow for the individual personality
variation and freedom of expression experienced by upper- and middle-
class whites.

These prejudices and stereotypes are especially problematic when they
lead to differential treatment in the workplace. As Peter, a U.S. military
veteran and federal special agent of Mexican descent, puts it:

> I think it does hinder me in ways because people judge me, the first thing,
> when people look at me. There's times when I'll go to the mall and I see a
> woman grab her purse as I'm passing by. Or people get either intimidated

by me, that does tick me off. Has it affected me, yeah, currently it does affect me at work sometimes. Cause people have misperceptions of you, stereotypes of you, it's something that's hard to fight or do anything about. You try what you can but it's extremely difficult. And if I get flushed when I talk it's because it does get emotional.

Peter describes a similar experience that countless African Americans, especially men, will recognize all too well—women grabbing their purses as he walks by. While we will return to these stereotypes of criminality in the next section, this respondent makes clear that the cloud of intimidation that this kind of prejudice carries with it spills over into the professional arena. Interestingly, he is apologetic in the interview about the level of emotion he expresses about the issues we discuss (which, to me, is barely noticeable), perhaps due to these exact negative perceptions he has previously experienced about seeming intimidating when he is simply speaking passionately. His quote includes a sense of helplessness that he is unable to realize his full potential at work because a college-educated Mexican American male who is as well spoken and as well trained as he is seems threatening to those around him.

Another on-the-job annoyance some respondents discuss is the perception of coworkers that they are not fully deserving of their position, following from the faulty assumption that affirmative action programs require employers to hire "unqualified" applicants. Many pieces have been written shattering such myths, so I will not present all the evidence to counter such claims here, but suffice it to say that employment law is quite clear on the point that "unqualified" minorities cannot be hired over qualified nonminorities, no matter how much the employer wants diversity in the workplace. Multiple college-student respondents attest to confronting such assumptions about their own spots at their current universities. (One of my student interviewers created the rapport that brought forth these examples by recounting her own story—every time someone questions her right to be at our university due to her minority status, she has to let them know that she was also credentialed enough to get into Harvard but she turned them down!) One Thai-Filipino American college professor, Charlene, finds this kind of questioning of her right to hold her position even more problematic than being assumed to be foreign:

You do have people like to point you out when they show that they're being diverse, and that's very annoying, when that's not the way you think about yourself, and you kind of, I feel like I'm being made a tool when that happens. I feel like that undermines who I was and why I should have been hired by this university. So, I think that's probably the thing that bothers me the most about it, and then, then the sort of perception of being foreign, but that's more like, I could deal with it.

Again there is a sense of dehumanization that is explored more earlier in the interview when a supervisor holds his hiring of her up to prove he is not racist or sexist because "we hired you and you have two check marks" (one for nonwhite and one for female). Charlene resents that her existence and professional credentials have been reduced to check marks on a page about her race and sex rather than her ability to do her job. Because of her southern U.S. upbringing and what she feels as a cultural disconnect from both her parents' native countries, she feels she could not bring nearly as much of a "diverse" perspective as potential others, and she does not appreciate the assumption that she is "exotic" when it serves an administrator's purposes.

If respondents feel that, once they have secured a position, their race/ ethnicity sometimes seems to overshadow their capabilities in the eyes of their coworkers, one can only imagine how many positions are never secured or even offered because prejudices toward a surname or an ethnic appearance forestall the hiring process. The more-frequent tales of workplace-related discrimination actually do come from experiences during the application or interview process. Indeed, one Puerto Rican American respondent who appears white to many, with no detectable accent, has actually experimented with taking the "s" off the end of his Spanish last name on resumes and found it made a big difference in how often he got called back for an interview. Other respondents have noticed similar repercussions in the job-seeking process. When asked if her ethnicity ever hinders her, Joy, an Indian American filmmaker with a master's degree, states: "It definitely hinders you the minute you want to work outside of your culture, the minute that I start applying for jobs that are like having to do with, you know, just regular sitcoms or just like mainstream white America, obviously, the white-bread culture, I think that they—that it's much harder to get jobs in mainstream America." She makes the interesting point that jobs within a tiny specialized market for one's own racial group might be easier to get, but once competing in the "mainstream" market, racism becomes more manifest. This kind of discrimination leads to the marginalization of talented nonwhites into racial/ethnic specific markets and subfields rather than in the larger markets that are more prestigious and lucrative.

Rebecca is a Macanese American college student who makes a similar realization as she compares two of her summer employment experiences. When reflecting on her position with an Asian firm, she begins with a sunny framing of her experiences. She uses the "it helps" minimization strategy. As she progresses to a more mainstream business, however, she realizes some hiring discrimination:

> In terms of jobs, I feel like it [my race/ethnicity] does help me, like this summer I worked for a . . company . . . they don't even have to interview me like twice, they were just like, "Oh," you know, "You have a good resume," and, you know, "It *helps to be of your background*, so, cause, with Asian businesses, it's—the communication part is crucial especially within your own ethnicity" and stuff like that. [Interviewer: Do you feel that's only a plus with Asian firms, or—] I think sometimes in general, sometimes it can hurt me, like I tried to interview for the [large marketing] agency two years ago, and it was totally totally quiet . . . it was for editing, sort of like, brochure material and stuff like that. . . . I did an interview and they completely left me . . . for two hours, and had forgotten about me. So I was trying to find the supervisor or whatever to hand in my—my papers and everything, and they're like, "Oh, OK, OK," you know. So I find that a little discouraging. [emphasis added]

Rebecca describes a sense of invisibility that is commonly experienced by African Americans, Asian Americans, and other minorities, which in this case had institutional consequences—she did not get the job. Another college student, a Guatemalan American young woman, Edita, also expresses a generationally consistent pattern—wanting to believe that one's racial/ethnic background helps in certain employment situations, but understanding that it is never altogether clear in which establishments it might help and which ones it would hurt: "It *does sort of help* to be a minority like you can get chances that other people don't. And then, I don't know because it sometimes hurts like if you're applying for a job and you just, your application ends up in the wrong hands and someone sees your background and you don't get it just because of that and people underestimate you both as a woman and then as a minority" (emphasis added). Sometimes the younger generation has not yet had enough employment-related experiences to be able to assess the extent of discrimination that may befall them there. Yet it is easy to sense from this quote the anxiety that comes from not knowing where "the wrong hands" would be.

Other respondents have faced prejudicial assumptions about themselves during the job-seeking process but feel they were successfully able to prove that these stereotypes did not apply to them. These accounts are indicative of that enduring faith in the American dream, despite major evidence to the contrary. We have no way of knowing how many other times these respondents were never allowed the chance to prove such naysayers wrong. Elisa, an Argentinean American teacher with multiple college degrees, explains:

> When I have to look for a space for a school, if I didn't get to meet with the people, and they heard me on the phone . . . it could take [your] importance away from a talk on the phone. It's different when you meet with someone and they get to feel, not only to hear what you're saying, but—looking for a space for a school, I think it was a little more difficult for me being from Argentina, or from a foreign country . . . just hearing the accent, [they wonder,] "OK, where is she coming from, why is she looking for a space for a school, who is she in this society?" . . . I think in those cases it doesn't favor me.

Most of the respondents do not have a detectable accent, so potential interviewers often reacted to last names or appearances; Elisa is one who did have an accent, however, and obviously encounters problems because of it. This demonstrates the faulty assumptions explored earlier in this chapter about the link between languages spoken and intelligence/ability level. Because Elisa is one of a few in the sample who is most often mistaken for white (white European), she had better experiences when she got to "meet with someone," most likely because she was able to cash in on some degree of white-skin privilege. Those hearing a Spanish accent on the phone may have expected someone darker skinned and not bothered to follow through. Those many other Latinos and Asian Americans who would have actually had the "feared" phenotype in question here may not have made it past the first interview stage, given the attitudes this respondent confronted in her own experiences. Her experience is interesting because it is the exact reverse of that often described by African Americans and other visible minorities. Many appreciate being able to secure first steps to employment over the phone where they can "sound white" and placate potential employers, because, as actual audit studies have shown, once employers discover they are black it can negatively affect their job prospects from that point onward.[6]

Like Elisa, Kali, the Indian American statistician with a master's degree, believes that she has effectively been able to neutralize employers' negative racial/ethnic preconceptions about her during the interview process. This sunny framing seems highly illogical, because it is unlikely, and indeed illegal, for employers to actually make known such biases to the interviewee. So these incidents in which the respondent *is* made aware of such employer biases in time to correct for them are undoubtedly a small fraction of the times such biases actually exist. Notice how Kali also uses the "other groups have it worse" minimization device to further downplay the treatment:

> But I think after 9/11 things have changed. [Interviewer: Towards you or —] Not towards us at all. On the contrary. If anything, towards Muslims. [Interviewer: You don't think people sometimes, do you think a lot of people sometimes associate you with Muslims or was that the first time?] They'll ask me. They'll ask me, sometimes for interviews, if I go to interview and they see I'm Indian, from my name they don't know when I apply but when I go in to interview they see me that I'm Indian and it's kind of in conversation they want to know if I'm Muslim and people will not hire you if you are but they won't tell you that directly because they are not allowed to ask. So they try to get it out of you indirectly but I get asked that very often, "Are you Muslim?" Sometimes directly, sometimes indirectly. [Interviewer: Does that ever offend you?] Not really because I'm not [Muslim]. But I can't imagine how, if I had been Muslim it would, of course it would. That's racism.

Kali's logic is fascinating. She believes that she has not experienced racism in these multiple incidents she describes because she is not Muslim, even though they assume she is. She believes that if she assures potential employers that she is not Muslim, no penalties will occur. Further, she has neglected to imagine all of the employers who at first glance thought she was Muslim and never gave her the opportunity to correct them because their biases thwarted that process before it could happen. I found this example of minimization to be the most striking of all the interviews.

Besides the minimization strategy, this quote also demonstrates how post-9/11 anti-Muslim and anti-Arab stereotypes powerfully affect these Latino and Asian American (not-black-not-white) respondents, even though they are not Muslims or Arabs. Several respondents stated that they often got mistaken for someone of Middle Eastern descent, particularly those who were biracial and had one non-Hispanic white parent. Because this post-9/11 stereotype carries with it the profile of a violent terrorist criminal, and it is fueled by the irrational flames of fear, now it seems all those in the not-black-not-white racial middle are caught in its racist snare.

Assumptions of Criminality and Terrorism

Although most of the above themes are shared by respondents whether they are Latino or Asian American, when examining the interviews for stereotypes about criminality, two distinct racial patterns emerge. The prejudices that Latinos describe are more similar to those faced by African Americans—they are assumed to be drug dealers or to somehow make the neighborhood so criminal as to be unsafe for whites. On the other hand, when Asian American respondents described assumptions about their criminality, they were referring to crimes of terror. Although we generally think of this as a post-9/11 stereotype, actually one respondent goes as far back as the Iranian hostage crisis and still was targeted by the same racial profiling. Notably, those of South Asian descent tend to mention these experiences. As with the stereotypical assumptions about jobs, there appears to be a distinct split between East Asians and South Asians in which the latter become the recipients of more negative stereotyping.

Some may immediately indict South Asians' darker skin color as the explanation for this difference, but this difference is hardly universal as there are many skin-color gradations in both Eastern and Southern Asia. Further, there are historical and political factors affecting the most popular stereotypes at any given time. For instance, in the mid-1940s—a point at which anti-Japanese sentiment was most severe in the United States— Asian Indians began to be classified as whites on the U.S. census, a privilege never experienced by Japanese Americans despite their socioeconomic standing relative to whites. This "white" racial categorization continued until 1980 when a separate Asian Indian category was established, and people were allowed to self-identify their race on the census for the first time.[7] Because Islam is one religion found commonly in certain South Asian countries, the post-2001 War-on-Terror climate could be having an impact on this historical shift from the more positive to the more negative images of Indians. Moreover, I have already presented evidence to show that white Americans are often not all that savvy about determining the particular ethnic background of any given Latino or Asian American individual, so it may not even be an actual connection to India that the stereotypers are perceiving. Stereotypes are seldom reducible to clear logic. Whatever the reasons, there are clear differences in the particulars of the types of crimes that Asian Americans and Latinos respectively are suspected of committing in the eyes of those who fear them.

Latino respondents' experiences expose several assumptions of criminality, particularly stereotypes that they are drug dealers or gang members. Because Claudia lived in a predominantly Dominican neighborhood in New York City at the time of this incident she recalls, she encountered such negative assumptions from white coworkers:

> I was speaking with these white ladies, and she [one of them] said, "Oh, I was invited to a birthday in Washington Heights"—and at that time I was living in Washington Heights—she said, "But I don't want to go there." I said, "Why you don't want to go there?" She said, "Because it's a danger[ous] community," and I said, "But I live in that community," and I said, "I'm not a danger[ous] person." And she said, "No, no, you're different, you're different." I got so offended. Because just because you come from this place does not mean all of them are criminal. I've been here for like seventeen years, and I've been breaking my back to try and get in the position that I'm in now. . . . I attain what I want in an honest and decent way. And you're going to find criminals in all communities! It doesn't matter! [laughs] So sometimes if you have this closed mind—and like, she said, "No, no, it's not you."

It is painful to work all of one's life in "an honest and decent way" yet still be perceived as "dangerous" to others because of something out of one's control. Besides the stereotype itself, the other part of this interaction that is offensive to her—enough for her to say it twice—is the perpetrator's cleanup attempt: "no, no, it's not you." Like the assumption of danger and criminality, this isolation of one "token" out from the rest of the negatively judged group is something that African Americans commonly experience. Rather than questioning one's own racist assumptions when confronted with evidence to the contrary, the speaker instead separates one person out from the rest of the group as an "exception." As one African American sergeant in the U.S. Air Force once told me, when referring to his frustration with being constantly told by whites "you're not like them," he says, "But I *am* them!" He learned how to speak and treat others from everyone else in his family who is also African American, so he wonders why he should be seen as "so different" from everyone else in the group; in his eyes, everyone in the group is no less deserving of this "special" designation than him.

Clearly, this "cleanup" tactic is not really about noticing anything particularly unique about one isolated individual of color. Rather, it reflects more the speaker's own experience: either the speaker has had limited interactions with members of the negatively evaluated group, so an interaction with a real person from the group is notably different than the generalized stereotype, and/or the speaker is working hard to retain the stereotypical image in his or her mind and is therefore separating out any evidence to the contrary. Sometimes it is emotionally jarring for individuals to realize that the world is not as they thought it was. Thus, it is easier to preserve the old and familiar ways of thinking than to admit one is wrong and take the opportunity to adjust accordingly.

Although Dominicans have many skin tones, often they are associated with being darker skinned and similar to blacks, especially in New York City, where the above respondent resides. It is not only Dominicans and blacks, however, who share these experiences with assumptions of criminality. As we saw in an earlier quote, a Mexican American respondent regularly experiences women clutching tightly their purses when he passes them. Another respondent, a young Salvadorian American man living in the Washington DC area, where a gang named MS-13 received media attention, is conscious of assumptions that he is a gang member. Monica is a white Cuban American who recalls assumptions that her Cuban father, and by extension, the entire family, were drug dealers as she was growing up:

> There is that assumption that if your father is Cuban then you must be a Communist, or that you must be a drug dealer. There's that assumption about Cubans or even Latinos in general that they deal drugs, and we did have that happen a couple times. No, I don't think they're accurate. [Interviewer: Where do you think that comes from, where do they?] From, with Colombia you hear about all the DEA [Drug Enforcement Administration] stuff in Latin America with people driving drugs and opiates. It's just a very—especially back in the eighties with the whole Iran Contra thing and the fact that there was drug dealing going on with that. It was just, there was just a perception, and because we were Cuban and *we moved to a place where people did not know a lot of Cubans or even*

Hispanics, there was just an assumption that we were drug dealers. Or that my father was a drug dealer or that he was a Communist. Or—I don't know why they—*I don't think that still persists today*. Maybe it does to a degree. [emphasis added]

Elsewhere in the interview Monica describes more at length the culture shock that her family experienced when moving from Miami to a Midwestern U.S. state. Her Polish mother and Cuban father eventually divorced, and her father returned to Miami because the racism they faced outside of Miami was so pervasive. In a region of the country like Miami where people are more familiar with Latinos, and Cubans specifically, her father knew he would be much less likely to encounter what he did in the Midwest. Because she is one generation removed from all of this, and has a white, blond-haired appearance, this respondent distances herself a bit from the experience, describing racism as more painful for her father than for her. This is evident in some of her minimization strategies, also used by other respondents, that this only happens in certain parts of the country, and that it does not happen anymore. She actually backpedals from this "only in the past" stance a bit towards the end, however, when she acknowledges that "maybe it does" still happen. But clearly her more vivid memories of the hostility come from when she was younger and lived with her father.

Other respondents also mention the drug dealer and gang member images attached to the Latino community, and they often blame the media for the misleading portrayals that lead to these stereotypes. The label of "illegal immigrant" comes up in some of the interviews as well. In contrast, Asian American respondents mainly mention stereotypes that they were intelligent and good at math. Responses to these so-called positive stereotypes are mixed—some find them useful in certain situations, while others feel they are problematic because they cannot live up to them. Whether respondents' backgrounds are in East Asia or South Asia, they mention stereotypes that had to do with such intellectual pursuits. It is solely respondents with South Asian backgrounds, however, who discuss facing stereotypes about criminal activity, and it mainly involves terrorism, rather than gang or drug activity.

While younger respondents (or more recent immigrants) characterize this "terrorist" stereotype that they face as a post-9/11 construction, David, who also grew up in the 1980s, recalls being cast as a suspicious terrorist even then:

The only weird thing was, I was in high school during the Iranian hostage crisis and because I don't look pure—I kind of more than now, kind of have a chameleon look for a lot of range. Everybody would think that. A lot of people thought that I was Arab, Middle Eastern, and so forth. So that was a period where I lot hassled more for being ethnic to begin with because they thought I was Arab or Persian or whatever. Basically they thought Iranian. . . . And so, going back to the original thing, in my upbringing, I think I stuck out as nonwhite in Irvine, but *I don't think it affected me except when* there was kind of like these situations like the Iranian hostage and so forth. [emphasis added]

David grew up with an Indian father and mother who is a Polish Jew, so he describes throughout the interview his "chameleon" experience in the racial middle, whereby he is often mistaken for a lot of different groups, depending on the area and the context. (He has lived and traveled worldwide.) His age at the time of the interview (forty) provides an important, wider historical lens, demonstrating that "terrorist" stereotypes of those in the racial middle extend well before the events of September 11, 2001. The minimization devices used here ("the only . . . thing" and "except" for that one time) are common throughout the respondents but are so striking here because the respondent also happens to teach college courses on race, so his interview is understandably lengthy and includes multiple examples of confronting racism assumptions like this. The fact that these rhetorical strategies are spoken even by someone who is clearly more aware of the pervasiveness of racial discrimination indicates just how deeply ingrained this compulsion to at least give lip service to the idea of the American dream is in the U.S. racial ideology. As we will see in chapter 6, racial ideology is so hegemonic that it infuses the worldviews of even the most racially progressive in society.

Elsewhere in David's interview, he shares an anecdote that reveals how deeply another one of the minimization strategies ("other groups have it worse") affected his consciousness:

I've never, like, regretted my ethnicity. But I've regretted the hassles, especially that I've had traveling. And the worst place is the United States. Whenever I come back from abroad, like, my favorite incident was . . . [pause to flip tape] but, I got back to the United States and there was a line of people going through customs and we were on line for U.S. citizens.

And I saw this really well-dressed African American male—this is in Los Angeles airport—and I just go, so the security guard came and I go, "They're gonna nail him!" And they went right to him and took him out to do, you know, check through his stuff more carefully. And I was just like, "Back in the United States . . ." and as they walk by me they pulled me out too, [laughs] and I was like "Oh! I forgot about me!" [laughs] So both of us you know, got to have the, you know, more-detailed search. And part, for me it was, I had no hassle too much about it because . . . [I was] . . . unshaven. But here's this guy who's dressed in a suit and stuff and so it was kind of funny because I should have received it—I would be the obvious other choice for that.

Like Charlene's assertion that her experience facing stereotypes about Asians is "better than being black," this quote also shows how another Asian American respondent expects an African American male to get worse treatment than himself. It takes being singled out for the "more-detailed search" to remind him that he also fits the phenotypical profile of a terrorist/criminal. This quote is also reminiscent of the double-consciousness moments in other interviews: the respondent experiences a momentary naivete where he or she expects to be seen as an individual and then is jolted back to the reality that he or she is also being perceived through the lens of a negatively stereotyped group.

One of the points raised by several South Asian respondents about the terrorist stereotypes is that they are "misplaced." First, it is important to note that, by definition, all stereotypes are misplaced. Even if these were actually respondents with Middle Eastern ethnicities and/or Muslim religions, it is faulty logic to assume that they would be more likely to be terrorists based on their background alone. Still, there is a feeling of added injustice expressed by these respondents, because not only do they know they are not terrorists, but they are not even members of the group from which the stereotypes originated. As Raj, who is decades younger (twenty) with an Indian father and white mother, points out: "More ignorant Americans, who just really don't know and haven't been aware, classify like Indians, Pakistanis, Arabs, all these groups, pretty much that India's in the Middle East. No, so like, when like September eleventh happened, a lot of Indians with turbans who weren't even Muslim got beat up in Texas. And it's just, that's just ignorance, but maybe that's a stereotype, Middle Easterner." Again it is attributed to American ignorance that many nations are lumped together into one conceptual rubric to which negative stereotypes are then applied. It is interesting that the word "terrorist" is not even mentioned in this anecdote. The stereotype associated with the turban in this anecdote is simply summarized as "Middle Easterner."

Other Indian American respondents, however, have described their experience with this misplaced stereotype as being attached to a "Muslim" rather than "Middle Easterner" identity. Recall Kali, who says she has experienced "no racism" because she has been able to reassure prospective employers that she is not Muslim. While she groups those experiences with potential employers together in one collective narrative, she also relates a more detailed and violent confrontation that occurred in a bar, fueled by this same Muslim/terrorist assumption:

My only encounter with racism was actually in New York, of all places, where someone thought I was Muslim, which was pretty bizarre. And I didn't bother to deny it but I'm sure Muslims face a lot now. [Interviewer: And what happened, were they just—] It was really bizarre. I was sitting at a bar and these two women walk in, you know white women and sit next to me. And I was sitting there with a friend of mine and this woman starts, the one next to me, she starts chattering with me. She says, "Where are you from?" and before I could say anything, she said, "Are you Muslim?" So I was like, oh. I said, I didn't say anything. Why, I don't have a religion. And then she started, she started, she was like—I don't actually have children, but [she said,] "For every white woman like me who has one child a Muslim has eleven children," and on and on, "And why don't you go back to your country?" and stuff like that. It was really bizarre and that really got me mad. And just to pick on someone. [I] tried to give her the benefit of the doubt. I thought maybe she had lost someone in nine-eleven, so I asked her, and she said, "No," she was just like that. She was getting into me, but I gave it back to her as well. I said, "Obviously you are not very well educated." And then she got mad at me and eventually she kind of reached out and scratched me. Can you believe it? It was really bizarre. So I took my drink and I threw it in her face. And then she got mad and she called the bartender, the owner, and she said call the police, [saying] "I want her thrown out of here." I've [been] going to that bar, it's my neighborhood bar, for four years, so there was no way he was going to throw me out. So he said, "You can call the police if you want." But she didn't. . . . It's sad. *I can't imagine what Muslims go through,* honestly. [emphasis added]

Keep in mind that even though Kali describes this as her "only encounter with racism," she reports multiple times when potential employers question whether she is Muslim during job interviews, and also recounts hostile stares both while living in Ohio and in Germany with her German husband. She minimizes the Germany incidents by saying that because she was with her German husband she did not experience anything. This reflects a recurring pattern among the sample whereby an incident is not deemed racist or discriminatory unless it is exceedingly blatant.

At every step of this anecdote, Kali is clear to point out the inaccuracy of the perpetrator's assumptions: she is not Muslim, she is not even religious, she does not have any children. These facts about her, however, unfortunately do not shield her from the prejudices that may be applied at any time in a racist society to those in the racial middle. In fact, 16 percent of the sample (8/50) reports that they are often misperceived as being Arab, Middle Eastern, or "Muslim," as in the above case. So it is a recurring pattern that they may experience such "terrorist" stereotypes even if they do not technically fit the profile in their own minds. Keep in mind that the most common misperception they report is actually being mistaken for Latino when they are Asian American, or for Asian American when they are Hispanic. So this cognitive "lumping together" in Americans' minds of the not-black-not-white middle occurs frequently, despite the fact that the most common answer respondents chose when singling out a group they feel they have least in common with was Asian Americans (for Latino respondents) or Latinos (for Asian American respondents). The respondents obviously have a clearer picture of just how many differences actually exist among all the groups Americans seem to interchange in their minds in the racial middle, but this does not prevent the mix-ups from happening to them.

Conclusion

It is evident there are similarities and differences between comparable studies on black experiences with racial discrimination and the present study on Latino and Asian American experiences.[8] These similarities and differences can be separated into two main categories of conceptual interest: (1) the specific type of prejudice and/or discrimination and the actual form that it takes, and (2) the way the targeted person frames and describes those experiences. This sample of Latinos and Asian Americans shares with blacks the experience of being perceived as only fit for certain jobs and not others (although the particular job in question differs among groups) and of being used as a "tool" on the job to prove diversity instead of being valued for one's unique contributions. They also share the experience of being targets of suspicion as potentially lawbreaking, although the specific type of law they are expected to break differs depending on race/ethnicity. Latinos across the board seem to share the experience of facing stereotypes that they are drug dealers, gang members, thieves (all of which other work shows that African American males commonly face), while Asian Americans, largely South Asians, face the stereotype that they are terrorists.

Although African Americans have also been shown to face negative stereotypes about their intellectual abilities, this sample of Latinos and Asian Americans face questions about their capabilities that seem qualitatively different. Specifically, they are assumed not to speak English. While this assumption could conceivably be rectified the minute the person speaks, it is evident that nonetheless this stereotype has had serious institutional consequences for respondents—from being placed in a low-ability track in school to not receiving college scholarships to not being asked to a job interview because of one's last name. Further, while African Americans certainly experience the "misrecognition"[9] in predominantly white environments of both being invisible and sticking out like a sore thumb because of negative judgments about their "skin color" and other physical features, most American blacks do not repeat the "all the time" constant annoyance of being asked "where are you from?" or, worse yet, "what are you?" It seems that most white Americans at least have a baseline understanding that slavery occurred in the early history of the United States, even as they perpetuate misinformation that slavery and other forms of disenfranchisement were "so long ago." In contrast, Americans seem to have less of an understanding that there were early presences of Latinos and Asians in the United States—that indeed, part of the United States *was* Mexico, and that many Latinos and Asians share family histories of being in the United States and speaking English longer than some non-Hispanic white Americans. While all of this questioning of people of color's "right to be here" in "our space" falls into a larger rubric of othering behavior, regardless of the nonwhite racial group being targeted, I maintain that the "where are you from?"/"what are you?" questioning, as well as the "you speak such good English" complimenting, are a more unique part of the racial middle's experiences with discrimination.

I have already explored at the opening of this chapter how research on African Americans has shown that they often may not be fully aware of the extent of racial discrimination they encounter in their everyday lives.[10] Further, other research reports that blacks also may tend to give a person the repeated benefited of the doubt before they admit that negative actions they experience at the hands of others might be racially motivated.[11] No study to my knowledge, however, has uncovered African Americans so frequently stating that they experience "no racism" or racism "only one time," despite evidence to the contrary. I would argue that the extent to which those in the racial middle minimize their accounts of racial discrimination, prejudice, and exclusion is qualitatively different than that typically reported by African Americans. The "where are you from?" questioning they experience places them in a relatively disadvantaged position from which to cope with racist assumptions and experiences. They are in a double bind, being already deemed as apart from the typical American dream narrative by others, despite the fact that their own accounts place themselves squarely within it. Based on their appearance alone, without saying a word, most of the respondents face this misplaced stigma of being "foreign." Should they speak out and criticize the United States for not being the "equal playing field" that it purports itself to be, they face further ostracism by engaging in supposedly un-American speech. While racism is something troublingly out of an individual's control, one can control the extent to which he or she is further deemed un-American by adapting one's worldview to champion the American dream rather than appear to be criticizing it by "dwelling" on racial discrimination. Thus, while respondents may appear to be engaging in passive denial, they may indeed be actively practicing a resistance strategy by which they refuse to be further deemed as un-American. The respondents' defiant choreography in the "where are you from?" dance (responding with the name of their hometown in the United States) bears witness to the purposefulness behind their minimization techniques. They are determined to let "ignorant" Americans know that they can lay claim to the American dream just as much as the next white immigrant.

Even for those respondents who do not employ such strategies of defiant resistance, instead insisting that it's all "no big deal" or even beneficial to them, research demonstrates that merely the mention of these ethnic-specific stereotypes can negatively affect individuals' performance. Claude Steele's social psychological experiments have consistently documented what has become known as the "stereotype threat." When people

are informed that members of their specific ethnic group tend to perform poorly on a particular test, they tend to score more poorly on that
test. Their scores recover when they are not given such negative information about their group.[12] Considering one of the persistent stereotypes
of Asians as passive or as not good English speakers, for example, being
cognizant of these assumptions on the part of Americans could negatively
affect their public speaking performances. Indeed, Mya, a Taiwanese-
Chinese respondent is aware of Steele's research (although the specifics
of the study are not clear in her quote, the implications of its findings are
not lost on her), and she passionately discusses how it applies to her own
experiences:

> What I wanted to say is, that I do believe, this is what I heard, I do
> believe it represents somewhat, some true scenarios, they say that, they
> use black as experiment. They give the black people a set of tests, and
> on the top of the test, they ask them, first time they ask them what is
> their answer, and second time they give exactly same test to the same
> group of people, black people, but then this time they ask the group their
> race, and guess what? The results came up, it shows much lower average
> number for that set of tests then all the other group people then all the
> other set of tests that did not ask the group their race. I totally agree
> with that, and that story is only one instance. And when they take it to
> the classroom and they're taking a test. But it's not only one instance,
> it's every day, every time, any situation, any event, you could run into
> the people who make sure you are a minority, and make sure you know
> you are Asian female, and make sure you know they are inferior than
> they are! [said loudly and on the verge of crying] I'm sorry. [Interviewer:
> No, that's fine.] There are the people like that. And when they are in the
> position of power or influence and are able to make your life miserable,
> and that was the only reason. And where do you go? Can you tell them,
> I knew he did that, or I know she's doing that because I am not com-
> municating at the same level as he expected. Who are you going to take
> back on a case?

Elsewhere in the interview Mya laments the fact that she experiences
many such slights in life but does not perceive that U.S. civil rights law is
set up to handle "a case" of what she deems as less than overt discrimination. She also reveals during the course of the interview that she is well
aware that, in being so outspoken about these and other issues, she is

stepping outside of the bounds of what is expected from both a female and an Asian American in U.S. society.

Whether one is a member of the majority or minority group in a racially divided society, both groups absorb the dominant racist ideology and internalize it to varying degrees, as discussed in chapter 3. That said, there are elements of white dominant culture that keep Latinos and Asians from speaking out against or even recognizing racism, as the above respondent identifies. Members of minority cultures themselves, however, have also internalized the message that they should not speak out, complain, or make a big deal about the racism that they face in the United States. To make it all a big joke is one way to survive in the culture without further repercussions. In another passionate moment from the interviews, Neva, who is Mexican American, explains:

My male cousins would tell Mexican jokes, and it didn't used to bother me when I was younger. But now, it's like, "So what are you exactly saying? Do you really believe that about the group and about yourself?" So, I do get uncomfortable now, when they tell jokes like, "What do you call a bunch of Mexicans running down a hill? A mudslide. Ha ha ha ha." Like, shut up. . . . For me, it's mostly my family who tells it. I'm like, "Could you please not be like that?" [begins crying] It's been hard . . . I mean, my brother tells these jokes and he claims that he doesn't believe them, but he tells them like so much, like even if you don't believe that you believe them, how do they not become part of your thinking? So I'm uncertain about him. And my mother, she just doesn't like, tell him to stop it or, it's been like, "Oh, [name] has gone off to college and now she's become sensitive about these issues and now she's like Ms. Cultural and she can't tell these jokes anymore," and it's like, well, maybe it's a good thing!

It often takes some kind of shift in one's frame of reference to realize, as a member of a stigmatized group in society, that the everyday racism one faces is severely problematic. Sometimes even those in one's own group cannot bear to hear about it. If one risks not only negative consequences from whites in power but also ostracism from one's own ethnic group, it is no wonder that many Latinos and Asian Americans opt not to speak out about the discrimination they face or to dwell much on it. Although a majority of this sample chooses to minimize the discrimination they experience in one way or another, a sizeable proportion of the sample (20/50) (including the brave young college student quoted above) treads a more progressive path. As we shall see in the next chapter, experiencing intimate and deep shifts in racial/ethnic perspectives (such as being brought up in a mixed-ethnicity home, or forming such a home oneself) is one of the ways that Latinos and Asian Americans slough off the dominant racist discourse and boldly call out the discrimination they face, unencumbered by apologies or disclaimers.

Scott, a Taiwanese-Chinese American respondent, with a white wife and two biracial children, has the potential to gain that kind of shift in perspective through his new family, but he decides to continue to opt for minimization instead. Perhaps because of his life partner's comparative lens—having been the recipient of white privilege all her life, she points out to him times when they are getting the stares, looks, and cold shoulders—he readily acknowledges that there is probably more racism directed at him that he is picking up on his radar. While many respondents may say there was no racism, this man is willing to concede that it may have affected him, but he prefers to continue to view the world through the lens of the American dream. Scott's quote so powerfully illustrates clinging to the American dream despite exclusion that I use it to close the chapter:

> I tend to think of myself as an individual so I don't pass the reactions that people have to me through the ethnicity filter. If somebody doesn't like me, I don't necessarily think, "Oh, is it because I'm Chinese?" It's more like, "I must have made a bad impression, I shouldn't have said that about their hair." [laughter] You know what I mean, or whatever, you know. I mean, just like this incident. [an incident described earlier in the interview where his family car was followed and various profanities, including racial epithets, were shouted by the driver] At the time that it happened, I didn't think, "Oh, I'm Chinese," or "oh, I'm a mixed-race couple, and that's why." It was "cranky old man," you know, and we just happened to be in the wrong place. So, even if it has hindered . . . me, it hasn't crossed my mind to say that's the reason why. Even if that was the reason.

6

Progressives

Seeing Race through Multiple Lenses

We have seen that the dominant ideology of race in the United States—color-blind racism—has a pervasive impact on those in the racial middle, supporting the thesis that the racial middle is "whitening" in some ways. They have also perpetuated racism in ways that are more unique to the "middle" than the whitening thesis accounts for. There is also a sizeable minority of this sample, however, that consistently rejects various components of color-blind ideology. Rather than rely on naturalizing stereotypes about other groups, or minimizing the impact of racial discrimination on their own or others' lives, they seem to reflect the optimist version of the browning thesis by articulating common concerns that they share across various groups, including Latinos, Asian, Middle Eastern, and African Americans. Most of them seem to have arrived at this position through one of three major ways, not necessarily mutually exclusive: (1) through intimate connections (usually in one's family of origin, procreation, or both) with persons outside of their own racial/ethnic group, often whites; (2) through moving between geographic areas with significantly different ethnic compositions or racial ideologies; and (3) through seeing themselves less as members of any particular racial/ethnic category at all—instead, as part of a multiracial, even global/international community. In all three cases, respondents have acquired multiple lenses through which to view race and ethnicity, and thus have developed critiques around the arbitrariness of race-based thinking and complicated their understandings about race.

In this chapter, I explore how this subsample of twenty arrived at these racially progressive outlooks, and what their progressive ideologies look like. As with the rest of this book, my aim is *not* to make statistically significant generalizations about which Latinos and Asians are most likely to be progressive, because I am unable to do so with these data. By definition, this highly educated sample that voluntarily gave of their time to discuss their racial/ethnic identities is already perhaps less likely to subscribe to color-blind racism than all Latinos and Asians as a whole. Furthermore, without comparison groups of whites and blacks within this study, it is impossible for me to speculate on whether the likelihood of progressivism (about 40 percent for this sample) in the racial middle is more like blacks or like whites. This sample's willingness to engage in talk about race, ethnicity, and culture with the interviewers, however, allows us some insight into racial progressivism in the racial middle, and an opportunity to consider how progressivism in the racial middle is qualitatively similar and/or different to that which has already been studied in whites and blacks.

Characteristics of Progressives

In order to narrow down this subsample of twenty progressives, I employed the same criteria used by Eduardo Bonilla-Silva in his multiple-method study of color-blind racism in white and black discourse. He defines racial progressivism as approval of racial intermarriage, approval of affirmative action programs, and belief in the reality of persistent discrimination as it affects the lives of people of color, especially blacks. In his sample of hundreds of whites, only about 15 percent met this criteria, and they tended to be working class and female.[1] No other study to my knowledge investigates to this extent these ideological components of Latinos' and Asian Americans' racial belief systems.

There are some studies, some of which I cite in this section, that examine Latinos and Asian Americans' views on particular political issues and/or the likelihood that they will be Democrat or Republican, or conservative or liberal. While most quantitative research on political attitudes of Latinos and/or Asian Americans has utilized the conservative/liberal or Republican/Democrat distinction, it is important to note that I do not use these traditional categories in this work. I use the categories of progressive and nonprogressive to focus on the race-related aspects of the respondents' views. Indeed, a few respondents counted for this study as "progressive" actually identify themselves as politically Republican or conservative, or occasionally as "moderates." Likewise, there are several self-identified liberals or Democrats in the study who are not categorized as racial progressives. Thus, the more traditional political affiliation categories (Republican/Democrat, liberal/conservative), while sometimes

TABLE 6-1
Influence of Cross-Racial/Ethnic Intimacy on Progressivism

	Ethnically Different Family of Origin	Ethnically Different Partner/Family of Procreation	Both
Total Sample (n = 50)	14 (28%)	16 (32%)	10 (20%)
Progressives (n = 20)	10 (50%)	11 (55%)	8 (40%)

overlapping, are not synonymous with the concept of racial progressivism used for this study. The advantage of these qualitative data is that we are able to examine the discursive elements of racial ideology that hide behind the more simplistic pro/con answers to policy questions. They have an interesting story to tell about how a segment of the racial middle views themselves vis-à-vis other U.S. racial groups.

In this sample, the one trait shared most consistently across the twenty progressives, and one that most clearly separated them from the non-progressives in the sample, was their involvement with cross-racial and/or cross-ethnic intimacy in their immediate families and partnerships. Interestingly, this finding runs counter to what the whitening thesis would predict. The whitening thesis uses intermarriage with whites as an important indicator of assimilation. It expects that identification as Latino or Asian American will decrease with increased intermarriage to whites.[2] The patterns displayed in table 6-1, however, challenge this prediction. It became evident to me on reading the interview transcripts that having an ethnically mixed family experience was an important experience shared by many progressive respondents. This was, in all but two cases, experienced by either having one white parent or being adopted by white parents (three out of four of the adoptees in the sample are progressive). In the other two cases, respondents had ethnically different parents—Thai/Filipino and Macanese/Hong Kong—who were both still Asian. Respondents discuss developing a critical eye on race and racism due to their family experiences. Having to understand themselves through the lenses of more than one racial and/or ethnic group simultaneously, they began to realize the limits of race-related stereotypes and overgeneralizations.

Further, being able to compare the more privileged experience of the whites in their families with their own allowed them to get firsthand experience with the differential treatment that whites and people of color routinely face. There were also respondents whose choice of a white spouse was consistent with a more color-blind and white-identified ideology;

TABLE 6-2

Demographic Characteristics of Progressives (n = 20)

Race/Ethnicity

Latinos (n = 23)[a]	9 (39%)[b]	Asians (n = 27)	11 (41%)
Mexican (n = 7)	5	Indian (n = 5)	3
Puerto Rican (n = 5)	3	Korean (n = 3)	2
Cuban (n = 2)	1	Filipino/Thai (n = 3)	2
		Macanese (n = 2)	2
		Bengali (n = 1)	1
		Chinese (n = 8)	1

Gender

Males (n = 22)	7 (32%)	Females (n = 28)	13 (46%)

Age

Under 30 (n = 16)	10 (20%)
30–50 (n = 25)	6 (12%)
Over 50 (n = 9)	4 (8%)

Generation

First (n = 16)	3 (19% of first-generation respondents are progressive)
"1.5" (n = 13)	7 (54% of 1.5-generation respondents are progressive)
Second (n = 18)	8 (44% of second-generation respondents are progressive)
Third/Fourth (n = 2)	2 (100% of third/fourth-generation respondents are progressive)

[a] (n = x) indicates number of respondents from the total sample that fit that category
[b] percentages indicate percentage of total sample that fit that category (for race/ethnicity, gender, and age)

these, however, were in the minority in this sample. For most, these inter-racial intimacy choices were made through race-conscious lenses, where the respondent was fully cognizant of the differential experiences that various members of their family would have due to their race and/or ethnicity.

Most of the other characteristics of this subsample reported in table 6-2 seem to be consistent with prior research. Previous studies have indicated that generation plays a crucial role in the racial attitudes and ideologies of immigrants. Those who are foreign born typically are more likely than the second and subsequent generations to embrace antiblack stereotypes and to characterize the United States as a meritocratic, open playing field.[3] That is, the longer time spent in the United States, the more they realize that the United States does not guarantee as much racial equality to its citizens as they had expected, and the more they potentially have in common with African Americans. As Portes and Rumbaut point out, such findings are counter to what assimilation theories predict—that the longer time spent in the United States, the less trouble immigrants will have with discrimination. Indeed, these scholars find that the amount of reported discrimination *increases* with subsequent generations.[4]

In this subsample of racial progressives, consistent with prior research, those who came to the United States as adults are much less likely to be progressive than the rest of the sample, with the exception of Puerto Rican Americans. The two second-generation Puerto Rican Americans in the sample are actually not racially progressive, while their first-generation counterparts are. Aside from this handful of Puerto Rican Americans, though, the majority of the sample who came here as adults is quite unlikely to be progressive. In this sample, however, I found it crucial to separate out two categories of foreign born—those who were raised in other countries and came here as adults I consider first generation, while those who were foreign born but raised and educated primarily in the United States I consider the "1.5" generation. As Jean Kim notes, this 1.5 generation tends to exhibit the patterns of the second generation, due to spending the vast majority of their lives, particularly the formative years, in the United States.[5] We can indeed see this in table 6-2. While only 19 percent of the sample who immigrated as adults is progressive, fully 54 percent of the 1.5 generation and 44 percent of the second generation is progressive. The two members of the sample who were third or fourth generation were also both progressive, but these numbers are so small that no major claims can be made about the patterns. Clearly, the biggest generational difference in progressivism in the sample is between those who were born and raised elsewhere and those who were raised in the United States (whether born there or not).

This generational pattern is not necessarily correlated with age, because the oldest members of the sample were all progressive (and interestingly, three out of those four are Puerto Rican American). The most striking age pattern here is the approximately doubled likelihood of being progressive if under age thirty. Those who were the oldest (over fifty) in the sample were slightly more likely than the middle aged (thirty to fifty) to be progressive; but again, this is likely to be more of an ethnicity effect, because most in the oldest group are Puerto Rican American (except for one who is Chinese American). Clearly being under the age of thirty makes the most difference on progressivism than any other age category, consistent with prior research. Similarly, gender appears to have the effect that most social scientists would expect. Females are a bit more likely to be racially progressive than males. This is consistent with Bonilla-Silva's analysis of white progressives[6] and bears out when analyzing political liberalism and conservatism by gender in the United States as a whole. Social scientists elsewhere have theorized that women's experiences with gender-related discrimination positions them to be more empathetic with other oppressed groups.[7]

Considering race, the persons represented in table 6-2 are spread fairly evenly between Latinos and Asian Americans, given the slightly higher ratio of Asian Americans to Latinos in the overall sample. This runs against findings from other work that Asian Americans are typically more politically conservative than Latinos.[8] I found Asian Americans no less likely to be progressive as a group than Latinos were as a group. There are, however, some important ethnicity patterns to take into account within these groups that could be affecting the patterns that are reported on a national scale. Notice that all six of the Central and South Americans in this sample are notably absent in the subsample of the twenty progressives. Likewise, only one of the eight Chinese/Taiwanese American respondents is represented in the progressives. Nationally, all Central and South American ethnicities taken together make up only a quarter of the total Hispanic population, while the Chinese Americans by themselves make up 28 percent of the Asian Pacific Islander total population. The latter group is also more likely to be registered and voting due to their longer generational history in the United States. Thus, if the Chinese Americans in general are a group that is likely to be conservative, then they are weighting the "Asian" total toward conservatism, when it is clear from this particular sample that the smaller Asian groups—South Asians, Southeast Asians, and Pacific Islanders—are more likely to be progressive. This is a case where overgeneralizations about panethnic racial groups can mislead us, without taking into account the particular ethnic differences within the group. Likewise, while Mexican and Puerto Rican Americans are the two largest ethnic groups for Latinos, and they tend to be politically more liberal, Central and South American groups (and also Cuban Americans) may not always follow the pattern of those larger groups.

Because most of the South Americans in the sample categorized themselves racially as white, I investigated the differences in progressivism among Latinos by their racial identification—white, black, or other. While six out of fourteen of the respondents who checked "other race" (43 percent) are progressive, only two out of eight (25 percent) who checked "white" are progressive. Not surprisingly, the one black Puerto Rican American in the sample was racially progressive. It is evident that racial identification with whiteness decreases the likelihood that one would be progressive, a pattern substantiated by other work[9] and one that would be predicted by the whitening thesis.

While the age, generation, gender, race, and ethnicity patterns in this subsample of progressives are interesting in light of the whitening thesis, ultimately with such a small and highly educated sample it is not possible to decisively confirm or disprove national patterns through these data. What we can glean from these interview data, however, are the stories that respondents tell tracing their routes to progressivism. Ultimately, their stories do not highlight their age, generation, or gender as much as they focus on the meaning of racial/ethnic identities in their lives and how those meanings shifted as they acquired multiple, critical perspectives on race from their life experiences.

Seeing Life from "The Other Side": The "Mixed" Route to Progressivism

Being able to observe life from "the other side" of racial and ethnic dividing lines is a common theme in the narratives of several Latino and Asian racial progressives. Whether these influential observations were collected at home growing up in a "mixed" household, in one's current mixed family of procreation, or both, they seem to be influential in shaping respondents' critical perspectives on racism. In one case, it seems that such observations can even be gained at the highest levels of a predominantly white corporation—a setting to which most of one's ethnic peers did not have access. As scholar Peggy McIntosh points out, we all live raced experiences in this society—whether consciously or not—and they become like water to a fish for us.[10] That is, it becomes almost inconceivable that there could be any other way but that to which we have grown accustomed. If those "other ways" are constantly a part of one's day-to-day lived experiences, however, and it becomes evident that there are multiple racial realities existing simultaneously (some with higher degrees of racial privilege than others), then it is easier to adopt a critical lens on the racial status quo, as progressives do.

Charlene, who is Thai and Filipino, has both an ethnically mixed family of origin and of procreation. Her parents experienced strong disapproval from their own parents when they got married, so she herself is a product of forbidden ethnic border crossing. After getting over their fears that a white man would not take as seriously the commitment of marriage as an Asian man, however, her parents were able to accept her white husband. Charlene has a keen understanding of what it means to be in the racial middle and have chosen a white, as opposed to a Latino or black, husband:

> [As an Asian American,] you sort of sometimes get to be counted as diversity, but you also are very easily accepted by whites' community. So that, like, my husband readily admits that it was a big enough stretch for [our] parents to be okay with him marrying me; they would never have accepted it if I were black. [Even] if my personality were completely the same, if my family were completely the same, they would have never accepted it. And so in that sense, being Asian helps me be able to be married to him and have a relationship with his parents that they can accept.

At every stage of her marriage—from the decision to marry to their decision to have children—Charlene has taken note of how racism has functioned to constrain their experiences as a family. On what seems a daily basis she and her family run into prevailing erroneous assumptions about race from the general public. She shares one such example from a recent shopping trip:

> I was standing next to my husband, and he was carrying my son in one of those little baby backpacks, and the salesclerk looked at me, you know, she looked at him and my son was making faces at her, and she's just like, "Oh, he's really cute. Is he adopted?" And she said this to my husband, and he said, "No, he's my son." And she was [like], "Oh. But I meant is he your adopted son?" He said, "No, he's my biological son." And she's just like, "But he doesn't look anything like you. He's got those strange Asian eyes." She goes, "Where did he get that from?" He's like, "From his mother," and he pointed like, right next to me. And she goes, "Oh, I didn't even see you." [Interviewer: Oh wow, and you were right there the whole time. Oh my gosh.] Yeah. Yeah. That was probably the most bizarre, memorable incident so far. But, yeah, I think it is pretty common for people to make comments.

Multiple layers of racial othering by the white clerk are evident in this example. First, the clerk assumes that a white man could not have a biological child who looks Asian. Second, the sales clerk describes her son as "cute" but also exoticizes him negatively by referring to his "strange Asian eyes." And perhaps most disturbing of all, the clerk treats Charlene as invisible even as she is standing right next to her husband and child.

Throughout her interview, Charlene is critical of how she is used as a tool or a token to demonstrate "diversity" when it suits her workplace, yet she is treated as more familiar and less suspect than her African American peers. Her experience with a white spouse and biracial child has allowed her to observe firsthand the more-valued treatment that whites in this society receive relative to her own experiences. At the same time, having grown up in a southern city in the United States, she is cognizant of how those experiences of marginalization that she faces regularly pale in comparison to those faced by black Americans. (Recall her quote from the last chapter that having to face Asian stereotypes is "better than being black, if you want to be frank about it.") Thus, she is aware of racism's pervasiveness and does not blame blacks or other people of color for racial inequality, she obviously supports intermarriage, and she supports affirmative action in principle, though she is critical of the "bean-counting" way it is administered and would prefer a more meaningful look at diversity in its implementation.

Another difference between the narratives of progressives and nonprogressives in the sample is the way they assess the relative diversity of their neighborhoods and social networks. Those who are not progressive tend to emphasize one or two token "black friends" to accentuate their own open-mindedness, while progressives tend to evaluate the same level of diversity (one or two nonwhites in a predominantly white environment) as inadequate and express their desire for change to a greater level of diversity. Rosa, who is quoted above, compares her more diverse living experiences of Mexico (early childhood) and San Diego (formative years) to her current predominantly white residence in North Carolina, and she is not pleased with that aspect of her neighborhood now:

My neighborhood now is predominantly white. . . . I would say ninety-five percent. . . . I would prefer that it wasn't this way. . . . The people who aren't white are actually from other countries. Like we have a house with a lot of immigrants from Africa, I'm not sure where they are [from] 'cause I don't talk with them that much. And then we have an Argentinean family, we got a couple, a couple who are Japanese, from Japan. I think we have one African American couple or young man who lives on the street. But it should have a little bit more diversity than that. I would say that the neighborhood overall is ninety-five percent white.

The respondents who are not classified as progressive in this study would typically take the examples of these four "nonwhite" families in their neighborhood as evidence of high diversity, while most progressives would find this inadequate. This is a pattern similar to the differences between progressive and nonprogressive whites in Bonilla-Silva's study. The majority of whites tend to overemphasize the amount of racial diversity in their surroundings and also try to point out someone they know who is a "real racist" in order to distance themselves from racism. On the other hand, progressives tend to be more candid about the levels of racism in their own lives.

Similar to the above respondent, Monica is currently married to a non-Hispanic white man; she was raised by interracial parents of Cuban (father) and Polish (mother) descent. She also grew up in the more diverse environment of Miami before moving to her current small southeast city and is displeased with the level of ethnic diversity, particularly as it affects her son's experiences:

> I would like to see more Latinos and African Americans in my community, Asian Americans and Filipino, all of that is so important to me. Because I grew up with that and it helped me become broader in thinking with different cultures, and customs, and different ways of thinking. My son unfortunately, has not been exposed to that in his short three years of life. In fact, he was at a primarily white school early on and even now he has one African American little girl that he plays with. And I hope that as he transitions up to some of the older classes he'll be exposed to more cultural diversity, but our community is growing to the point where in my neighborhood we're starting to see that, but not to the degree that I would like to see it. And I guess it's important because I want him to know that there's more out there than the white American that you see all the time. And I want him to understand the differences, and really try to learn from other people. Because I think so much of who I am came from my father being from, an immigrant from another country. . . . And I want [son's name] to be exposed to that as well. So if there was someone who needed his help, he would not be hesitant to do it because they're from another country.

Monica characterizes herself as someone who "roots for the underdog" when reflecting on her own political philosophy. Elsewhere in the interview, it appears that growing up with one white parent in the house was influential, in her case, because she identified with her white mother as someone who "rooted for the underdog" by marrying her father, considered a minority in society. While culturally, Cuban and Latin American cultural influences were most dominant in her home (her mother learned Spanish and spoke fluently with her father and his family), ideologically her mother's frame of reference on the world seems more intimately connected to her than her father's. Her mother did not approach her own interracial marriage with a color-blind outlook—she did not depend on their shared language of English, but rather educated herself on the language and customs of her husband's heritage and strived to make it all part of her children's upbringing. By identifying with her white parent, in this case a progressive white parent of the same gender, she internalized a worldview that is critical of racism and other forms of injustice.

Monica's experience raises an important point about intimacy with whites and its potential to either "whiten" or "brown" (make racially progressive) someone in the racial middle. By predicting that intermarriage with whites "whitens," the thesis assumes that the white person holds a color-blind outlook and seeks to minimize attention to race. In the case of racial progressives, however, the whites in their intimate circles can often be whites who grapple with race in decidedly non-color-blind ways, as in the case of Monica's mother. Thus, looking to clarify further research on "whitening," it might be interesting for future researchers to ask respondents about *which* whites they feel most comfortable—those who de-emphasize race or those who actively and regularly engage outside their racial comfort zones in meaningful ways.

In contrast, other progressive respondents seem to have been affected by their white parents in the opposite way. That is, rather than identifying with a racially progressive white parent, they defiantly and deliberately chose a worldview that was clearly opposed to that of their parents. This is particularly the case with progressive respondents who were adopted by two white parents. One Korean respondent who was adopted and raised by white parents realized early on that she could not expect her parents to understand the prejudicial and discriminatory experiences she encountered as an Asian American. Because shortly before this interview I had interviewed another Korean respondent whose adoptive parents tried to expose their children to Korean culture in their home and took trips to Korea, I asked the present respondent, named Sarah, if her parents had tried to do the same kinds of things. She found this question laughable and responded:

No, in fact, I think, yeah, they don't get it. . . . I mean whenever I explain it . . . [her objection to the word] "oriental," instead of going "oh, OK," they're like, "Whatever." [Interviewer: So they approached it in a really color-blind way, the cultural difference in the adoption process, OK. Did you, so, your position now is kind of like to try and educate them about it, or how do you deal with that?] No, I mean, I tried since I was like three years old, it's kind of long past. I think the thing for me now is to work with my [infant] son. . . . My husband, because he is Caucasian, is very white male, and he hasn't got much [awareness]. . . . I've had to explain to him that, you know, there's a possibility that our son might encounter something, and he's gotta know how to react to it. My niece and nephew are mixed, they're Amer-asian [*sic*] and my niece has dealt with it some at her school, and I don't think my brother knows how to deal with it.

Clearly, Sarah has given up on the possibility that her parents could ever understand the impact of racism on her (and her other Korean American adopted brother's) life. Since as young as three years old, she figured out that her white parents did not have the tools to help her to navigate through the racism she faced in her life, nor were they interested in believing or validating her own experiences. This is poignantly described in her narrative in just a few short words: "instead of going 'oh, OK,' they're like, 'whatever.'" Not only were they unwilling to be proactive in educating their children about their country of origin and American racial realities, but when they had the opportunity to be educated by their own children about it, they still were unwilling to accept the information. As an adult, she has made the choice to not waste her energy on that education process for her parents, but instead to focus on her newborn son. Refusing to let history repeat itself, she uses the opportunity to turn around the same ignorance she found in her parents in her own white husband, letting her husband know adamantly that her son "might" face racism and "he's gotta know how to react to it." Having observed her niece's experience, she knows that by an early age, children will face some racism when they do not fit into the accepted white mold.

Notably, Sarah is somewhat ambivalent about an education on Korean culture itself. She expresses a willingness to explore that with her own son if he should indicate an interest: "I think that if it's something he wants to explore, then I have to do it with him. I don't know how well I would though, considering I don't know a whole lot about Korean culture. But I think there are books out there that I could buy him, and we can read together." Here we can see the difference between "Korean" as a cultural identity or ethnicity and "Asian American" as a racial experience in the United States. While a Korean cultural identity is not particularly salient for Sarah (but she would be willing to "explore" it with her son, if interested), giving her son the tools to cope with the racism that Asian Americans face in the society is treated in a totally different voice. In the first quote from Sarah, her word choice and tone suggest that her son *must* know about coping strategies for racism, whereas an education about a culture that seems foreign to all of them is less essential, in her view. Being cognizant that she and her own brother suffered because their own parents were not able to prepare them for the reality of the racism that they would face, she is determined not to let that cycle continue with her own child.

Similarly, another adopted respondent, Caitlin, recalls that by early childhood it was clear that her own white parents had a much different outlook on race than her own. Caitlin, who grew up in Puerto Rico and did not move to the mainland until adulthood, describes an early vivid memory:

> My parents made a comment one time to say that these neighbors of ours were black, sort of like surprised that we didn't get it. [laughs] You know, and we all looked at them like, "What are you talking about?" And my mother says, "Well, they're black!" And I'm like, "There's no color in Puerto Rico!" I mean, she never made a statement about any other people of any other, you know, that we had [met]. So we didn't understand why all the sudden *these people* were black! Because, why weren't *these* people black, you know what I'm saying? So they were the African Americans and she *definitely*—we didn't understand why she was—first of all, why we had to be told that. Second of all, we didn't comprehend it. [Interviewer: Yeah, do you remember how old you were?] I was probably seven. And I remember that because I think she was surprised that we didn't know what they were, and she was like "honey, well they're black" and I'm like, "No they're not!" You know! I mean, how can you say that in Puerto Rico? Everybody's all a range of colors!

Having known nothing but a Puerto Rican American frame of reference on "race," Caitlin realized early in her life that her white parents, who had grown up in the mainland United States, had quite a different view on race than her own. Caitlin was operating from a Latin American perspective on race, where categories are more fluid, and there is often not a clear dividing line between categories of "white" and "black" but rather many in-between shades. It was a vivid memory for Caitlin that her parents made a clear distinction of difference based on skin color, one that she clearly rejected as untrue. Further, she also took note of the fact that her parents treated these racial distinctions as natural, by expressing shock that their children were not somehow automatically aware of them. In recognizing that her parents viewed "race" as such a natural and clear system of differences, she knew that her own outlook was quite different.

Her parents had moved to Puerto Rico for economic reasons during Operation Bootstrap—they felt their business had growth potential on the island. Thus, they had no family ties and little cultural knowledge of Puerto Rico upon arrival. Caitlin feels that there was therefore some ambivalence on the part of her mother about Puerto Rico in general that translated into some perhaps unintentional but nonetheless influential cultural racism passed down to her children. Caitlin's progressive ideology thus was shaped by having to navigate around her own mother's negative impressions of the only culture she had known. Her mother's perspective also influenced her preferences for who was the most ideal mate for her daughter. She remembers that her mother was "ecstatic" when she dated "an American boy with blue eyes and blond hair" but was less enthusiastic about her dating Puerto Rican Americans. Her mother not only had skin-color preferences, but relied on stereotypes about cultural gender roles to justify her rejection of Latino men. She relied on a progressive critique of these stereotypes, however, by pointing out that there is just as much sexism prevalent in North American men; they are just not as overt in their expressive styles so it may be harder to detect at first:

> Well, I used to tell my mom, I used to say, "Mom, in five minutes you know what you're going to live with. Here it takes you six months!" [laughs] You know, I'm like, "We had this conversation already." I said, "It takes me six months to figure out if he's controlling whereas with a Latino you know in five minutes, that you can either live with this or you don't! You make your choices, you know. It takes you six months—six months of wasted [time/energy]." . . . So to me that's the difference. Everything's much more controlled, emotions are more underneath.

Clearly, Caitlin had to constantly work against the racist ideas of her own parents, and especially her mother, about "her own" culture, and thus developed a progressive critique of her mother's positions that came out of her own experiences.

She observes that her "North American parents," her relatively advantaged socioeconomic status, and her lighter-skin tone have combined to result in a relatively privileged experience for her, despite being a "person of color." Indeed, like the Mexican-Russian respondent quoted earlier, because people often assume Caitlin is white, she is exposed to some assumptions and discourses that perhaps her darker-skinned Latino counterparts do not so overtly hear. She recalls one such incident from her recent past:

> Somebody made a comment in my home about hurricane Katrina and how they didn't think it was racial, the pieces of not going to aid the people immediately. And I was like, "Oh you did not say this at my kitchen table!" [laughter] So you know, I had to say, "As a person of color, I am *totally* offended by this because I don't agree," and she, I don't think she was surprised or offended by it because, by me saying "I'm offended" as much as she was—that I was a person of color and that I was willing to say that. And I said, "And I'm only saying I'm a person of color because I have to say it in this country, because in my country I am not a person of color." OK, so, I can't tell you how many times, I have had people argue with me that say I'm not a person of color. . . . I think growing up, having an American name made it hard for me to be accepted in my culture. I was called the *gringa*, and I wasn't *gringa*. I wasn't born in the United States, I never grew up in the United States, never lived in the United States. I just happened to be born and someone adopted me who happened to have an English name. And I have that name. . . . But having had that experience makes me *just* a little bit more like, "Wait a minute, don't make an assumption because you don't know." So I'm much more aware of that since it happens to me constantly.

Caitlin feels that she is "more aware" of racist assumptions people make because of her borderline appearance. It is not necessarily the case, however, that respondents who are able to "pass" as white are any more progressive than those who are not. Indeed, Latinos who chose the "white" racial category in this study were actually less likely to be progressive than those who did not. For Puerto Rican Americans in particular, the factor that seems to separate progressives from nonprogressives is not skin tone as much as amount of time spent in Puerto Rico. Caitlin's other counterparts in the sample who spent part or all of their growing years in Puerto Rico shared the "continuum" view of race with their parents, who were also born and raised in Puerto Rico, so they will be discussed in subsequent sections. The key formative aspect of *this* respondent's progressive outlook is clearly the experience of the conflict between her white parents' and her own racial views. She has had to assert her Latin-ness despite her lighter appearance, English surname, and North American parents, in order to contrast herself with her parents' (and the dominant) racial ideology.

Another respondent who also grew up outside the United States has gained some insights into the dominant racial ideology of whites, but not actually through his own family experiences. This Taiwanese-Chinese respondent named Tim is the only progressive Chinese American in this sample. He supports affirmative action because "the negative side of no affirmative action would be greater." In other words, he feels people would racially discriminate against minorities if left to their own devices and not legally expected to not discriminate. He speaks from personal experience, having attained a senior position in his career, but not without encountering racial stereotypes and double standards along the way. At one point he discusses, although not in first person, the stereotypical assumptions that Asian Americans are not assertive enough to be good leaders, and how this solidifies a glass ceiling in the workplace:

> Generally [for] East Asians, the culture requires people to be humble or more inward, in a way, so generally people feel that Asians are quiet and not outspoken and they probably work hard, but not as a leader type because . . . in East Asia, when in business, you cannot be aggressive. . . . And in this country, somewhere you have to be aggressive or assertive, and if you are not, then you are not a leader. . . . So in a way that does affect [one's] career, and it's part of the stereotype, but it's hard to say this is a stereotype because it's part of the culture. But for people who doesn't understand . . . then they see this person in the office, they might not know enough about this, so the first impression, this person they find these kind of stereotypes.

Tim feels that Asian Americans' careers are sometimes unfairly limited because many Americans observe in them the culturally learned behavior of humility and thus assume they are incapable of being good leaders.

Tim makes clear, however, that East Asians are not somehow naturally less aggressive, but rather are simply exhibiting the respectful behavior that "the culture requires."

In the workplace, Tim has observed not only these major assumptions that limit career advancement, but the supposedly more subtle everyday conversational assumptions that he knows his white counterparts do not have to face. He shares one such example that he experienced when working on a project out of state:

> This is for a project at the University of [name] and the engineer said, "Oh yeah, my daughter has a friend who is Chinese." And so when he says that, it means like, oh I know somebody who is Chinese. Something I don't think he would say, my daughter has a good friend who is Chinese, if [it were] somebody here, [who] would [not] have even mentioned, it . . . but I guess over there, there are not many Chinese.

Evidently, Tim feels singled out and stigmatized, as his coworker draws attention to his race in an awkward manner. Unlike the respondents discussed in chapter 5, who tend to minimize discrimination or claim there was only one such incident, Tim has a multitude of examples to offer. In another example of conversational racism, he recalls:

> One particular person that I used to know, so he [would] always make certain type of jokes, not necessarily to all, but certain ethnic groups. . . . I remember when he heard my daughter, I think she was playing hockey, and he was like, "Oh that's great because she'll be the only Asian playing hockey, ice hockey," and oh he'd say, "That's good she's the only one so the college will recruit her." Something like that. . . . [The] reality is [this is] not true because there is an Olympian who is Chinese. So occasionally . . . a lot of times they use this as joke.

Clearly, Tim does not believe that these "jokes" are funny; rather, they unfairly and unnecessarily single him and his family out because of their race or ethnicity. He points out that people "use" their racist assumptions by attempting to pass them off as jokes. He also critiques the generalization that Asian Americans are not athletic, or at least do not play hockey, pointing to at least one example to the contrary. Like most progressives, he deconstructs naturalist generalizations about members of his racial/

ethnic group, and perhaps because of his ample experiences with discrimination, does not blame blacks for racial inequalities. Indeed, when asked which groups face the most discrimination today, he names "Hispanics" and "African Americans." Like other progressives in the sample, he places the discrimination he faces into context with members of other groups in society that may be darker skinned and/or have it worse than his own, without necessarily minimizing his own.

Likewise, Tim is approving of intermarriage. Moreover, even though he reports that he and his wife would answer the U.S. census race/ethnicity questions the same (Asian Pacific Islander as race and Chinese/Taiwanese as ethnicity), from the perspective of their native countries, he considers himself to be part of a mixed marriage. He states: "my wife and I have different ethnic background[s] because her parents were born in China and my parents were not." His own parents were born in Taiwan, which he describes as a source of political tension between him and his wife. Like Charlene (the Thai-Filipino American respondent), whose ethnically different parents would be both considered Asian American by U.S. racial categories, Tim and his wife would also be categorized as a racially homogenous marriage by U.S. standards. Yet both of these respondents in our progressive sample from ethnically "mixed" marriages may come to the U.S. racial status quo with a fully honed critical eye due to their own "border-crossing" backgrounds.

Another aspect of Tim's parental history that may be relevant to his progressive ideology is that he describes his parents' socioeconomic background as highly elite (in his native country). Indeed, he characterizes both his mother's and his father's families as "very rich," and his grandfather was a "state senator appointed by an emperor." Thus, when he observes the extra hassles he goes through in his own everyday life just to obtain a senior-level position in his own company, and he compares it to the experiences of his parents, for whom being "Asian" and "less aggressive" was not an issue in obtaining their high status, he may feel some sense of inequity or relative deprivation. Most quantitative studies of Asians' "becoming white" process would observe that Tim's income, education, and occupational status is above average, and in this he is more like whites than like blacks. Yet a qualitative look at his situation reveals that he faces many of the same glass-ceiling experiences of other minority groups, and that he is critical of the racism that does not regard him with the same degree of humanity of his similarly situated white counterparts.

Like the other progressive respondents analyzed in this section, he has been able to observe the U.S. racial social structure from other, more privileged vantage points and has contrasted it with his own experiences, resulting in a critical perspective on the racial status quo.

Geographic Moves as Catalysts of Progressive Conversions

While the above respondents do not seem to pinpoint a set time when they "became" progressive, as if they had always been so, others identify particular moments in their lives when they stepped out of one environment and into another, enabling them to adopt a newer progressive lens. Like the above respondents who had ethnically mixed and often part-white intimate environments, the respondents who move also get to see the racial social structure from a new vantage point, but one that comes a bit later in their lives, and sometimes puts them more directly at odds with other family members.

France Winddance Twine's article "Brown-skinned White Girls" discusses young women of African descent who grew up in predominantly white suburban neighborhoods with white parents; these women did not begin to see themselves as people of color until leaving for a more diverse college environment, at which time they developed more racially progressive points of view.[11] Although Twine's article suggests that people of color must move out of white suburbia and into more diverse environments to experience such an awakening, the present study demonstrates that progressive awakenings can actually occur when moves happen in either direction. That is, not only did the respondents in this sample have awakenings when they moved from predominantly white to more diverse environments, but also when they moved from racially diverse to more homogenous/white environments. Either way, the respondents adjusted by embracing new racial frames of reference to make sense of their new environs.

Two second-generation progressive respondents—one Latino (Mexican) and one Asian American (Filipino)—were not taught their parents' native language in their homes and experienced a sort of ethnic revival when arriving at college and finding student ethnic organizations. These narratives are not unlike those from Twine's study. Neva, a young Mexican American woman, becomes emotional and cries at several points in her interview when contemplating her own family's level of shame around being Mexican; she reflects here on how that internalized racism affected the amount of cultural information they chose to transmit to her:

> I think I've always—at least from my dad's side, it was always, "Yeah, *viva la raza*" [a motto of Chicano pride], but like I said, I haven't had much contact with him, so I didn't get that too much. But my mom's side, I still see some of the elements she was taught when she was growing up, like it being shameful to be Mexican. She never said it was shameful, but it's one of the things you can tell that she's [begins crying] ashamed. Like, she doesn't think there's anything good about the culture, herself, so consequently, she didn't really teach me about the culture. Most of the stuff I learned about the culture was from school.

Neva grew up in California in a neighborhood that was predominantly Mexican American until she was nine years old, and then moved to a predominantly Asian American neighborhood for the rest of her childhood. Coming to college, she was immersed in the "whitest" environment she had ever experienced, and she connects this shift with her shift in racial consciousness. In answer to an interview question about how important being Mexican American is to her, she responds:

> It's definitely become more important to me since I've come to college. In the past, it wasn't important to me at all. For others, especially, where I'm from, it's very important. It's like the most important thing for them. Like where I used to grow up, and the neighborhoods around where I live now, they're proud to be Mexican. They put up the Mexican flag, they're into "*la raza*" and it's an important to their identity. For me, more so in the present . . . [Interviewer: What do you think triggered this change the most? Like, why now?] Being in this school! Yeah, the sea of blondes. And the people here always see my last name and ask me if I know Spanish, and I really hate being called upon for like, some people are curious because they don't know a lot, but in class there's like "the girl with the Hispanic point of view, and let's hear what she has to say," and I'm like OK, and I don't really know anything about the Hispanic point of view, so I'm trying to learn.

Neva reports regularly encountering a form of racism similar to the experiences of African Americans at predominantly white colleges and universities.[12] They are called on to be the spokespersons for their racial group on days when race enters the discussion, and then routinely ignored on most other topics. Having faced this kind of stigmatization in a predominantly white environment has actually inspired her to identify more with the category "Mexican" than she had in the past when inhabiting more racially diverse environments.

Consistent with a progressive ideology, and with the browning thesis, Neva also perceives more similarities between herself and African Americans than she does with whites. She feels that what unites them is their common experiences with oppression, even if they are not often able to come together across their differences to recognize it:

> Well, I know at least where I'm from, there's a lot more similarity between blacks and Hispanics, but in those two groups in my city at least have been so antagonistic to each other for so long, and I'm like, "You guys have very many things in common," sometimes I have this conspiracy theory that like they were purposely turned against each other to get rid of both of them because they don't want either of them. Yeah, I'd say [the groups most similar to each other are] black and Hispanic. Farthest away? That's hard. I guess I'd have to say white. I personally feel an affinity with my Asian friends, but I know a lot of Mexican Americans that don't at all. [Interviewer: What aspects of black culture make it similar, and what aspects of white culture or Asian culture make it so difficult?] I don't know if it's that the culture is similar as much as we're similarly treated. Yeah, similar experiences. Especially like black and Hispanic culture in, the way that the white culture reacts to perceived black and Hispanic culture. I feel a very strong message from that.

While some respondents would focus more on cultural differences between groups, it is evident that progressives are more likely to stress racial identities over cultural ones, by emphasizing the common treatment different groups receive from the white majority. Recall that in chapter 3 respondents who were not racially progressive were much more likely to naturalize perceived cultural differences between themselves and members of other groups than the progressive respondents analyzed here. Thus, while Neva perceives shared experiences with both blacks and Asian Americans, she acknowledges that others may be too preoccupied with the cultural differences to be able to notice the racial similarities between them.

Unlike the above respondent, Jon, a Filipino American student respondent, grew up in a predominantly white neighborhood, so his college environment was no less diverse than his previous milieu. Yet he still had the similar experience of not really identifying much with a Filipino identity until college: "I lost my language at the age of five. . . . I feel a little cheated in that." He characterizes it as a total accident that he would eventually develop a "passion" for learning more about his culture when he arrived at college: "My dumb luck, my person helping me move in, my greeter was actually the president of the Filipino organization." Like other progressives, Jon sees many connections among himself, African Americans, and other nonwhite groups, even as he is aware of the ways that racism works to keep them from recognizing those similar experiences. When asked to consider the stereotypes Americans have about Filipino Americans and/or Asian Americans, he reflects:

I think white people think that Asians are the model minority. You know if Asians can do it, then how come the blacks and Latinos can't do it too? So that's the stereotype for Asians, they have very subservient, smart, skilled, passive, that's the stereotype I've gathered that white people have about Asians, at least from the media . . . so I think blacks and Latinos would kind of believe that Asians are passive and such. But here's the caveat: I know that blacks and Asian Americans have worked together during the civil rights movement, so there is an understanding between those two sides as to what we really are, not just these stereotypes. And for Latinos—Filipinos and Mexicans—we've shared a lot of the same problems in the early nineteen hundreds and eighteen hundreds when it came down to things like antimiscegenation laws or any type of laws against minorities because Americans, or whites would just see Filipinos and Mexicans as like the same. You know, they're brown.

Again, we see how progressives prefer to stress the ways that the white majority has applied racism similarly to the different groups despite their differences.

The college environment was also an influence on another Mexican American respondent's racial ideology, even though unlike the above two respondents, he did speak Spanish and felt more connected to Mexican culture at home. At home, however, his parents did not speak critically of white racism, despite their work in manual labor–type jobs, and only had positive things to say about white supervisors. Thus, Roberto was shocked to encounter a more critical ideology when entering college in California that challenged his previous worldview: "I was definitely a Mexican American up until high school. And then I entered college and my world was turned upside down, and I learned about the Chicano movement . . . and I identified myself as a Chicano." Analogous to the distinction between Latino and Hispanic, the term Chicano is typically used to indicate an ideological position that is more critical of white racism than either Mexicano or Mexican American.[13] College ethnic studies were highly influential in the transformation for this respondent, who is one of the respondents discussed in chapter 5 who changed his name (from Roberto to Bobby) to make life easier. He later encountered a college professor who encouraged him to "decolonize" himself by changing his name back to Roberto. In discussing how college ethnic studies helped him to become more critical of anti-Latino stereotypes, he references the name change as a symbol of a sort of ignorance-as-bliss former life:

I know that I felt it a lot, the stereotypes they hurt me a lot when I was an undergrad. A huge emotional impact of how, when I was going through the Chicano studies program, I learned a lot of literature on what America thought about Mexican Americans—lazy, uneducated, here to take our jobs. Immigrant issues that Mexican Americans are here to take jobs of working-class Americans are always very emotionally laden, and so that does bother me a lot. In Arkansas there was actually a billboard on immigrants coming over and taking our jobs, and it was sponsored by this organization, it was very offensive, so those stereotypes are offensive and it's personal, and it hurts me to see that. And so sometimes I even feel ashamed, not that—not at the stereotype, but I feel ashamed of not wanting to be Mexican because I don't want to be a target of that. And so I tell myself that it would probably not hurt me as much if I distance myself from my culture, in that sense. And so yeah there have been times when I say, God, I can't stand this, constantly everywhere I go, I'm ethnicized [*sic*] and I hear the stereotypes, and I'm just going to become Bobby again to avoid all that. [laughter]

There is a substantive literature in racial identity development that identifies stages of racial identity that people of color (and also whites) experience that could potentially transform their worldview, as happened with several of the above respondents.[14] The immersion stage, as it is sometimes called, can often be experienced by college students who "immerse" themselves in readings, groups, and experiences having to do with their racial identity in order to develop some pride around a culturally devalued identity. Many such racial identity development models posit a later stage of incorporation or integration whereby the person emerges from immersion with a greater self-confidence and pride that no longer has to be reinforced by always surrounding oneself with co-ethnics. Perhaps due to his more advanced age (thirty-nine) relative to the above-quoted students, this respondent, although still named Roberto, is not as identified with Chicano as he once was, and now seems to be in the incorporation stage:

> Is it important to me to be Mexican American? Not as much as it used to be. I used to be a person that needed to have cultural artifacts of Mexico everywhere. Like in my office I would have the Aztec sun, and then I'd have a little pot, a traditional pot that they make beans in on the stove, a Mexican flag, T-shirts, very ethnicized, [*sic*] and I think I outgrew it, I just no longer feel that that's that important in my life. And so I think it's a way of trying to be comfortable with just being a person. . . . Now for example if you go to my office, I have nautical stuff. I have like boats, fishing, shells, lighthouses, so I let people know that I have other interests, not just ethnicity, and I really love that, ocean stuff. So I decided to surround myself with things that I love as opposed to things that define me. . . . Most of the time I think it's important to others, others do see me as a minority, as a Latino. I don't think there's a time when it's ever deemphasized.

Roberto recounts many incidents of discrimination and prejudice he has faced, including work-related examples, reported in chapter 5. Thus, just because he has moved away from a more-politicized Chicano identity personally (and also identifies as politically moderate, much to the chagrin of his more radical Puerto Rican American buddies from college) does not mean he is any less aware of the impact of racism on his everyday life, as are progressives in the racial middle. While Roberto has a white spouse, his progressive conversion seems to have predated that relationship, and he definitely ties his ideological position to his college experiences.

Other respondents attribute their progressive outlooks to non-college-related geographic moves where the racial/ethnic makeup of the area changed significantly from what they had previously experienced. One Korean American adopted respondent named Jessica describes such a transition, which resulted from her move to Texas from Maryland when she was eleven. There were a lot more Asian American students in her school in Maryland than there were in Texas. Even though she did not hang out with them because they spoke their native languages and she spoke only English, she thinks that the simple fact of having more Asian Americans around meant that her peers were less likely to rely on simplistic stereotypes about Asian Americans:

> When I moved to Texas, I was the only Asian in like a lot of my classes, and there wasn't a big Asian population in the part of [city] that I grew up in. So, that's when I started actually realizing that they've seen my differences 'cause sometimes I would look in the mirror in Maryland and not even notice that, like, I was Asian. [laughs] So in Texas I realized who I was and then I knew that coming to college I wanted to learn more about my heritage and diversity issues, 'cause you couldn't really talk about that in high school. [Interviewer: So it was almost the fact that there being fewer Asians around and therefore perhaps encountering more, just, maybe misinformation, stereotypes there?] Uh-huh, and people would like, be like, "You look exactly like this one," and get us confused, and that's how they would classify [me], as "the Asian girl" or "the Chinese girl." Also, I was in a relationship with [a boy] he was Filipino and Mexican, and he was really strong about being Asian . . . being with him also showed . . . how proud I was to be Asian, and he brought that out in me.

Interestingly, it was not moving to an area with more Asian Americans but into an area with fewer Asian Americans that activated Jessica's progressive outlook on race and racism. Although Jessica was never particularly connected to Korean culture, and had mainly white friends in Maryland, just the fact that there were more Asian Americans around meant that people were less likely to approach her with racist comments and stereotypes. Once she moved to an area where more Asian American stereotypes abounded, she became the brunt of dehumanizing language that she had not before experienced. Facing such race-based treatment and being able to articulate progressive (and prideful) arguments to challenge it was for her more salient than necessarily having any specific education about Korean culture.

Jessica repeatedly brings up counterexamples to challenge naturalist assumptions about Asians—for instance, the expectation that she would be naturally gifted academically (she is not and has to work hard for As and Bs) and that all Asians are short (bringing up professional basketball player Yao Ming, who is "like seven foot"). Further, like other progressives, she sees connections between herself and other nonwhite groups: "I see it as all together, because definitely you don't see many Latinos here, so I think here I connect more to African Americans and I'm like dating an African American here. It's weird in the summer I connected more with Hispanics and Mexicans and actually I dated a Mexican there, so I never really realized that, but I think it's the geographic [difference]." Through her dating partners, Jessica has explored the common connections among her own and other people of color's shared experiences with racism. At the same time, she does not think her own situation in the racial middle can be reduced to "black and white." She admits that being Asian American she feels "more accepted among the races," and during campus discussions of race relations, she tries to interject a racial middle perspective because she is often frustrated by the tendency of such conversations to only deal with "black and white."

Another respondent, Wanda, experienced an early-childhood move from Puerto Rico to New York City that shifted her racial consciousness. This move occurred in 1949, when she was almost ten years old. Due to the pervasive racial segregation in New York City at that time, she soon found herself in Harlem public schools and allied with black Americans:

I've always identified quite a bit with the black community because when I came to the States, I was in a Spanish environment with Spanish kids, but there was a period that we lived in, and I went to a school in Harlem. And I didn't speak English, and my biggest helpers, or the people who helped me the most to learn at that time, were black kids. Because there were just three of us in the school who were Spanish speaking, all the others were black kids. And there was some white, but mostly everyone were black kids. So they taught me how to jump double Dutch, they taught me how to play dodgeball, and one of them took me under her wings and kind of was my protector when they'd look at me and say, "How come . . ." and I could tell that they were like, "You look just like us, why don't you speak English," and I would then, smile and say, "No speak English, no speak English." [in accent] And then she would say something them, because she was in my class, the teacher had asked [about something], and so she would talk with them, I noticed, and then after that everything was OK. And then they taught me how to go, on lunch time we'd sneak out and go across the street to the grocery store and buy hot dill pickles, well you know, they were hot, that was attractive to me, because I was used to eating hot various foods. And I always remember that as being a very happy, welcoming kind of feeling. And so, I identify with the plight of racism in this country.

Due to her darker-skinned phenotype, and the 1950s New York City environment, a racial/cultural bond with the city's black community seemed like the best fit. Clearly, this is a different experience from that of Caitlin, light-skinned Puerto Rican American respondent, who rejected her white mother's white/black, binary racial mindset. Because Wanda was actually residing in the mainland United States, as a child, it was the path of least resistance for her to fall into the country's black/white divide, on the side that she more closely resembled, at least phenotypically.

As an adult, however, Wanda has more vociferously resented people's insistence that she "choose one"—black or Puerto Rican American/"Spanish"—and maintains that she is most certainly both/and. In her career in higher education administration, she has encountered many situations where she has had to confront such dualistic thinking:

I went for an interview . . . and one of the questions that the [black] principal asked me, "What do you consider yourself? Spanish or black?" And that was the first time I was asked that. And then when I was working at the university, a Spanish professor who was very Spanish, or Puerto Rican-esque, walked in the room, in the meeting, and he says, "Well [respondent's name], we're having a discussion here, so, what are you? What do you consider yourself?" And it was some argument about how the Spanish-speaking countries were represented in the curriculum of the Latin American and Caribbean Studies Program. But the Caribbean, like Trinidad and other English-speaking islands, were not being represented in the curriculum, in the classes we would offer. And so he wanted to know how I was going to vote. . . . And it took me aback, because I did stop and think, and I said to him, I said, "Well you know, I've never had that kind of schizophrenic personality where I split myself to one or the other, you see this skin has always been this way. I've never known it to be any different, and I've always felt that I was black. And as far as Spanish, I was born talking, you know, and I learned to ask for food and everything else in Spanish. And I didn't really know English until after I was ten, probably more like thirteen, fourteen. So I can't separate the two, and I never have and I don't think I'm going to start at this stage in my life! [laughs] So when I see what is there then I'll have to make a judgment based on how I feel." But, it took me aback, it made me angry, and I had a whole lot—a mixture of emotions—because, "How *dare* you make me choose. How dare you. It's not for me to do that."

Wanda echoes the findings of Rodriguez, who writes that Latinos typically can vary in how they answer the "race" question, depending on the context of the question, who is asking the question, and why.[15] This position is exemplified by Wanda's statement: "so when I see what is there then I'll have to make a judgment based on how I feel." Although she is sometimes treated as African American, other times whites have separated her out as "better than" African Americans, and she has been privy to racist comments in much the same way that the border-crossing respondents of the previous section have been:

> When I first came and I was in this country, a lot of the times, Puerto Ricans would try to make sure that white people would know that they weren't black Americans. And I scorn that. . . . I'm not shunning being black, or being considered black American, that's OK. But I do have my pride in being Puerto Rican. And so—[Interviewer: But you're not going to do it to the extent of denigrating another group?] Another group, yeah. And that's what it becomes. . . . I worked in a place where the bookkeeper treated me nicely because she knew I was going to college and because I wasn't "one of them [African Americans]." And it *bothered* me, but, that's just one time that I guess I didn't attack it and I didn't confront it because I needed the job. I had to have a job. . . . I had lost some other jobs. I was working in an office, and office jobs had been hard for me to get. And I was getting good money and I could work over time, so I can't tell you how tough that was.

Although Wanda did not really have to "take sides" racially as a child in Puerto Rico, this became increasingly an expectation of her when she moved to the mainland. She has never felt comfortable, however, having to deny her connections to African Americans because of the prevailing racist mindsets in the United States. Having to do so in the above-mentioned job situation was clearly an uncomfortable experience for her. While her geographic move was the initial catalyst for her progressive worldview, her narrative also has elements of respondents' experiences from other sections. Having a foot in each world—Latino and black—has allowed her to develop a critical eye on racist ideology in general, while being a part of multiple communities means that she does not necessarily have sole allegiance to one. Such a "post-race" consciousness is most typical of the progressive respondents in the following section.

"Racial Chameleons": Transcending Racial Categories from the Middle

While some progressives develop their racial ideology through experiencing the vantage points of more than one racial category, and others do so in the context of a major identity-developing geographic move, a third group (the remainder) are less likely to see themselves of members of any particular racial/ethnic group at all. This seemingly race-less position, however, is not a color-blind one where the pervasiveness of racism is denied or an allegiance to the norm of whiteness is internalized. Quite the contrary, these progressives see themselves as part of a multiracial, even global/international community that opposes racism and the reification of whiteness as hegemonic. They usually discuss being uncomfortable with all white spaces, and they visualize their children (both real and imagined) as becoming part of such a multiracial community where no one part of their identity is stressed over any other. They are chameleons in that they feel like they can move in and out of various racial/ethnic groupings without necessarily becoming beholden to any one in particular. Such a vision is quite arguably only possible in the current (early twenty-first century) era, and indeed, of the seven respondents that most closely fit this category, only two are over the age of thirty. Thus, this pathway to progressivism in particular is one that members of the growing racial middle may increasingly experience.

There is also an ethnic pattern in this "chameleon" subgroup of progressives. Almost all of them are South Asian or Pacific Islander, except for one Puerto Rican American. Three out of five of the Indian Americans in the sample are progressive, and all in this subgroup. The one Bengali American respondent in the sample espouses this multiracial/global worldview as well. Interestingly, both Macanese American respondents fit into this category—one of them has two Asian parents, while the other has one white/Irish parent. It seems that all of these particular Asian respondents do not fit into the prototypical East Asian ethnicities (Chinese, Japanese, Korean) that formed the earliest history of Asians in the United

States and set the stage for others to come. Thus, they are already a bit on the outskirts in two ways—being nonwhite, they are not part of the racial majority in the United States, and being from the lesser-known Asian ethnicities, they are marginalized within the Asian Pacific Islander panethnic racial group. This dual-marginal status may make it feel easier to "rise above" the various categories by not feeling fully included by either.

Although Puerto Rican Americans are not similarly marginalized in their Latino panethnic racial category, we have already seen in previous sections how Puerto Rican American concepts of race in particular are much more fluid and continuous than those predominant on the mainland United States. What the three Puerto Rican Americans in the progressive subsample share in common is that they spent at least part of their growing years in Puerto Rico (two moved to the mainland as adults, and the other migrated at age ten but did not learn English fully until her mid-teens). In contrast, the two nonprogressive Puerto Rican Americans were born on the mainland and never experienced the more fluid racial outlook of the Latin American island. They are fully habituated to the racial dividing lines of the mainland United States. Although the other two progressive Puerto Rican Americans in the sample were more deeply affected by adopted white parents and a mid-childhood move to the United States, respectively, all three Puerto Rican American racial progressives brought with them this more globally affected conception of "race" that transcends the limiting U.S. boundaries.

The progressive Puerto Rican American I will discuss in this section is married to a non-Hispanic white spouse. Alfonso is a medical doctor, and thus quite conversant with the limits of "race" as a category of genetic meaning, and the fallacy of any clear dividing lines between "black" and "white." On the use of race as a category in medical research, he explains:

> Yes, there are some conditions that are more likely to show up in people that are mixed race or black race or white race, but there are more differences, say, between people who classify themselves as white, there are more genetic differences, than say between overall people that are black and people that are white. So, what happens is that the race tends to be used as a surrogate or as a proxy for socioeconomic conditions. So we talk about esophageal cancer being prevalent in black people. Well it's because some black people in certain neighborhoods may smoke a lot, drink a lot, and have poor diet based on their socioeconomic condition and their education, and will therefore be more susceptible to these

things not because of their race as such. So if you use these categories for medical research, it's all wrong, I think.

He draws on his experiences in Puerto Rico of the variety of pheno-types even within one family. From there, he arrives at the same multi-racial, chameleon concept of race that is most prominent in the younger generation:

> There's a famous Puerto Rican actor, Raul Julia, and he was quite light skinned, but his younger brother who was in our same school, he was black, completely black. And I think one of his parents was of mixed race, one was white, so you have some kids who are born darker than others. So, I think that many people, like my parents' generation, much more so than now, I think there's more acceptance now of whatever you are, and this concept of mixed race is something that is very attractive to many people, that they don't have to—I say it like that because it's the way I feel. I feel that because I'm Puerto Rican and because I'm American, I have a better preparation, or better, different sets of values and things that I've learned, so somebody that is a mixed race rather than stuck with the one drop of blood and I'm black, they can say well my mother is Cherokee, my great-great-great-grandfather was an African slave, I have somebody else who comes from France, and this idea, I think it's better. [laughs]

Alfonso believes that in truth, everyone is multiracial if one goes far enough back into the genealogy. He is involved with a Hispanic genea-logical society where he discovers this truth through his examination of various family records. He also draws on the optimistic version of the browning argument, when he makes the claim that people who can claim multiple backgrounds actually have "better preparation" for everyday life than people who are "stuck with" the idea that they must be only one "race." Although he admits that on the census he would check white for race and Puerto Rican American for ethnicity, he discusses the Spanish and African components of his heritage during the interview. Like other respondents in this section, when discussing the ethnic makeup of his ideal neighborhood, he prefers neither a predominantly Latino or Puerto Rican neighborhood, nor a neighborhood where "most people are white." Instead, he prefers an area that has a little bit of everything.

Also like other progressives throughout the sample, Alfonso puts his racial middle experience in perspective. As a light-skinned Puerto Rican

American, he understands that even though he shares some "African blood" with black Americans, his experience of the U.S. social structure has not been akin to theirs:

> I've learned in the studies of my family that on my father's side my great-great-great-grandmother was a slave in Puerto Rico, something that my parents didn't know, and that maybe my grandmother knew, but she wasn't telling. I remember looking in the census, two of her brothers were marked as mulatto, and then she was marked as white. [pause] But you know we went back in some of the documents that her grandmother was a free black, and her great-grandmother was a slave. I tell that to my mother and she doesn't believe it. [laughter] I think it's very different. I don't think I can claim to—I don't think it would be fair for me to say, "Oh, I am black like you, my brother," because I haven't suffered discrimination like they have suffered. [Interviewer: Right. So the distant genealogy is less important than the everyday lived experience.] I think so. Sure. No, because in some ways, if you want to use a term that's used commonly, my grandmother, my father, pass as white, whereas if we go by these definitions of one drop, we really aren't [white]. So we really haven't suffered the same way as other people have.

Drawing on one's mixed heritage is a way that several other respondents in this section justified their perspectives that they were not beholden to any one racial group. David was the other over-thirty respondent in this category; he comes from an Indian father and a "Polish Jew" mother yet does not refer to himself as either Indian or Jewish much during the interview. Instead, he feels most included in international or multiracial communities. Although he was born in New York, he had lived in both Israel and India by the time he was two, and from there on out rotated every few years living in India, Japan, and the United States, until they settled fairly permanently in California when he was thirteen. As a result, he seems to feel most affinity to people with similarly eclectic backgrounds rather than to Indian or Jewish Americans per se. Indeed, David prefers to describe himself as multicultural rather than biracial, seeing biracial as too limiting and not encapsulating the full variety of his habitus:

> One of my good friends . . . [the reason] we kind of have very similar backgrounds is his mom was a Polish Jew. And unlike my mom, who

ended up in the United States, his mom ended up in Mexico. And so, he's half Mexican, half Polish Jew. And he speaks Hebrew. And his best friend growing up was Japanese. And he went to a private Japanese school for eight years and language school in Mexico. And so he's fluent in Japanese and doesn't look at all Japanese. And I speak Chinese and there's no reason for me to except for my academic interest. So we both have these kind of weird things where we speak an Asian language that has no relationship to our ethnicity. We both don't look like one of our two identities—he doesn't look Jewish, but he actually lived in Israel, studied Hebrew in Israel, probably is much more seasoned part of his identity. And so . . . here are these two Jewish guys sitting at a table but neither of them–like anyone wouldn't perceive them as Jewish.

David describes this type of background that he shares with his friend as "being foreign in multiple locations," and this vantage point has "shaped" his racial ideology. He also discusses another friend who is "half Japanese, half white" but "looks Native American" and, like himself, had lived abroad for some time. His friend did not feel welcomed by the Japanese student association, so he joined (and eventually became president of) the Filipino student association, which he gravitated toward because he had several Filipino friends. This constant traversing of boundaries is the kind of existence to which he can relate most, dubbing it a "foreign-slash-Asian background." Likening this status to that of a "chameleon," he explains how he inhabits a type of catchall perceived ethnicity wherever he goes:

I . . . kind of have a chameleon look for a lot of range. A lot of people thought that I was Arab, Middle Eastern, and so forth. . . . So, I have a lot of Persians come up to me and say, "Oh . . .," and you know start speaking to me and asking me where restaurants are, and stuff like that. When I've traveled in Guatemala they consider me to be whatever, they considered me Hispanic but not of whatever country they're in because I didn't speak Spanish well, so I must be from some other Spanish-speaking country. And in Italy, . . . I was in Bologna for a year and I spoke Italian well enough to kind of get along and people would consider me to be from the South because I always looked so stupid. [laughs] So, I always kind of had this thing where people wouldn't automatically assume that I'm American in the countries that I've lived, they would just assume I'm from some other place.

David attributes the combination of his ambiguous ethnic appearance and his extensive travels abroad to this outlook that places him outside the bounds of any one ethnic or racial group. Interestingly, he has experienced all three categories of progressive influence reviewed in this chapter: a mixed family of origin and a current white partner; several influential geographic moves; and certainly the sense of being a racial chameleon. Although other respondents have traveled abroad quite a bit and have mixed parents, most other well-traveled respondents did most of their traveling as adults and have not acquired multiple languages unrelated to their ethnicities the way this respondent has. Because many of his formative years were spent having to "blend in" to many diverse settings, these experiences seem to have solidified his progressive worldview.

There are two other (younger) progressives with at least one Indian parent—one has an Indian father and a white mother, and the other's mother and father are both Indian. These two respondents both share a sense of belonging to a larger grouping of people of color rather than Indians per se. For example, Raj, a twenty-year-old biracial Indian-white respondent, like other progressives, says his ideal neighborhood would not be all Indian or all white: "I don't like places that are all one thing, you know what I'm saying? You know, mixture's good." Raj admires what he views as the mixing of Latino and black culture through music and the arts, and he echoes the optimist browning perspective already seen in this section that posits a multicultural society as a "stronger society":

> I think affirmative action is pretty important, actually. I think coming from, people forget that the civil rights movement only happened like thirty, forty years ago when America was strictly segregated, and thirty, forty years ago is not a lot of time. I mean, like even I hear that a lot of African Americans saying "oh, we don't like affirmative action," but like affirmative action isn't just there to help you as a minority. It's overall there, it's a policy implemented to help overall society, you know what I'm saying? It's not there, like that's what a lot of people don't understand about affirmative action, it's not there just to help minorities and hurt white people. It's there to build the strongest society by having people of different ethnic groups in these positions.

Raj's supportive outlook on affirmative action is clearly not based on whether he can benefit from it (unlike some nonprogressive respondents discussed in chapter 3), but rather on its fit with his own vision of

a "stronger" multicultural society that will benefit everyone, "not . . . just
. . . minorities."

Already on the outskirts of the "Asian" community because he has one
white parent, Raj (along with Crystal, another twenty-year-old progressive
who is Macanese-Irish) feels more comfortable in a more diverse multicultural environment. In Asian groups sometimes they may feel like they
are "not Asian enough," as discussed in chapter 2. Recall that even some
respondents whose parents are both Asian, however, could sometimes feel
as if they do not fit in with the more traditional aspects of Asian communities. Such is the case with two other respondents—one Indian American (though she prefers "South Asian") and one Bengali American—both
are of the "1.5." generation because they are foreign born but moved to the
United States at a young age. Joy, the South Asian American respondent,
discusses why she feels a more global bond with people of color (due to
their collective experience with marginalization) than solely to Indians:

> A lot of my friends are all either from different cultures and stuff, but it
> definitely like strikes me that every time I'm like involved in something,
> like at a meeting or in class, that I'm like the only Indian person in the
> room, or the only person of color in the room. But generally for me it's
> not an issue for me of me being Indian and them not Indian, it's an issue
> of color and not, and if I'm there and there's black people around, His-
> panics around, I feel generally much more comfortable, but every time
> you're around people that are all white, it's not that I feel uncomfortable
> it's just the reality is that that situation happens pretty much all the time
> but it's definitely noticeable and it's an issue. And I think it's also prob-
> lematic because of the way that you feel like you're perceived.

As a filmmaker, Joy discusses in chapter 5 the various forms of work-
related discrimination and pigeonholing that she has faced. She is fully
conscious not only of the racial discrimination she faces, but of how nonwhite groups are pitted ideologically against each other to the benefit of
the majority:

> I think black people have suffered racism like no other, I think a lot of
> Latinos also suffer from great racial hardships, I think Asians do and
> South Asians do as well. But I also think that it becomes often times very
> complicated because all the minority groups generally use each other as
> scapegoats, so it's not like we're only suffering racism from white people,

we suffer racism from black people and black people suffer racism from Asian people, and I think that that becomes harder. Especially after the Patriot Act. Blacks were so happy to see that somebody else was taking the blunt of the racism. And yeah. That type of racism is kind of hard. And I think that that's definitely gotten worse over the years, about scapegoating between minority groups

Rather than blaming blacks or Latinos for the "racial hardships" they face, Joy's progressive outlook is that African Americans (and others) may scapegoat each other because they may be relieved to have the wrath of the majority distracted from themselves. This is quite different from suggesting that "blacks are just as racist as whites" and other such rhetorical strategies common to color-blind ideology.

What Joy also shares with Reena, another progressive South Asian (Bengali) American respondent, is a sense of disconnect from the more traditional aspects of their ethnic communities. Both Joy and Reena are under thirty and describe themselves as being more "Westernized" in terms of dress and expected roles of women than the older generations in their families and ethnic communities. Thus, both discuss feeling not as much allegiance to an "Indian" or a "Bengali" identity per se as they do to a larger segment of multicultural America. Still they harbor no illusions that they are incorporated fully into the fabric of "America"—as Reena comments: "the more I grow up, the more disillusioned I become with 'we're all equal,' and stuff like that." While Joy is a bit older (mid-twenties) and has experienced more of the work world, so has honed her analysis of such inequalities to a greater degree, but both Joy and Reena share this general sense of a connection to a larger community of people of color rather than either to whites or to "their own" ethnic group.

Conclusion

While there are certainly Latinos and Asian Americans who live racially segregated or isolated lives, this chapter describes a subsample of them who have clearly traversed many racial boundaries and as a result gained a critical perspective on the dominant, and perhaps overly restrictive (from their vantage point), racial ideology. Although racial intermarriage with whites is often taken to be an indicator of "whitening" from the perspective of traditional assimilation research, if we examine the racial ideology of progressives, we can see that many of them have gleaned a non-color-blind critique of whiteness as the norm through those very experiences with whiteness. Further, in contrast to those respondents discussed in chapter 3 who use color-blind ideology to distance themselves from African Americans, the respondents discussed in this chapter frequently see connections between their own experiences with racism and that of African Americans, even as they acknowledge qualitative differences. Thus, even as they acquire some of the structural correlates of whiteness (e.g., education, income, occupational status, residential patterns), they may nevertheless possess a racial ideology that is quite different from that of the majority of white Americans.

Perhaps most interesting is the last group of progressives, who seem less concerned with stressing the power of the white majority over people of color (in the traditional African American racial progressive vein), but more interested in stressing the global advantage of a multicultural society where no one racial or ethnic identity needs to be stressed at all. While a civil-rights-era progressivism stresses racial/ethnic pride as a healthy antidote to white racism, this particular group of racial middle progressives sees little need to accentuate their own racial/ethnic pride. Instead, they characterize the dominance of whiteness as almost passé. While they acknowledge the racist barriers they continue to face in everyday life, they are also convinced of a future where those barriers will soon not matter as much. They are determined to be part of creating a society where "difference" is an asset, and no one racial/ethnic identity is emphasized over any other. Perhaps such a utopia is only visible from the vantage point of the racial middle, where the racial "rules" of society are already somewhat less clear. Many of them are the voices that will be shaping the next generation, so it could behoove us to listen to their predictions.

7

The Potential of the Racial Middle

My interest in studying Latinos and Asian Americans together was sparked while I was working on another book on elite white men's racial views.[1] I became struck by the juxtaposition of these white men's glaring antiblack stereotypes with their overwhelmingly positive characterizations of both Latinos and Asian Americans—they saw them as good workers, highly motivated, having a strong sense of family, unwilling to "make excuses"—the opposite of everything negative that they attributed to African Americans. These initial experiences with elite white racial views created a predisposition in me toward accepting the whitening thesis. Indeed, from the perspective of elite white men, it seemed that Latinos and Asian Americans were much more "like them"; they could relate to them more than they could African Americans. I found compelling Yancey's thesis that there would be an impending black/nonblack split in the country as Latinos and Asian Americans grew to be a sizeable proportion of its population.[2] I even set out conceptualizing this project as a study of the processes by which Latinos and Asians were becoming white. Indeed, the fact that the sample selected for this project is more highly educated than U.S. Latinos and Asian Americans as a whole reflects this original intention of studying just the process of whitening.

As I moved forward on the project and began listening to the voices of these respondents themselves, however, it became evident that a more complex pattern had emerged from these data. While certain demographic indicators—educational levels, marriage patterns, residential choices—may point toward Latinos and Asian Americans appearing "more white than black," in-depth conversations with a sample of those in the racial middle who share these demographic characteristics reveal that their experiences hardly approximate those of white Americans. Roberto, a Mexican American college professor who has assimilated to whiteness by most demographic variables considered by such research, perhaps puts it best: "I can become white, but they will not allow me to." Eduardo Bonilla-

Silva and his colleagues have proposed one of two paths for members of the racial middle—either becoming "honorary whites" or becoming a part of the "collective black." While my data do lend some support to this bifurcated pattern, they also suggest additional experiences that cannot be reduced to either of these options. Indeed, even the progressives discussed in the previous chapter do not approximate honorary whiteness, but nor do they seem to connect to a notion of "collective blackness." These data suggest that in order to make room for the expanding racial middle, our society will need to look further than the limiting, phenotype-based concepts of white, brown, and black, to the more global perspective of the so-called Third World diaspora and their collective experiences in the globalizing economy of the postcolonial world.

Support for Whitening

Certainly the data do point to some ways in which Latinos and Asian Americans are "whitening," lending further empirical support to patterns found elsewhere. As table 2-1 illustrated, after their own group, white Americans are the group toward which most Latinos and Asians tend to report feeling the closest. Further, Latinos and Asians are twice as likely to report feeling most distant from blacks than they are to say they are the closest to blacks. These patterns, coupled with the antiblack racism exposed in chapter 3 (whether explicitly stated or implicitly "veiled" through discussions about other racial middle groups), convey a greater social distance between the racial middle and blacks than the relatively smaller social distance between the racial middle and whites. The racial middle would seem to have a comfort level with whites that, on average, they do not tend to have with blacks. This is certainly affected by residential segregation, occupational segregation, and the sheer greater numbers of Americans considered "white" than Americans considered "non-Hispanic black."

Further, those in the racial middle are ideologically affected by racism, as evidenced by their attraction preferences for mates, their minimizing of the extent of racial discrimination in society, and their reduced likelihood of racial progressivism when they identify racially as white. We saw in chapter 4 that while both Latinos and Asian Americans are more likely to be partnered with whites than any other group when out-marrying, Latinos in particular subscribe to the notion that white partners are the most ideal choice—a modern carryover from the colonialist ideology of colorism applied to enslaved communities. Again, while available numbers of whites play a role in these intermarriage patterns, these in-depth interviews reveal the racist ideology that influences the behaviors. For instance, those who are from families who claim they are opposed to outmarriage not on racial grounds but because they are worried about losing their language and cultural practices, are more willing to make exceptions for white partners (who speak Spanish, and so on) than they are for hypothetical and real African American mates.

When considering how they will interpret and make sense of the racial prejudice and discrimination that they face, we can see that the whitening thesis does play out for members of the racial middle. Just as whites tend to minimize the extent of racial discrimination that currently exists in society, so does the racial middle minimize it, but in this case it is self-effacing because they are minimizing what is happening to themselves (whereas when whites use minimization they are doubting the trustworthiness of African Americans). So even here the racial middle has lent its own "twist" to the dominant racial ideology. Moreover, those who are willing to take the more progressive stance that racism is everyday and frequent tend not to identify as much with whiteness. They are less likely to identify as white Hispanics and more likely to say they feel a connection to African Americans. Thus, we see more "white Hispanics" espousing the particular components of racial ideology discussed in chapter 3. It would be interesting for future researchers to examine to what extent members of the racial middle from less-educated backgrounds adopt the dominant racial ideology by downplaying the discrimination they face.

Support for Browning

Those who advocate a browning perspective do not expect the racial middle to identify to such an extent with the dominant racial ideology. Instead, they point to the coalition potential among the broader category of "people of color" that will include not only African Americans, but Latinos, Asians, Middle Easterners, and Native Americans as well, among others. They argue that racism is pervasive enough to have shaped a progressive consciousness even among the racial middle that leads them to share experiences already well documented among blacks.[3]

The Latinos and Asian Americans in this sample are hardly exempt from the racialized stereotypes and everyday racism that routinely target African Americans. For instance, the reports in chapter 2 from respondents who feel criticized for being "not Asian enough" or "not Latin enough" because they only speak English or do not consume certain Latino/Asian cultural products are similar to reports from African Americans who are sometimes labeled as "not black enough" if they listen to music other than R&B/hip-hop, are too focused on their studies, and so on. These nonwhite groups share the experience of being hemmed in by essentialist notions of race and ethnicity that characterize the majority group as well rounded in contrast to subordinated groups, who are falsely assumed to be more limited in their interests and capacities. When respondents discussed in chapter 5 face stereotypes that members of their groups are better suited to certain fields than others (e.g., Latinos as landscapers, Asian Americans as nail technicians) or worse yet, under suspicion of criminality (e.g., Latinos as illegals or drug dealers, South Asians as terrorists), the parallels with African Americans' experiences are evident. Whites are more or less excused from being pigeonholed into such limited racialized roles by society. Because the higher-than-average educational levels of this particular sample might insulate them to some extent from certain job-related forms of discrimination, it would be interesting for future research to examine these patterns in other segments of the racial middle.

Further, while there is much ambivalence in the racial middle on the subject of affirmative action policies, very few respondents (nine) actually outright oppose the policy. This pattern is similar to African Americans, who tend to be highly supportive of affirmative action as compared with whites.[4] This could be an area of potential political coalition, as it has been in the case of the movement to repeal affirmative action in higher education in California and elsewhere.[5] As they discuss affirmative action and other issues in chapter 3, members of the racial middle are also regularly engaging in articulate and insightful critique of the racial and ethnic stereotypes that are applied to them, not unlike African American respondents in other qualitative studies of racial discrimination.[6] While they are not always able to apply these same critical reasoning skills to stereotypes about other groups (as we will discuss more in the next section), they appear to be more willing than average whites to engage in such critiques. Given that socioeconomic status is an influential variable on support for affirmative action (although not as influential as "race"), it might be worthwhile for future researchers to explore whether support for affirmative action is as consistently high among the lesser-educated members of the racial middle.

Like their support of affirmative action, the racial middle also seems to be similar to African Americans in their overwhelming support for intermarriage, much more so than the average figures for whites.[7] While people of color in general may "prefer" (in the "it would be nice" fashion) mates for their family members and children who would preserve and continue the cultural patterns to which they have become accustomed, they rarely reveal the talk of disowning or disavowing their intermarried family members the way that whites do. In other words, the racial middle's intermarriage preferences seem to be more flexible and less rigid than those of their white counterparts, which makes them not unlike African Americans in that regard. Some of the racial middle seem to share with African Americans some fears about potential cultural disrespect and loss that could occur through out-marriage, particularly to whites. This is not enough to drive them to disapprove entirely intermarriage, however, but rather they adopt more of a wait-and-see attitude about the level of acceptance that the potential partner would have of their culture. No one in the racial middle expresses the "concern for the children" and the worry that multiracial children would be discriminated against, which is so commonly expressed by whites. It remains to be seen whether lesser-educated members of the racial middle would be more or less approving of intermarriage than those respondents analyzed for this study.

Finally, while not reflective of the majority of the sample, a sizeable number of persons (especially younger respondents) see points of connection between their own experiences and those of other people of color (both African Americans and other racial middle groups). Five respondents discussed feeling a specific bond with the experiences of African Americans, while six others see themselves as connected to a larger "people of color" category, although they tend to use terminology like "diverse," "global," or "international" to refer to that community. Nine others empathize with the collective experience of discrimination faced by African Americans and other people of color through a racially progressive ideology. While often this lens on race brings them to a uniquely "middle" perspective rather than a "browning" perspective, it still is not a lens typically utilized by whites. Although I can only speculate, it seems plausible that, because shared experiences with discrimination would likely only be more pronounced among the less-educated members of the racial middle, we could expect that other more diverse studies of the racial middle might find even more support for various aspects of the browning thesis.

Patterns beyond the Racial Poles

Although the findings outlined above are enlightening enough, the most interesting patterns in these data tended to emerge outside of what would have been predicted by either the whitening or the browning theses. For example, while the whitening thesis would have predicted that respondents identify with whites, and the browning thesis would have expected them to identify with blacks, the respondents actually identify most with their own racial middle group, and also tend to be mistaken for other racial middle groups when they are perceived by outsiders. That is, Asian American respondents tended to be mistaken for Latinos or Middle Easterners, and Latinos tended to be mistaken for Asian Americans or Middle Easterners, before being mistaken for blacks or whites. Further, while the whitening thesis has some credence when we look at the group that respondents feel furthest away from—African Americans—of at least equal importance is the finding that the respondents also tend to see "the other racial middle group" (Latinos when they are Asian American, and Asian Americans when they are Latino) as that from whom they feel the greatest distance. Thus, as scholars continue to focus on the question of whether blacks or whites will become the reference group of Latinos and Asian Americans, they risk missing the possibility that their reference group might actually be found in the racial middle.

Again, when examining racial ideology, we find that whitening and browning theses do not necessarily allow for the complexity present in the racial middle. When combing this sample for the kind of explicit antiblack racism that other scholars have found in white interview data,[8] results were few and far between. Yet by analyzing not just for antiblack discourse, but also for racist discourse about the racial middle, some respondents seemed to be casting a negative light on *those* groups in the same way that whites tend to target African Americans in other studies. Ecuadorians were seen as too close to blacks, some Filipinos were seen as too "ghetto," certain Latinos were seen as too "hip-hop." While in the end these comments have the same ideological effect as the more explicit forms of antiblack racism, the complexity of the way this racism is discursively practiced would most likely be missed by the conventional survey methods of other studies.[9] These studies tend to use standard questions that ask respondents to evaluate behaviors typically negatively associated with blacks, but less frequently if at all do these questions attach the same behaviors to other racial middle groups. Beginning conceptually with the racial middle in order to study the racial middle would be a radical departure from the above-cited studies, but these data suggest that such an approach may be fruitful.

This ideological complexity in the racial middle continues when considering affirmative action, another popular topic of focus for studies in the bipolar race-relations model. The whitening thesis expects that Latinos and Asians would reject affirmative action, while the browning thesis would predict they would support it. While in this case the browning thesis is supported more than the whitening thesis in our particular (and not completely representative) sample, because over half of the sample supports affirmative action and very few oppose it, the most innovative racial ideologies emerge from somewhere in between. A number of respondents are ambivalent about affirmative action, in that they want to embrace the color-blind ideology of American society but recognize that the reality is somewhat different. More to the point, even those respondents who are either ambivalent or opposed to affirmative action defiantly state that they will nonetheless claim its perks whenever they can. These respondents creatively shape the dominant color-blind ideology to portray themselves as motivated, good-capitalist players who are doing as any American should —seizing an opportunity. While some feel comfortable stating their opposition to affirmative action despite this "seize the opportunity" practice, others lean more toward an ambivalent position on the policy due to the dissonance that this personal practice may introduce. To my knowledge, the survey research on Latinos and Asians has not allowed for these kinds of complex positions on affirmative action, and it would be interesting for future research to tap into their views further on a larger and more diverse sample (especially with respect to education levels), particularly given the changing demographics of the United States.

When considering how racial ideologies are expressed in the form of attitudes about racial and ethnic intermarriage, the whitening and browning theses present two options: either Latinos and Asians will intermarry primarily with whites, practicing marital assimilation, or they will marry with members of their own and other nonwhite ("brown") groups. Certainly the mating behaviors of our sample, at first glance, would support a whitening perspective. Another component of the whitening perspective, however, would be that respondents would see white cultural values as superior and black cultural values as inferior. When considering Asians in particular, some of our respondents defy this simplistic expectation. There are a handful of Asian American respondents who would (or did) outright oppose intermarriage with whites in their family, and still others who would *prefer* their family members to not marry whites (or even to be too influenced by their white friends) due to some aspects of white cultural values that are seen as troubling. Specifically, some Asian Americans fear that their children would not be as respectful of their elders, nor of education, if they became too heavily influenced by what they see as some self-indulgent aspects of American culture. Thus, when considering the bipolar racism framework, a visual graph might depict an upward slope as we move from black to white on the continuum of mate acceptability, yet with Asians we might see a peak of acceptability in the middle, flattening out on both the poles of black and white. Neither a whitening nor a browning perspective fully captures this complex evaluative framework among Asians.

When we consider the racial middle's experiences with discrimination, the results again defy the simplistic predictions advanced by either whitening or browning arguments. The whitening argument would suggest that Latinos and Asians are experiencing some degree of white-skin privilege, while the browning argument would suggest that Latinos and Asians experience roughly the same types of discrimination as other people of color in the United States. Because conceptualizations of what discrimination is have often been shaped by the cultural understandings of what African Americans have experienced in the past, however, there are types of discrimination unique to the racial middle that such a popular conception of discrimination might miss. Respondents often characterize the many instances when their citizenship status, "American-ness," or English-language ability is questioned as innocent ignorance, or curious questioning, on the part of the observer, rather than as discrimination "with a capital D." Yet these are blatant examples of the barriers to full acceptance that members of the racial middle must overcome on a daily basis. Although many of them have known no other country but the United States, they are deemed suspect strangers in their own land. While some respondents have certainly also faced some of the more "traditional" forms of exclusion—in jobs, housing, education, and everyday slurs and taunts— there are other forms of discrimination being faced by the racial middle that may not be tapped by traditional measures of racial discrimination.

Members of the racial middle are hardly the only ones who hold ideologically complex positions on matters of race. Even on the racial poles, there are subgroups that hold equally intriguing positions—for example, black conservatives, white antiracists who use color-blind discourse, and blacks who employ color-blind discourse.[10] I do not mean to suggest that those in the racial middle have a corner on the market of ideological complexity when it comes to race. These findings suggest, however, that future research should proceed with extreme caution when simply transposing measures that have worked with blacks and whites onto racial middle groups.

Transcending Race from the Middle: Cheerleaders for "Tolerance" or Leaders of Worldwide Antiracist Struggle?

The relations between the racial poles in United States have not only shaped our collective understandings of what "discrimination" is, but also our understandings of progressivism, antiracism, or what is needed to eradicate racism. Antiracism has often, although not exclusively, been defined by those who seek to end antiblack racism. Dichotomous notions of the oppressors and the oppressed have worked well to form revolutionary and reform movements, but members of the racial middle can sometimes be left wondering where they fit into this bipolar framework. As an educator who has attended and led many workshops on race, racism, racial privilege, and antiracism, several times I have witnessed the confusion of Latinos, Asian Americans, biracials, and others when workshop leaders ask them to choose either the "white" group or the "person of color" group (or worse yet, the "black group"). Well-intended racial progressives and antiracists may be perpetuating misunderstandings about the racial middle even as they seek to eradicate the very racism that the racial middle faces.

It is the existence of this very bipolar framework of racial progressivism/antiracism that may lead members of the racial middle to reject explicit antiracism altogether and instead create new languages for challenging the racial status quo. Several respondents do not see their primary allegiances as much to their particular racial or ethnic communities as they do to a broader community of multiracials or to a global/international community. For example, Roberto is a progressive Mexican American man married to a German American woman. When asked what cultural traditions he would pass down to his future children, he does not as much desire that his children would learn to speak Spanish as he wishes that they would learn some other language so that they are bilingual citizens of a global community. Monica, a progressive Cuban American woman married to a white American, also consciously attempts to surround her son not just with other Latinos, but with many other "hyphenated Americans"—others who, like them, are "not just white." These respondents seek to challenge racism, but not necessarily by aligning with a "people of color" or "collective black" community as the browning thesis might predict. This solidarity is formed not in opposition to whiteness, for it includes whiteness to some degree. Yet it is not reducible to whiteness.

Take the example of Rebecca, a progressive Chinese-Macanese-Portuguese student who grew up in New York City. Rebecca had a working-class upbringing (her father was a police officer) in racially and ethnically mixed neighborhoods where she felt more comfortable with African Americans and Latinos than she did with Asian Americans (other than her own family) or whites. She describes herself as part of an "in-between culture," a "very well-rounded multicultural kind of person," as opposed to a person of color. As a young adult who is romantically involved with a Dominican American now, she envisions herself as the parent of even more "in-between" children. When describing the future society that she expects her children will inhabit, she states: "By the time they grow up, I doubt that there's a distinct Asian identity they can identify with, or . . . [a] distinct Hispanic identity they can identify with or anything. I think I just want them to be well rounded individuals and . . . a multicultural person."

Rebecca's dream for her children is not unlike April's. As a Korean American Californian who was adopted and raised by a white family, now married to a Mexican man and speaking Spanish (but not Korean), April hopes that her future children would see themselves as "children of the world." Respondents who hail from New York City and California, two U.S. areas with sizeable populations of both Latinos and Asian Americans, are perhaps closest to being able to forecast for us what this future society might look like. As members of the racial middle, they have not only begun to socialize with each other and recognize commonalities, but they also feel hemmed in by limiting stereotypes of what "being Asian" or "being Latino" is supposed to be. While a bipolar conceptualization of race would tell them that if they're not "acting Latino or Asian," then they must be either "acting white" or "acting black," they have defiantly characterized themselves as children of a multicultural society where an allegiance to one particular race is no longer necessary. Indeed, some feel such an identification may even become obsolete within their lifetimes.

These racial categories, however, have been crucial to the ongoing struggle against racism in the United States. Those who have advocated "erasing" them have mainly been those who desire to further the racial status quo. Indeed, scholars of "color-blindness" as the dominant racial ideology of the contemporary United States have consistently demonstrated how it actually functions as a form of racism.[11] In a society so deeply structured by racism, it becomes a "sincere fiction" for members of the society to actually claim they "do not notice" race.[12] In reality, color-blindness most often orients itself in an off-and-on, "now you see it, now you don't" approach to race.[13] Advocates of color-blindness may claim to ideally "not notice" race, but instead make reference to various race-related (and often antiblack) stereotypes by use of code words such as "ghetto," "hip-hop," "urban," "at-risk," and other such phrases that we have seen some of the respondents in this book using. Thus, color-blindness allows racist assumptions to continue unabated in forms that are more difficult to pin down because the language is less racially overt. Moreover, it serves the ideological function of blaming the victim—that is, if race is really no longer an issue, as color-blindness suggests, then the extent to which any racial inequalities remain, those who struggle must be "bringing it on themselves," irrationally seeing racism where there supposedly is none. As discussed in chapter 4, because such an ideology most clearly serves the interest of the dominant group (whites) it should come as no surprise that whites use color-blindness with much greater frequency than nonwhites.[14] Language like "children of the world" that we see some of these respondents begs careful analysis to assess whether this racial middle position of "transcending race" serves the ideological function of color-blindness yet again, or whether it offers a new vision of antiracism, more inclusive than its bipolar predecessor.

The word choice of "multicultural" by some of the respondents raises the same question. The "multiculturalist" movement has been criticized for failing to take power into account. Particularly in education, being multicultural has meant teaching about the food, customs, and practices of various cultural groups without a systematic analysis of the discrimination that some groups have faced historically and contemporarily. Although all groups may share the fact of having a "culture," society has consistently valued certain cultural traits over others, and has legally

TABLE 7-1
Respondent Perceptions of Racialized Behaviors

Latino	Asian American
Speak Spanish	Prefer eating only Chinese food
Don't speak English well	Don't challenge/disobey parents
Physically expressive	Major in math/science

White	Black
Conservative/Republican	Like hip-hop/rap music
Upper class/advanced degree	Follow urban ("ghetto") trends
Westernized (culturally)	of style, dress, and speech
Consume U.S. popular culture	Complain too much about
(music, film, clothes)	racism
	Politically organized/strong

excluded certain cultural groups from many benefits, to the advantage of others. In order to educate students about such institutional and structural discrimination, critics have argued that an antiracist education is preferable than the typical multicultural approach.[15] Antiracist education also empowers students with strategies for challenging contemporary discrimination, bringing home the point that the struggle is ongoing.[16] This stands in contrast to the "cheerleaders for tolerance"[17] approach, which applauds the status quo and does not suggest the possibility that any additional struggle for a better society is necessary. From a multiculturalist perspective then, full equality has already been achieved. Of course, such a perspective stands in stark contrast to most empirical social science evidence. Thus, multiculturalism alone offers little more than a sincere fiction, much like color-blindness.

The word choices that these respondents make as they consider the future clearly deserve careful analysis. Some of their word choices, as they attempt to carve out a niche in the American racial mosaic that includes them, may emanate from a general dissatisfaction with society's expectations of what it means to be "Asian American," "Latino," "black," or "white." Examining table 7-1, which I created as a summary of various statements made throughout the interviews, we can see just how limiting these racial expectations come across to the respondents. In the top two boxes, respondents often resented that if they did not conform to the behaviors listed, they were not considered to be "Asian enough" or "Latino enough," despite being grounded in other cultural aspects of their race or ethnicity. Likewise, if they appeared to conform to any of the behaviors in the "white" box, they resented that this seemed to cancel out their ethnic identities in people's minds. They maintained they were not "white" just because they exhibited one or more of these seemingly non-ethnic behaviors. Perhaps viewing all of these "boxes" as equally limiting, some respondents select language like "multicultural" and "children of the world" in order to create a conceptual space where people of many different backgrounds share their experiences of racial/ethnic complexity. If they choose these terms, however, because they are searching for something more benign and palatable to the white majority in the face of the social stigma that the "Latino," "Asian American," and "black" boxes carry, then their vision of the future becomes stagnant, without much hope of transforming current social arrangements.

The transformative potential of the idea of transcending race from the middle lies in its ability to draw connecting lines between the struggles faced by Latinos, Asians Americans, Middle Easterners, and others in the United States to the struggles of colonized peoples worldwide. Some scholars have begun to theorize about such a racialized hybrid space, particularly as the political economy becomes globalized and an international division of labor has resulted. In Los Angeles, for instance, Darder, Torres, and Ngin have identified a "Spanish-Pacific" network whereby "Spanish speaking retailers in the Los Angeles garment district are often ethnic Chinese and Koreans from Peru and other Latin American countries who have established their businesses in the section dominated by other immigrants."[18] Their study opens with the case of Young Suk Lee, a fashion retailer in Los Angeles who grew up in Peru, speaking Spanish, not Korean. Lee's experiences defy the simplistic notions of conventional racial/ethnic categorization. She is one of the "children of the world" about whom our respondent, April, speaks. Darder, Torres, and Ngin argue that the complex racial space that these Los Angeles residents occupy is due not to their racial or ethnic identities, but to their shared relationship to the international political economy. Immigration and welfare reform bills, for example, target them on this basis and not solely because of their racial identities. Whether Lee speaks Korean or Spanish is less relevant than her location in this economic configuration. By focusing on how the globalizing economy has forged bonds of connection among the working class across racial/ethnic lines, this research suggests that it is not only with the educated (as in this sample) but also in other strata of the racial middle that this idea of transcending racial/ethnic boundaries has emerged.

At its transformative best, members of this Spanish-Pacific network would not avoid terms like "Latino" or "Asian American" in order to whitewash themselves, but rather to leave open the possibility of coalition across and beyond these two limiting categories. To see itself not necessarily as a "multicultural" community, but as a global community with an understanding of racism that goes beyond just one country, is a vantage point from which the racial middle could offer society the greatest possibility for social change.

Subverting the Bipolar by Looking beyond the United States

Latinos, Asians, and other members of the racial middle are uniquely situated to bring the United States into the twenty-first century by broadening our understanding of racism beyond the U.S. borders. Many of them have recent collective memories of colonialism and the deleterious effects it can have on a culture and its economy and peoples. While many American blacks and whites may see black-white relations as the prototypical model of racial dynamics, some Latinos and Asian Americans may prefer to see the U.S. civil rights struggle as but one of many larger global struggles against worldwide racism and colonialism.

Latinos in particular have a collective history of European colonization, through which colonial powers enforced the messages of European superiority and African-diaspora inferiority. As they became part of the United States, the darker-skinned among them already understood through this history the parallels they shared with some African American experiences of subordination. Yet the "pigmentocracy" they carried with them from Latin America was never quite as rigid as that within the United States,[19] as we see for example in Wanda's interview. Wanda identifies as a black Puerto Rican American and sees ranges of color and relative privilege even within her own family. Further, Latinos of all skin tones face cultural racism that bears some resemblance to what some white ethnic groups, such as Mediterraneans (e.g., Greeks, Italians), historically faced in the United States, characterized as perhaps too passionate and emotional for Western/Anglo-Saxon standards. These "inferior" characterizations from a colonial perspective continue to be experienced today by Latinos as they are selectively incorporated into the United States.

In addition, Latinos share with Asian Americans the perception of foreignness/otherness that we saw so poignantly illustrated in the testimony of respondents in chapter 5. As nativist treatises like Samuel Huntington's make plain, Latinos have been viewed as a threat to American identity and security for having the alleged audacity of "holding on" to their language and culture.[20] In the worldwide political climate of "War on Terror," such "suspect ethnicity" and perceived foreignness from a Western perspective carries with it a social stigma that can sometimes result in life-threatening consequences, whether in the United States or in other Western nations across the Atlantic. South Asians in particular have faced the assumption of "potential terrorist" in the United States and elsewhere, which connects them to this global experience of unfair and alarmist suspicion.

Asian Americans in general carry the additional stigma in the United States of having formerly been enemy combatants. Military-based anti-Japanese, anti-Korean, and anti-Vietnamese sentiments still loom large among some Americans and their global allies. Thus, while Latinos may sometimes be painted as culturally inferior via assumptions of being too loud and expressive, Asian Americans face characterizations of cultural inferiority instead for being perceived as too quiet and therefore potentially secretive, cunning, clannish, and dangerous. In the contemporary context, however, some East Asian nations (e.g., Japan, China, Hong Kong) have gained a greater degree of respect worldwide from an economic standpoint and are less likely to face the stigma of being from "backward" or "less-developed" nations in the way that Southeast and South Asians are more likely to be viewed.

Additionally, while East Asian nations are certainly not strangers to struggles with colonial powers, Southeast and South Asians (especially Indians and Filipinos) share with Latinos the understanding of European colonization and the phenotype-based assumptions of inferiority that accompanied it. This in part explains why more of the progressive respondents discussed in chapter 6 were Indian or Southeast Asian than Chinese. Also, reexamining table 7-1, it is interesting to note that while most of the behaviors deemed "black" carry some negative stereotypical assumptions, some respondents—notably only East Asians—somewhat admirably characterize African Americans as being more politically organized. Relative to Latinos and other Asian Americans, East Asians have had less of a historical necessity to become acquainted with counter-ideologies that challenge European colonialist hegemony. Thus, as the largest and most visible voice of antiracism on the U.S. scene, African Americans and their struggle to end white supremacy may symbolize for some Asians a coherent "frame" through which to begin to make sense of their own experiences of being shortchanged out of full access to the American dream. For other Asian Americans already schooled in European colonialism from their "homeland" experiences, however, the discrimination they face in the United States is simply another shade of something they have seen before.

Yet while the black civil rights struggle in the United States offers a useful framework through which the racial middle can advocate for racial justice, we know that an interesting subsample of progressives in this study find it limiting and not necessarily directly applicable to some of their experiences. In framing their allegiances not necessarily with "people of color" or a "collective black" community, but rather as "racial chameleons" or as "being foreign in multiple locations," they suggest the potential of an antiracist space that is not defined primarily by phenotype identification. In Rod Bush's study of the Black Power movement, he identifies two major factions: (1) a more conservative nationalist wing for which "blackness" was a primary criterion for membership and whose goal was success in the capitalist framework (e.g., Nation of Islam), and (2) a more progressive wing that formed coalitions with Red Power, Yellow Power, Brown Power, and working-class white movements and whose ultimate goal was world redistribution of wealth and power (e.g., the Black Panther Party). Bush effectively demonstrates that the latter faction's ability to frame the problem of racism as worldwide white supremacy is what allowed it to so effectively build alliances with disenfranchised peoples of many different racial/ethnic identities.[21] To the extent that the racial middle is able to frame its unique racial/hybrid space as part and parcel of many other such international struggles, it has the potential to create a powerful multifaceted antiracist force. It cannot settle for a "we are the world" multiculturalism terminology, however, if it expects to do anything other than reproduce the contemporary racial status quo.

The Future of Race

As scholars have worked to make sense of what racism-as-we-know-it will become with the impending growth of the Latino and Asian American populations, we have often reverted back to the bipolar modes of thinking that have served us fairly well in the past. Many socioeconomic indicators suggest that the experiences of the racial middle are quickly becoming more like those of whites than blacks. Other experiences, particularly in the political sphere, are indicative of a collective "people of color" experience that members of the racial middle are being folded into along with blacks. To some extent, depending on the area of life upon which we concentrate, both perspectives can be true. Yet these two perspectives are hardly capturing all of what is occurring in the racial middle, missing how society can perhaps be transformed by those more unique experiences.

Even when scholars have attempted to further delineate possibilities beyond the dichotomous, they cannot help but revert back to bipolar language to sketch out their frameworks. For instance, Eduardo Bonilla-Silva and his colleagues have suggested that some members of the racial middle will become indistinguishably *white*, others will be located in a somewhat privileged but still tenuous "honorary *white*" category, and the rest will fall into a "collective *black*" space. Because this framework goes beyond a dichotomy, I sympathize with it the most, yet still I know that many of the respondents I studied would not choose to conceive of themselves as "honorary whites," nor would they align themselves with a "collective black." As we have seen, even outsiders' perceptions of these respondents would rarely place them along either one of these poles. Hardly any respondents are mistaken for black, a small minority is mistaken for white, but the vast majority is taken for some other racial middle group. Thus, whether we consider their own or others' perceptions, the categories of white, honorary white, and collective black do not seem to do complete justice for what is going on for this particular group of respondents. Even as many of them may collect what we in the field would consider to be "white privileges," this is hardly the end of the story. Both their claim to Americanness and their abilities are nonetheless questioned—these are neither fully "white" nor neither fully "black" experiences. So how are we to make sense of them?

I maintain that members of the racial middle themselves, particularly the youngest and the progressives, may be our best source yet for the new terminology and theorizing about the racial middle. The "children of the world," the "in-between culture," the "multiculturals," and the "racial chameleons" in the sample are pointing us to a new direction in theorizing about race. In adopting this language to describe themselves, they are not always abandoning their ethnic identities by trading them in for whiteness (as did Irish Americans and Russian Jewish Americans before them), nor are they visioning themselves as "people of color" or a "collective black." The terms they prefer do not use any sort of color coding or identify any particular ethnicity. Yet at the same time, these terms do not indicate a position of privileged whiteness or sanitized cultural identities typical of assimilation experiences. These respondents understand that Latino and

Asian American racial identities, in and of themselves, are highly complex. So it is this complexity that they tend to identify with most, rather than any homogenous identity, whether "white" or "mono-ethnic."

The future of race may be thus not in academic theories and racial terminology, but in the everyday experiences of the racial middle themselves, as they do the work of carving out a space that they can call their own. This space values bilingualism, even multilingualism, languages "of the world," whether or not they seem to correspond to one's particular ethnicity. This space values cultural traditions that do not emanate from the dominant culture, and welcomes the opportunity to celebrate multiple traditions simultaneously. It is a space where political candidates who look out for "the underdog" broadly defined are valued, especially when the "underdog" is not limited to one particular ethnicity. Indeed, as I write, a man named Barack Obama is running for the U.S. Democratic party presidential nomination, occupying this same type of hybrid racial space. Though the old bipolar habits of the United States die hard (as the one-drop rule still characterizes him as African American), Obama grew up with a white mother from the Midwest, knew of his Kenyan father, and lived for a time in Hawaii as well as Indonesia with a stepfather who was native to that area. His profile is not unlike some of the respondents in this sample who do not identify with the "basic five" U.S. racial categories as much as they do with the notion of being a "racial chameleon" or an American member of the international community.

At its best, the hybrid space that the new progressive racial middle seeks to create would be a space where whiteness is not the norm. Race would not be eliminated or forgotten about in color-blind/apathetic fashion, for the hegemony of whiteness would be vigilantly detested. Yet those who reside there would defiantly engage in many cultural practices that others might label as "white" while still claiming to be anything but. The racial middle, quite simply, would want to change the rules of the racial game. As their numbers grow and their voices get louder, they might very well succeed. While neither a "whiter" nor a "browner" nation will likely result from such changes, the result of a more racially inclusive society could perhaps be more plausible here, in this "color-nuanced" space, than with either of the other more explicitly color-coded predictions.

Appendix A
Interview Guide

We are interested in finding out the different factors that go into people deciding what race or ethnicity means to them. There are no right or wrong answers. We really just want to hear your thoughts and experiences about these issues. You may choose not to answer any question you do not wish to answer, or ask us to turn the tape recorder off at any time. Please feel free to ask any questions of me along the way as well.

1. The 2000 census asked people to choose from the following categories for "race": white, black, Asian, Native American Indian, and other. For the first time, people were also allowed to check more than one category. Then, people were asked to answer an ethnicity question where they could choose up to three nationalities that described their ethnicity (for instance, Chinese, Cuban, Irish, Puerto Rican American, Mexican, Vietnamese, etc.). How would you answer this question? Why? Would this have always been how you answered? [If more than one race or ethnicity is mentioned, probe for whether one is more salient/significant to them than another.]

2. Would anyone in your household have answered differently than you? How about anyone in your extended family? Was this always how the others would have answered?

3. Do you know people with the same heritage as you who might have answered differently to this question? If so, why?

4. What do you think about this categorization system? What is good about it, if anything, and what do you think needs improving, if anything?

5. Family history: Who in your family were the original immigrants? Where did they come from and how long ago? Why did they come? What

was their education and occupation? What about your own parents (or who raised you)?

6. What is your religion? Were you raised in it? How often have you attended religious services?

7. Did you speak a language other than English at home growing up? In what contexts was it spoken, and by whom? How about now?

8. Describe the ethnic background of the neighborhood where you live now (and where you grew up, if different). If there were/are people around of other ethnic backgrounds, how did you (and your family) feel about them? [Probe for other race/ethnic categories not mentioned by the respondent—another way to phrase this question is, did you get any messages from your family or others around you about the "others" different from you while growing up?]

9. How did your family feel about being _____? Did they talk about it often? Did they belong to any groups/clubs that were ethnic in purpose?

10. How did your family feel about you dating outside your ethnic group? How did you feel about it? Did you ever do it? What was the reaction? [Probe for racial/ethnic groups not mentioned.] What about outside your religion? Did any members of your family do so? What was the reaction?

11. Is it a common occurrence for people to ask or comment on your ethnic background? Can you recall the last time someone asked or commented on it? What are you most often perceived as (or misperceived as) by others? How do you respond?

12. Would you say that being _____ is important to you? Are there times when it is more or less important to you? What about to others? Do you feel there are times when it especially benefits you? Do you feel there are times when it particularly hinders you (such as getting a job, house/apartment, or anything else)?

13. Do you know of any people who have changed their name? What do you think about this? Do you think your last name has helped you assimilate easier? Would you ever change your last name to help assimilate? [Here you can help with examples, like some Asians go by an anglicized nickname rather than their given name, and/or some Latinos have anglicized their surnames . . .]

14. Are there people who are _____ that are more commonly perceived as white than others? Are there people who are _____ that are quicker to identify as white than others? Why do you think this is? [Probe for nationality, socioeconomic status, religion, etc.]

15. Do _____ jokes bother you? Does it matter if they are told by an _____ or an outsider? Do you ever tell jokes about other ethnic groups? If so, which ones?

16. Do you think Americans have a stereotype about what being _____ is like? If so, what is it? Is there any validity to it? Where do you think it comes from?

17. What do you think are the best things about being _____? The worst?

18. Do you feel more comfortable being around _____s than non-_____s at times? If so, when? Any idea why? Are there times when you are more comfortable around whites than _____?

19. If you had to move somewhere else, would you choose a neighborhood that had a good percentage of _____s in it? Why or why not?

20. What are special ceremonies like in your family (funerals, weddings, christenings)? Are there aspects of these ceremonies that are different from other Americans' that you know of?

21. What are some _____ customs or practices that affect your everyday life? Do you eat any ethnic foods regularly? Special holidays, or ways those holidays are celebrated differently due to your _____ background?

22. Do your children (and grandchildren) see themselves as _____? Is it less important to them than it is to you, or about the same? What would you hope they learn about being _____? Would you prefer they choose someone _____ to spend their lives with, or does it matter? Are certain groups more preferable than others?

23. Would you describe yourself as working class, middle class, or upper class? What about your family of origin? What class would you say most _____ people are? In your personal opinion, do you think your socioeconomic status or physical appearance places you closer to whites than to other ethnic groups?

24. Which group or groups would you say face(s) discrimination now? Have things gotten better, worse, or about the same for these groups in your lifetime? How so?

25. Are there certain ethnic groups you feel are close/similar to being _____? If so, which ones, and why? Are there other groups you feel you would have a harder time identifying with? If so, which ones, and why?

26. What do you think of bilingual education being provided in the nation's schools for students for whom English is not their first language? [For instance, some people are opposed to this because they feel a "total immersion" into the English language is necessary, while others feel it is important for the process to be more gradual so that students don't get behind in other subjects such as math due to a language barrier.]

27. Should individuals be able to get vouchers to attend private schools when they live in districts where the public schools are of poor quality, or should the government instead invest in improving schools for the entire area?

28. When you decide who to vote for, does being _____ ever influence you? What are some of the issues you look for a candidate to support? What party do you typically support?

29. Now I just want to ask your views on three other policies: (a) What do you think of current U.S. *immigration policy*? Do you feel things are too lax/too restrictive, especially with regard to your own or your family's own nation(s) of origin? (b) What about *welfare policy*? Some people feel that the two-year limit imposed by Clinton's Family Responsibility Act was too strict and provides only menial job training, while others feel there need to be stricter limits and that too many take advantage of the system. (c) What about *antidiscrimination policies*? Some people feel it is important to take affirmative action so that groups who are underrepresented in certain jobs and schools get preferred when all other credentials are equal, while others feel that one's demographic profile should have no bearing on such decisions. We also have the option to file a civil suit if we feel we have been discriminated against. Is this enough/too much—what do you think?

30. Finally, could you just give me a few little facts about yourself: What year were you born? What is your occupation? What is the highest level of education you completed?

31. Can you think of anyone else you know who is Latino or Asian that might be interested in being interviewed by us [especially those who do not necessarily identify with their heritage as strongly as you do, that we might have trouble recruiting through other means]?

Thanks so much for your time. If there is anything else you would like to add, or to ask me, please feel free to do it now!

Appendix B

Respondent Information

Name (Gender)	Race(s)	Ethnicities	Age	Generation*	Geographic background (origin/current)	Occupation	Education
Aldo (M)	Other	Brazilian	49	1	Brazil/NJ	Software developer	PhD
Alfonso (M)	White	Hispanic [Puerto Rican American]	60	1	Puerto Rico/NYC	Surgeon	MD
April (F)	API	Korean	30	1.5 (adopted)	CA	Math teacher	JD
Brian (M)	Other+	Japanese	30	4	CA/VA	Unemployed (field: drama)	Bachelor's
Bruce (M)	Asian	Chinese/ Taiwanese	52	1	Taiwan/ NJ	Manager, human resources	Master's
Caitlin (F)	Other	Puerto Rican American	51	1 (adopted)	Puerto Rico/VA	Social worker	Master's, some grad.
Cathy (F)	Other	Asian Indian Polish Jew	40	2	CA/VA	Professor	PhD
Charlene (F)	Asian	Filipino Thai	35	2	TN/VA	Professor	PhD
Christopher (M)	White	Honduran Dominican	41	2	NYC	Self-employed	Bachelor's, some grad.
Claudia (F)	Other	Hispanic [Dominican]	43	1.5	NYC/CT	Home-visit child specialist	Master's
Crystal (F)	White Asian	Macao, Portuguese (dad) Irish (mom)	20	2	VA	College student	Some college
Debie (F)	Asian	Filipino	20	1.5	NJ/NYC	University student	Currently in college
Dolores (F)	Other	Hispanic [Dominican]	38	2	NYC	Client advocate	Some college

Name (Gender)	Race(s)	Ethnicities	Age	Generation*	Geographic background (origin/current)	Occupation	Education
Edita (F)	Other	Guatemalan	20	2	VA	College student	Some college
Elisa (F)	White	Argentinean	39	1	Argentina/NJ	Teacher	Bachelor's, some grad.
Heather (F)	White API	Filipino White	31	2	VA/CA	Bartender	Some college
Joy (F)	Asian	"South Asian" or Indian	20s	1.5	NJ/NYC	Filmmaker	Master's
Jessica (F)	Asian	Korean (birth parents) Polish (adoptive parents)	18	1.5 (adopted)	MD/TX	University student	Currently in college
Jim (M)	Asian	Chinese	56	1	Taiwan/NJ	Computer administrator	BS
Joe (M)	White	Hispanic [Cuban]	38	2	Miami, FL/VA	FBI agent/ naval officer	Bachelor's
Juanita (F)	Other+	Hispanic [Mexican]	20	3	KY/VA	College student	Some college
Kali (F)	Asian	Indian	41	1	Bombay/OH/NYC	Statistician	Master's
Levan (F)	API	Cambodian	20	2	VA	College student	Some college
Lisa (F)	API	Vietnamese	20	1.5	Philippines/Virginia	University student	Some college
Luis (M)	White	Brazilian	47	1	Brazil/NJ	Professor	PhD
Ly (F)	Asian	Chinese	53	1	Taiwan/Brazil (3 years)/NJ	Homemaker (marketing)	Master's, MBA
Maria (F)	Other	Puerto Rican American	22	2	NYC	University student	Currently in college
Mateo (M)	Other	El Salvadorian	20	1.5	VA	College student	Some college
Michael (M)	white	Puerto Rican American	47	2	PA/VA	Electrical engineer	Master's
Monica (F)	Other	Cuban [also Polish]	34	2	Miami, FL/VA	Program director	Master's
Mya (F)	Asian	Taiwanese Chinese	52	1	Taiwan/NJ	Technology field	Master's
Neva (F)	Other	Mexican	20	2/3 (mom/dad)	CA	College student	Some college

Name (Gender)	Race(s)	Ethnicities	Age	Generation*	Geographic background (origin/current)	Occupation	Education
Peter (M)	Other	Mexican	34	2	CO	Special agent ex-military	Bachelor's
Raj (M)	Asian	Mother white father Indian	20	2	VA	College student	Some college
Rebecca (F)	API	Chinese Portuguese Macanese	19	2	NYC	University student	Currently in college
Reena (F)	Asian	Bangladesh	19	1.5	Bangladesh/ CA/VA	College student	Some college
Ricardo (M)	Other	Mexican	22	2	CA	University student	Currently in college
Roberto (M)	Other	Mexican	39	1.5	CA/VA	College professor	PhD
Rohit (F)	Other	Indian	39	1	India/NJ	Pharmacist	PhD
Rosa (F)	White	Mexican Russian	33	1.5	CA/NC	Librarian	Master's
Roxanne (F)	Other	Mexican	45	2	UT/VA	Loan officer	Bachelor's
Sarah (F)	Asian	Korean (birth parents) White-Irish (adoptive parents)	34	1.5 (adopted)	VA	Computer consultant	Bachelor's
Scott (M)	API	Chinese Taiwanese	35	1.5	TX/VA	Restaurant owner	PhD
Teddy (M)	API	Taiwanese Chinese	44	1	Taiwan/NJ	Computer programmer	Master's
Tiffany (F)	API	Filipino	19	2	Virginia	College student	Some college
Tim (M)	API	Taiwanese Chinese	52	1	Taiwan/NJ	Architect	Master's
Tomas (M)	White	Brazilian	49	1	Brazil/NJ	Researcher	PhD
Victor (M)	Asian	Korean	52	1	Korea/NJ	College professor	PhD
Vincent (M)	Asian	Chinese	56	1	China/NJ	Engineer	PhD
Wanda (F)	Black	Puerto Rican American	67	1.5	NYC/VA	Retired higher education administration	Master's and more grad.

+ would actually refuse to answer the race question
* 1 = moved to U.S. as adult; 1.5 = moved to U.S. as child; 2 = first to be born in U.S. (second generation);
  3 = third generation; 4 = fourth generation

Notes

NOTES TO CHAPTER 1

Epigraph: Big Bill Broonzy, "Black, Brown, and White," originally recorded Chicago 1951, appears on *Defiance Blues: Livin' in the House of the Blues*, Platinum Records, 2001.

1. Joseph L. Graves Jr., *The Race Myth: Why We Pretend Race Exists in America* (New York: Dutton, 2004)

2. Clara Rodriguez, *Changing Race: Latinos, the Census, and the History of Ethnicity in the United States* (New York: New York University Press, 2000).

3. U.S. Census Bureau, "Fact Sheet for Race, Ethnic, or Ancestry Group: Census 2000," retrieved at www.census.gov on October 5, 2006.

4. George Yancey, *Who Is White? Latinos, Asians, and the New Black/Nonblack Divide* (Boulder, Colorado: Lynne Rienner, 2003). Such predictions are based on current immigration and fertility rates remaining consistent until 2050.

5. Alejandro Portes and Ruben G. Rumbaut, *Immigrant America: A Portrait* (3rd edition) (Berkeley: University of California Press, 2006).

6. Edward Murguia and Tyrone Forman, "Shades of Whiteness: The Mexican American Experience in Relation to Anglos and Blacks" in *White Out: The Continuing Significance of Racism*, ed. Ashley W. Doane and Eduardo Bonilla-Silva (New York: Routledge, 2003), 63–79.

7. Yancey, *Who Is White?*

8. Portes and Rumbaut, *Immigrant America*.

9. Yen Le Espiritu, *Asian American Panethnicity: Bridging Institutions and Identities* (Philadelphia: Temple University Press, 1992).

10. Rodriguez, *Changing Race*.

11. Espiritu, *Asian American Panethnicity*; Jean Kim, "Asian American Identity Development Theory" in *New Perspectives on Racial Identity Development: A Theoretical and Practical Anthology*, ed. Charmaine L. Wijeyesinghe and Bailey W. Jackson III (New York: New York University Press, 2001), 67–90.

12. Kim, "Asian American Identity Development Theory"

13. Ronald Takaki, *A Different Mirror: A History of Multicultural America* (Boston: Little, Brown, 1993).

14. Rodriguez, *Changing Race*, 102

15. Joe R. Feagin, *Racist America* (New York: Routledge, 2000).

16. Richard D. Alba, *Ethnicity and Race in the USA: Toward the Twenty-first Century* (Boston: Routledge and Kegan Paul, 1985).

17. Takaki, *A Different Mirror*.

18. David Roediger, *The Wages of Whiteness: Race and the Making of the American Working Class* (New York: Verso, 1991).

19. Alba, *Ethnicity and Race in the USA*.

20. Takaki, *A Different Mirror*.

21. Ibid.; Alba, *Ethnicity and Race in the USA*.

22. Ibid.

23. Rodriguez, *Changing Race*; "Race: The Power of an Illusion," executive producer Larry Adelman (California Newsreel, 2003).

24. Takaki, *A Different Mirror*; Espiritu, *Asian American Panethnicity*.

25. Cheryl I. Harris, "Whiteness as Property" in *Black on White: Black Writers on What It Means to Be White*, ed. David R. Roediger (New York: Schocken Books, 1998), 103–18.

26. Alba, *Ethnicity and Race in the USA*.

27. Ibid.

28. Espiritu, *Asian American Panethnicity*.

29. Ibid.

30. Ibid.

31. Ibid.; Kim, "Asian American Identity Development Theory."

32. Espiritu, *Asian American Panethnicity*.

33. Ibid., 32.

34. Edward Said, *Orientalism* (New York: Knopf, 1979).

35. Espiritu, *Asian American Panethnicity*, 107.

36. Rodriguez, *Changing Race*.

37. Espiritu, *Asian American Panethnicity*.

38. Mary Waters, *Ethnic Options: Choosing Identities in America* (Berkeley: University of California Press, 1990); Mary Waters, "Ethnic and Racial Identities of Second-Generation Black Immigrants in New York City" in *Rethinking the Color Line: Readings in Race and Ethnicity*, ed. Charles A. Gallagher (Mountain View, California: Mayfield Publishing Company, 1999), 421–36; M. Patricia Fernandez-Kelly and Richard Schauffler, "Divided Fates: Immigrant Children in a Restructured Economy" *International Migration Review* 28 (1994): 662–89.

39. Rodriguez, *Changing Race*.

40. Elizabeth M. Grieco and Rachel C. Cassidy, "Overview of Race and Hispanic Origin," *Census 2000 Brief* (March), U.S. Bureau of the Census, 2001.

41. Rodriguez, *Changing Race*.

42. Portes and Rumbaut, *Immigrant America*; Murguia and Forman, *Shades of Whiteness*.

43. Portes and Rumbaut, *Immigrant America.*

44. Bernardo M. Ferdman and Placida I. Gallegos, "Racial Identity Development and Latinos in the United States," in *New Perspectives on Racial Identity Development: A Theoretical and Practical Anthology,* ed. Charmaine L. Wijeyesinghe and Bailey W. Jackson III (New York: New York University Press, 2001), 32–66.

45. Murguia and Forman, "Shades of Whiteness," 72.

46. Yancey, *Who Is White?*; Jonathan W. Warren and France Winddance Twine, "White Americans, The New Minority? Non-blacks and the Ever-Expanding Boundaries of Whiteness," *Journal of Black Studies* 28 (1997): 200–218.

47. Herbert Gans, "Symbolic Ethnicity," *Ethnic and Racial Studies* 2 (1979): 1–20.

48. Milton Gordon, *Assimilation in American Life* (New York: Oxford University Press, 1964).

49. Yancey, *Who Is White*

50. Murguia and Forman, "Shades of Whiteness," 75

51. Eduardo Bonilla-Silva, *Racism Without Racists* (Lanham, Maryland: Rowman and Littlefield, 2003).

52. Joe R. Feagin and Clairece Booher Feagin, *Racial and Ethnic Relations* (6th ed.) (Upper Saddle River, New Jersey: Prentice Hall, 1999).

53. Yancey, *Who Is White?*; Roediger, *Wages of Whiteness*; Karen Brodkin, *How Jews Became White Folks and What That Says About Race in America* (Rutgers, New Jersey: Rutgers University Press, 1999).

54. Samuel Huntington, "The Hispanic Challenge," *Foreign Policy* (March–April 2004): 30–45.

55. Portes and Rumbaut, *Immigrant America,* 35.

56. Feagin, *Racist America*; Joe R. Feagin and Eileen O'Brien, *White Men on Race: Power, Privilege, and the Shaping of Cultural Consciousness* (Boston: Beacon Press, 2003).

57. Murguia and Forman, "Shades of Whiteness"; Melanie Bush, *Breaking the Code of Good Intentions: Everyday Forms of Whiteness* (Lanham, Maryland: Rowman and Littlefield, 2004).

58. Portes and Rumbaut, *Immigrant America.*

59. Murguia and Forman, "Shades of Whiteness."

60. Portes and Rumbaut, *Immigrant America.*

61. Eduardo Bonilla-Silva, " 'New Racism,' Color-Blind Racism, and the Future of Whiteness in America" in *White Out: The Continuing Significance of Racism,* ed. Ashley W. Doane and Eduardo Bonilla-Silva (New York: Routledge, 2003), 271–84.

62. Edna Bonacich, "Class Approaches to Ethnicity and Race," *Insurgent Sociologist* 10 (1980): 11.

63. Sharon M. Lee, "Asian Immigration and American Race Relations: From Exclusion to Acceptance?" *Ethnic and Racial Studies* 12 (1989): 368–90.

64. See, for example, Yancey, *Who Is White?*; Murguia and Forman, "Shades of Whiteness"

65. Portes and Rumbaut, *Immigrant America.*

66. Ibid.

67. Ibid.

68. Kim, "Asian American Identity Development Theory."

69. U.S. Census Bureau, "American Fact Finder: Hispanic or Latino Origin by Specific Origin, Detailed Tables," retrieved at http://factfinder.census.gov on October 4, 2006.

70. U.S. Census Bureau, "Fact Sheet for Race, Ethnic, or Ancestry Group: Census 2000."

71. Portes and Rumbaut, *Immigrant America.*

72. Ferdman and Gallegos, "Racial Identity Development and Latinos in the United States"; Murguia and Forman, "Shades of Whiteness."

73. U.S. Census Bureau, "Table 50: Married Couples of Same or Mixed Races and Origins: 1980 to 2000," Statistical Abstract of the United States: The National Data Book (121st ed.), Washington DC, 2001; U.S. Census Bureau, "Table 57: Family Groups with Children Under 18 Years Old by Race and Hispanic Origin: 1980 to 2000," Statistical Abstract of the United States: The National Data Book (121st ed.), Washington DC, 2001.

74. The interview guide questions were adapted from Waters, *Ethnic Options.*

NOTES TO CHAPTER 2

1. Michael Omi and Howard Winant, *Racial Formation in the United States: From the 1960s to the 1980s* (New York: Routledge & Kegan Paul, 1994).

2. Edward Murguia and Tyrone Forman, "Shades of Whiteness: The Mexican American Experience in Relation to Anglos and Blacks" in *White Out: The Continuing Significance of Racism,* ed. Ashley W. Doane and Eduardo Bonilla-Silva (New York: Routledge, 2003), 63–79; Melanie Bush, *Breaking the Code of Good Intentions: Everyday Forms of Whiteness* (Lanham, Maryland: Rowman and Littlefield, 2004).

3. Yen Le Espiritu, *Asian American Panethnicity: Bridging Institutions and Identities* (Philadelphia: Temple University Press, 1992).

4. Clara Rodriguez, *Changing Race: Latinos, the Census, and the History of Ethnicity in the United States* (New York: New York University Press, 2000).

5. Murguia and Forman, "Shades of Whiteness"

6. Espiritu, *Asian American Panethnicity.*

7. Eduardo Bonilla-Silva, "Rethinking Racism: Toward a Structural Interpretation," *American Sociological Review* 62 (1997): 465–80.

NOTES TO CHAPTER 3

1. Joe R. Feagin, *Racist America* (New York: Routledge, 2000); Eduardo Bonilla-Silva, *Racism Without Racists* (Lanham, Maryland: Rowman and Littlefield, 2003).

2. Bonilla-Silva, *Racism Without Racists*

3. Ibid.; Leslie Carr, *Colorblind Racism* (Thousand Oaks, California: Sage, 1997); Ruth Frankenberg, *White Women, Race Matters: The Social Construction of Whiteness* (Minneapolis: University of Minnesota Press, 1993).

4. Frankenberg, *White Women, Race Matters*

5. Bonilla-Silva, *Racism Without Racists*

6. Leonard Steinhorn and Barbara Diggs-Brown, *By the Color of Our Skin: The Illusion of Integration and the Reality of Race* (New York: Plume, 2000).

7. Carr, *Colorblind Racism.*

8. Bonilla-Silva, *Racism Without Racists*, 153.

9. Bonilla-Silva, *Racism Without Racists.*

10. Ibid.

11. Thanks to an anonymous reviewer for this alternative interpretation.

12. Bonilla-Silva, *Racism Without Racists.*

13. Donald R. Kinder and David O. Sears, "Prejudice and Politics: Symbolic Racism Versus Racial Threats to the Good Life," *Journal of Personality and Social Psychology* 40 (1981): 414–31.

14. This is of course leaving aside the fact that it becomes ideologically inconsistent for whites who oppose race-based affirmative action to take advantage of a host of other non-race-based affirmative action policies (such as those based on gender, veteran status, alumni parents at universities, and so on), as they often do.

15. Charles Gallagher, "Transforming Racial Identity Through Affirmative Action" in Race and Ethnicity: Across Time, Space, and Discipline, ed. Rodney Coates (Boston: Brill, 2004), 153–70; George Lipsitz, *The Possessive Investment in Whiteness: How White People Profit from Identity Politics* (Philadelphia: Temple University Press, 1998); Karyn D. McKinney, *Being White: Stories of Race and Racism* (New York: Routledge, 2005).

16. George Yancey, *Who Is White? Latinos, Asians, and the New Black/Nonblack Divide* (Boulder, Colorado: Lynne Rienner, 2003).

17. Bonilla-Silva, *Racism Without Racists*

18. Joe R. Feagin and Eileen O'Brien, *White Men on Race: Power, Privilege, and the Shaping of Cultural Consciousness* (Boston: Beacon Press, 2003).

19. Edna Bonacich, "Class Approaches to Ethnicity and Race," *Insurgent Sociologist* 10 (1980): 11.

20. Eduardo Bonilla-Silva and David G. Embrick, "Black, Honorary White, White: The Future of Race in the United States?" in *Mixed Messages: Multiracial*

Identities in the "Color-Blind" Era, ed. David L. Brunsma (Boulder, Colorado: Lynne Rienner, 2006), 33–48.

NOTES TO CHAPTER 4

1. Mary Waters, *Ethnic Options: Choosing Identities in America* (Berkeley: University of California Press, 1990).

2. Ibid.

3. Eugenia Kaw, "'Opening Faces': The Politics of Cosmetic Surgery and Asian American Women" in *Sociology Readings: Exploring the Architecture of Everyday Life*, ed. David M. Newman (Thousand Oaks, California: Pine Forge Press, 2000), 315–29; Jean Kim, "Asian American Identity Development Theory" in *New Perspectives on Racial Identity Development: A Theoretical and Practical Anthology*, ed. Charmaine L. Wijeyesinghe and Bailey W. Jackson III (New York: New York University Press, 2001), 67–90.

4. Clara Rodriguez, *Changing Race: Latinos, the Census, and the History of Ethnicity in the United States* (New York: New York University Press, 2000).

5. Ibid.; Eduardo Bonilla-Silva and David G. Embrick, "Black, Honorary White, White: The Future of Race in the United States?" in *Mixed Messages: Multiracial Identities in the "Color-Blind" Era*, ed. David L. Brunsma (Boulder, Colorado: Lynne Rienner, 2006), 33–48.

6. Waters, *Ethnic Options*.

7. Kim, "Asian American Identity Development Theory"; Bernardo M. Ferdman and Placida I. Gallegos, "Racial Identity Development and Latinos in the United States," in *New Perspectives on Racial Identity Development: A Theoretical and Practical Anthology*, ed. Charmaine L. Wijeyesinghe and Bailey W. Jackson III (New York: New York University Press, 2001), 32–66.

8. See, for example, Eduardo Bonilla-Silva, *Racism Without Racists* (Lanham, Maryland: Rowman and Littlefield, 2003); Joe R. Feagin and Eileen O'Brien, *White Men on Race: Power, Privilege, and the Shaping of Cultural Consciousness* (Boston: Beacon Press, 2003); Joe R. Feagin and Hernan Vera, *White Racism: The Basics* (New York: Routledge, 1995); Ruth Frankenberg, *White Women, Race Matters: The Social Construction of Whiteness* (Minneapolis: University of Minnesota Press, 1993).

9. Bonilla-Silva and Embrick, "Black, Honorary White, White."

10. Rodriguez, *Changing Race*.

11. Bonilla-Silva, *Racism Without Racists*.

12. Yen Le Espiritu, *Asian American Panethnicity: Bridging Institutions and Identities* (Philadelphia: Temple University Press, 1992).

13. Ibid.; Rodriguez, *Changing Race*.

14. Paul Spickard, *Mixed Blood: Intermarriage and Ethnic Identity in Twentieth-Century America* (Madison: University of Wisconsin Press, 1989).

15. Rodriguez, *Changing Race*; Bonilla-Silva and Embrick, "Black, Honorary White, White."

NOTES TO CHAPTER 5

1. This is not to say that African Americans do not at all get asked "what are you?"—particularly those who are biracial, ethnically mixed, or light skinned —but it is not as characteristic of an experience for the entire group. Likewise, I acknowledge that often African Americans will be praised as being "so articulate" when they display a command of the English language, which is similar to Latinos and Asians being praised for having "such good English" when it is their first (or only) language. Most English-speaking whites leveling such "praise" at African Americans, however, do expect to be able to communicate with the blacks they encounter in *some* form of English that they would be able to understand, unlike when they approach Latinos and/or Asian Americans with this kind of stereotypical logic.

2. Philomena Essed, *Understanding Everyday Racism: An Interdisciplinary Theory* (Newbury Park, California: Sage Publications, 1991).

3. Eduardo Bonilla-Silva, *Racism Without Racists* (Lanham, Maryland: Rowman and Littlefield, 2003).

4. Deirdre Royster, *Race and the Invisible Hand: How White Networks Exclude Black Men from Blue Collar Jobs* (Berkeley: University of California Press, 2003).

5. W. E. B. Du Bois, *The Souls of Black Folk* (New York: Bantam Classic Books, 1989 [1903]).

6. Joe R. Feagin and Melvin P. Sikes, *Living with Racism: The Black Middle Class Experience* (Boston: Beacon Press, 1994).

7. Clara Rodriguez, *Changing Race: Latinos, the Census, and the History of Ethnicity in the United States* (New York: New York University Press, 2000).

8. See, for example, Feagin and Sikes, *Living with Racism*; Essed, *Understanding Everyday Racism*; Royster, *Race and the Invisible Hand*; Kenneth Bolton Jr. and Joe R. Feagin, *Black in Blue: African American Police Officers and Racism*; Joe R. Feagin, Hernan Vera, and Nikitah Imani, *The Agony of Education: Black Students at Predominantly White Colleges and Universities* (New York: Routledge, 1996).

9. Feagin, Vera, and Imani, *The Agony of Education*.

10. Royster, *Race and the Invisible Hand*

11. Feagin and Sikes, *Living with Racism*.

12. Claude M. Steele, "A Threat in the Air: How Stereotypes Shape the Intellectual Identities and Performance of Women and African Americans," *American Psychologist* 52 (1997): 613–29.

NOTES TO CHAPTER 6

1. Eduardo Bonilla-Silva, *Racism Without Racists* (Lanham, Maryland: Rowman and Littlefield, 2003).

2. This assimilation pattern happens over time, however, and is most evidenced by the increased likelihood of the offspring of these marriages to identify as white, and cannot be investigated with the present study. Here I focus on likelihood of progressive ideology, which the whitening thesis would generally expect to be low, particularly among those who are intermarried with whites and thus following the other assimilative patterns predicted by the theory.

3. Alejandro Portes and Ruben G. Rumbaut, *Immigrant America: A Portrait* (3rd ed.) (Berkeley: University of California Press, 2006); Melanie Bush, *Breaking the Code of Good Intentions: Everyday Forms of Whiteness* (Lanham, Maryland: Rowman and Littlefield, 2004).

4. Portes and Rumbaut, *Immigrant America.*

5. Jean Kim, "Asian American Identity Development Theory" in *New Perspectives on Racial Identity Development: A Theoretical and Practical Anthology,* ed. Charmaine L. Wijeyesinghe and Bailey W. Jackson III (New York: New York University Press, 2001), 67–90.

6. Bonilla-Silva, *Racism Without Racists.*

7. Joe R. Feagin and Hernan Vera, *White Racism: The Basics* (New York: Routledge, 1995).

8. Yen Le Espiritu, *Asian American Panethnicity: Bridging Institutions and Identities* (Philadelphia: Temple University Press, 1992).

9. Edward Murguia and Tyrone Forman, "Shades of Whiteness: The Mexican American Experience in Relation to Anglos and Blacks" in *White Out: The Continuing Significance of Racism,* ed. Ashley W. Doane and Eduardo Bonilla-Silva (New York: Routledge, 2003), 63–79.

10. Peggy McIntosh, "White Privilege and Male Privilege: A Personal Account of Coming to See Correspondences through Work in Women's Studies (1998)" in *Race, Class and Gender* (4th ed.), ed. Margaret Andersen and Patricia Hill Collins (New York: Wadsworth, 2001), 95–105.

11. France Winddance Twine, "Brown-Skinned White Girls: Class, Culture, and the Construction of White Identity in Suburban Communities" in *Displacing Whiteness: Essays in Social and Cultural Criticism,* ed. Ruth Frankenberg (Durham, North Carolina: Duke University Press, 1997), 214–43.

12. Joe R. Feagin, Hernan Vera, and Nikitah Imani, *The Agony of Education: Black Students at Predominantly White Colleges and Universities* (New York: Routledge, 1996).

13. Murgia and Forman, "Shades of Whiteness."

14. See, for example, Kim, "Asian American Identity Development Theory"; Bernardo M. Ferdman and Placida I. Gallegos, "Racial Identity Development and

Latinos in the United States," in *New Perspectives on Racial Identity Development: A Theoretical and Practical Anthology,* ed. Charmaine L. Wijeyesinghe and Bailey W. Jackson III (New York: New York University Press, 2001), 32–66.

15. Clara Rodriguez, Changing Race: Latinos, the Census, and the History of Ethnicity in the United States (New York: New York University Press, 2000).

NOTES TO CHAPTER 7

1. See Joe R. Feagin and Eileen O'Brien, *White Men on Race: Power, Privilege and the Shaping of Cultural Consciousness* (Boston: Beacon Press, 2003).

2. George Yancey, *Who Is White? Latinos, Asians, and the New Black/Non-black Divide* (Boulder, Colorado: Lynne Rienner, 2003).

3. See, for example, Philomena Essed, *Understanding Everyday Racism: An Interdisciplinary Theory* (Newbury Park, California: Sage Publications, 1991); Joe R. Feagin and Melvin P. Sikes, *Living with Racism: The Black Middle-Class Experience* (Boston: Beacon Press, 1994).

4. Yancey, *Who is White?*

5. See Antonia Darder, Rodolfo D. Torres, and ChorSwang Ngin, "Racialized Metropolis: Theorizing Asian American and Latino Identities and Ethnicities in Southern California" in *After Race: Racism after Multiculturalism*, ed. Antonia Darder and Rodolfo D. Torres (New York: New York University Press, 2004), 47–66.

6. See for example, Feagin and Sikes, *Living with Racism*; Essed, *Understanding Everyday Racism.*

7. See, for example, Eduardo Bonilla-Silva, *Racism Without Racists* (Lanham, Maryland: Rowman and Littlefield, 2003).

8. Ibid.; Feagin and O'Brien, *White Men on Race*; Karyn D. McKinney, *Being White: Stories of Race and Racism* (New York: Routledge, 2005).

9. See, for example, Edward Murguia and Tyrone Forman, "Shades of Whiteness: The Mexican American Experience in Relation to Anglos and Blacks" in *White Out: The Continuing Significance of Racism*, ed. Ashley W. Doane and Eduardo Bonilla-Silva (New York: Routledge, 2003), 63–79; Yancey, *Who Is White?*

10. On black conservatives, see Andrea Y. Simpson, *Tie That Binds: Identity and Political Attitudes in the Post–Civil Rights Generation* (New York: New York University Press, 1998); on white antiracists using color-blind discourse, see Eileen O'Brien, *Whites Confront Racism*: Antiracists and their Paths to Action (Lanham, Maryland: Rowman and Littlefield, 2001); on blacks using color-blind discourse, see Bonilla-Silva, *Racism Without Racists.*

11. Bonilla-Silva, *Racism Without Racists*; Leslie Carr, *Colorblind Racism* (Thousand Oaks, California: Sage, 1997); Ruth Frankenberg, *White Women, Race Matters: The Social Construction of Whiteness* (Minneapolis: University of Minnesota Press, 1993).

12. On society structured by racism, see Eduardo Bonilla-Silva, "Rethinking Racism: Toward a Structural Interpretation" *American Sociological Review* 62 (1997): 465–80. On sincere fictions, see Joe R. Feagin and Hernan Vera, *White Racism: The Basics* (New York: Routledge, 1995).

13. Frankenberg, *White Women, Race Matters.*

14. Carr, *Colorblind Racism*; Bonilla-Silva, *Racism Without Racists.*

15. Amanda Lewis, *Race in the Schoolyard: Negotiating the Color Line in Classrooms and Communities* (Rutgers, New Jersey: Rutgers University Press, 2003).

16. Barbara Miner, "Taking Multicultural, Antiracist Education Seriously: An Interview with Enid Lee" in *Race, Class and Gender* (4th ed.), ed. Margaret Andersen and Patricia Hill Collins (New York: Wadsworth, 2001), 556–62.

17. Special thanks to Dee Royster for offering up this useful phrase!

18. Darder, Torres, and Ngin, "Racialized Metropolis," 59.

19. Clara Rodriguez, *Changing Race: Latinos, the Census, and the History of Ethnicity in the United States* (New York: New York University Press, 2000).

20. Samuel Huntington, "The Hispanic Challenge," *Foreign Policy* (March–April 2004): 30–45.

21. Rod Bush, *We Are Not What We Seem: Black Nationalism and Class Struggle in the American Century* (New York: New York University Press, 1999).

Index

About the Author

Eileen O'Brien is Assistant Professor of Sociology at Christopher Newport University, Virginia, and resides in Williamsburg, Virginia, with partner, Kendall James, and children, Kaya and Kaden O'Brien-James. She is also author of *Whites Confront Racism* and coauthor of *White Men on Race* and *Race, Ethnicity, and Gender: Selected Readings.*